Croce's book is not only a c̲ It takes
a very special and courageous person to write a book condemning
animal experiments on purely scientific and methodological grounds.
*Dr André Menache BSc. (Hons), BVSc. MRCVS, President, Doctors and Lawyers
for Responsible Medicine*

Croce brings to his subject great experience, towering moral stature,
profound reflection and dignified reason. His thesis is in the title, of
which the book is proof. A truly human medical science cannot include
animal experimentation. Such practices are an alternative to science, a
dodge around the medicine licensing laws. We do not yet have a sufficiently precise notion of how animals and humans are distinct: only a
sorcerer's apprentice would trust the similarities. Methods for humane
scientific enquiry already exist that are perfectly adequate for human
need, if not for industrial greed. Case closed. *Dr Peter Mansfield, President,
National Pure Water Association*

Many books have been written concerning the ethical problems and
cruelty of vivisection. Only a few deal with the scientific errors resulting
from the extrapolation of results from animals to humans, especially
when healthy but deliberately injured animals are taken as models for
diseases occurring naturally in people. Who could better introduce us
to this perspective than Professor Pietro Croce, who for a long time
himself performed animal experiments until he eventually recognized
the harmful consequences? Professor Croce argues against vivisection
on scientific grounds and shows convincingly that it has nothing to do
with good science. *Dr Bernhard Rambeck, Head of Biochemistry, Epilepsy
Research Foundation, Germany*

Professor Croce's book is an immense contribution. Scientific veracity,
elegance and wit are its hallmarks. I highly recommend it to those who
care to know the truth about vivisection. *Dr Moneim A. Fadali MD,
M.Ch., FACS, FRCS (C), FACC, FACCP, author of* Animal Experimentation: A Harvest of Shame

A bold and challenging book that I very much hope will highlight the
many problems and dangers inherent in our continuing reliance on
animal experimentation. Ignoring this issue can no longer be an option
for any of us. *Michael Mansfield QC*

About the author

Dr Pietro Croce is Professor Emeritus of Pathology, University of Milan, a member of the American College of Pathologists, and Honorary President of Doctors and Lawyers for Responsible Medicine. He is a leading Italian medical researcher who for 30 years headed the Research Laboratory of the L. Sacco Hospital in Milan. International recognition resulted in various awards, including a Fulbright Fellowship. He has also worked in research departments abroad, including the National Jewish Hospital, University of Colorado and Toledo Hospital, Ohio as well as the Ciudad Sanatorial of Tarassa in Spain.

He is the author of a number of medical works in Italian and Spanish. His most well-known work, *Vivisezione o Scienza: La Sperimentazione sull'uomo*, in which, after many years of relying on the customary techniques of animal experimentation, he concluded that they led to results untenable in scientific terms, has been published not only in Italy, but also in Germany and Japan. The present book is an updated and revised edition of that classic work.

VIVISECTION OR SCIENCE?
An investigation into testing drugs and safeguarding health

Pietro Croce

Zed Books Ltd
LONDON · NEW YORK
in association with
Doctors and Lawyers for
Responsible Medicine

Vivisection or Science? An investigation into testing drugs and safeguarding human health was first published by Zed Books, 7 Cynthia Street, London N1 9JF, UK and Room 400, 175 Fifth Avenue, New York, NY 10010, USA in 1999

in association with Doctors and Lawyers for Responsible Medicine (DLRM), 104b Weston Park, London N8 9PP, UK.

The present work is a revised and updated edition of an earlier English-language version of the book by Pietro Croce, translated by Henry Turtle and published in a limited edition in Switzerland by Civis Publications, POB 152, Via Motta 51, 6900 Massagno, Switzerland.

Original translation from the Italian by Henry Turtle, revised and edited by Margaret Dain, Fiona Ford and Sian Mills.

Cover designed by Andrew Corbett
Set in Monotype Ehrhardt and Univers by Ewan Smith
Printed and bound in Malaysia

A catalogue record for this book is available from the British Library.

US CIP has been applied for from the Library of Congress.

ISBN 1 85649 732 1 cased
ISBN 1 85649 733 X limp

Contents

Editors' note

Although Professor Croce has not been in a position always
to update references, they are nevertheless still completely
relevant to his thesis.

Introduction

In this book I have deliberately juxtaposed science and pseudo-science, with the express purpose of producing a clash.

Pseudo-science, as with all mystification, arouses mirth or sarcasm. Such mirth is always cruel. However, just as one shouldn't laugh at a drunk, so also one should not laugh at that small band of researchers who, in *good* faith, persist in searching the entrails of frogs, guinea-pigs, dogs, cats and apes for the answers to human ailments.

But then there are the researchers in *bad* faith, who are legion. These are the people who manage to extract for themselves diplomas, honorary degrees, university chairs – and, of course, money – from animal viscera. Such is the subject matter of the first part of this book.

The second part deals with true science. The basic methods of biomedical research, including epidemiology, mathematical and computer and *in vitro* experimentation, are discussed.

I have tried to avoid any kind of tediousness that might discourage the average or lay reader. At the same time, there has been no sacrifice of scientific rigour, so that those who possess a suitable scientific background will be helped to take their first steps, perhaps, towards a science that is in need of radical renewal.

Pietro Croce

Introduction

I. Vivisection: the dangers to human health

1. My road to Damascus

I used to experiment on animals. For many years I obeyed the stale, positivistic logic that had been imposed on me during my university studies and had conditioned me to believe, for a long time afterwards, in the maxim 'Scientific positivism is the only possible logic in medical and biological research'. But to assert that the human mind can work with only one possible system of logic means admitting that it is unable to look in more than one direction.

With my head filled with notions handed down by the professors and gained from books and from practice in hospitals in Italy and abroad, I tried to put my thoughts in order. But it was like trying to assemble a defective jigsaw puzzle – the pieces did not fit together and produced distorted images, separated by spaces that could not be filled and forming a mosaic that fell apart at the least jolt.

I realized that there must be something wrong with medical thinking and practice – a false premise, both fundamental and elementary, capable of undermining the entire structure and vitiating everything built upon it – in other words, a methodological error.

Vivisectionist thinking arises from empirical science, which reached its peak in the nineteenth century and is based on the selection and construction of experimental models that reproduce freely those phenomena to be researched.

As an example, two condensers charged positively and negatively with electricity and placed near each other produce a spark. This is the experimental model for the natural phenomenon of lightning. But what is the appropriate model for the study of humankind, its functions, malfunctions and illnesses? The solution seems obvious (but for this very reason contains a deception that undermines it utterly), namely, the proposition that the animal be taken as the experimental model for the human being. Immediately, our first obstacle presents itself: which animal should we choose? There are millions of species of animal on earth – should we use the mouse? the dog? and why not the rhinoceros or the warthog?

In the physical and mechanical sciences, the researcher designs and constructs an experimental model that possesses the characteristics appropriate to his or her objective. On the other hand, the researcher in the biological sciences who takes an animal as an experimental model is obliged to accept something already formed by nature. It would be a strange and improbable coincidence if this animal's characteristics were appropriate for the purpose in view.

Even the choice between different species of animal is illusory: it is more a kind of fishing blindly among different possibilities in a haphazard way or – worse still – an opportunistic search for the most 'convenient' animal. The mouse, the rabbit, the guinea-pig are convenient, because they are easy to house, and so are cats and dogs, because they can be obtained cheaply. The one element that should be the deciding factor – that the animal should have morphological, physiological and biochemical characteristics applicable to humankind – is neglected. In fact, only a human being or a chimera can meet this criterion.

An experimental model of the human species does not exist. All species, all varieties of animals and even individuals of the same species differ from one another. No experimentation carried out on one species can be extrapolated to any other. The belief that such extrapolation could be legitimate is the main reason for the failures, and sometimes for the catastrophes, that modern medicine inflicts on us, especially where drugs are concerned. Too little is spoken or written about certain unpleasant facts, sometimes out of deference to a science that purports to be 'the saviour of mankind', but more usually to avoid provoking the huge economic and political interests that prop up this 'saviour'. For example, in August 1978, it was only Japanese newspapers that reported the procession through the streets of Tokyo of thirty thousand people paralysed and blinded by clioquinol, and it was only the trial and conviction of the firm producing the drug that brought the matter to public notice. (See Chapter 7 for details of the clioquinol tragedy.)

Issue No. 8, August 1983, of *Il Bollettino d'Informazione sui Farmaci* (Drug Information Bulletin), published by the Italian Ministry of Health and possessing the limited readership of all such publications, stated that 'Between 1972 and June 1983 the registration of 22,621 medicinal preparations was revoked' (in other words, their sale prohibited). Since drugs are usually manufactured in different formulations (tablets, suppositories, etc.), the preparations actually taken off the market numbered about five thousand. All of them had apparently passed, with flying colours, the animal tests required by law.

Another official report informs us that things are by no means improving. Between 1984 and 1987, side-effects (only reported ones, naturally) from medicines numbered 14,386, including 112 deaths (Miceli 1981). How many years must pass before it is realized that a medicine is dangerous – and how many will have fallen victim to it in the meantime? This question was answered by Professor Hoff at the Congress of Clinical Medicine, Wiesbaden, in 1976: '6% of fatal illnesses and 25% of all illnesses are due to medications.' Professor Dr Remner of Tübingen, at a meeting of German insurance companies, said: 'In the Federal Republic of Germany, about 30,000 deaths a year are due to medicines.'

If Germany bewails this situation, Italy is not exactly happy either: health statisticians report that 10% of hospitalizations are due to toxic drug effects, and 30% of hospitalized patients have their stay in hospital prolonged because of incorrect treatment. From the UK there are more of these alarming statistics: in 1977, 120,366 cases of toxic drug effects were reported in hospitalized patients (Mann 1984). And in the USA, one in every seven hospital beds is occupied by patients suffering such effects.

My demand for the abolition of animal experiments is based not on a love of animals but on a concern for the health of fellow human beings. Anti-vivisectionist thinking is much more scientific than the boasting of the vivisectors, who operate in a medieval climate of thought. They are too lazy or too greedy to break loose from a comfortable conformity and to apply themselves to the historical scientifically correct methods (for example, clinical observation) that are today largely in disuse, or to the numerous modern scientific methods, such as cell and tissue cultures, mathematical models, epidemiology and so on.

There are, then, many alternatives to vivisection. About 450 have been described, but their number is theoretically unlimited, since every piece of research presupposes a method specific to that research, able to guarantee a credible result that is compatible with scientific logic, freely reproducible and capable of satisfying Karl Popper's 'criterion of falsification'[1] – all of which are lacking in vivisectionist methodology.

Scientific progress is achieved only by small steps. I would prefer these steps to be tiny, but sure. Vivisectors like to present animal experimentation as a short-cut to biological knowledge, having failed to notice that it is a short-cut in the wrong direction. The claim that medicine must progress by trial and error is unacceptable. In medicine, 'error' means the sacrifice of a person – or, perhaps, thousands of people. I say one person or thousands deliberately, because one is of as much value as thousands. The vivisector says: 'But we work for the benefit of the majority.' Not so! They have no right to sacrifice a single human being for the hypothetical and entirely uncertain benefit of an indefinite number of others at some unspecified time in the future.

At 5.25pm on 16 November 1984, it was announced on the radio that Baby Fae had died. 'Baby Fae' was the nickname given to a baby girl born in California on 14 October 1984 with a heart malformation that meant that she could not survive for long. On 26 October, at the University Medical Center of Loma Llinda, Dr Leonard Bailey transplanted a baboon heart into the human baby. People marched in protest past the hospital. The small victim died, most probably due to rejection of the new heart, 21 days after the operation.

Baby Fae was a guinea-pig in a vivisection experiment. The primary objective of the experiment was (presumably) to establish whether rejection would take place even when the immune system was incomplete. It is an interesting scientific finding that rejection did occur, even though it was easily predictable. But scientific findings notwithstanding, human and medical ethics must also play their part, and no such torture can be justified in the name of scientific advance.

However, that is not all. There is a coda to this dreadful story, astonishing even at an elementary technical (I deliberately avoid the term 'scientific') level. Professor Bailey himself tells us that rejection occurred not because of the incompatibility of the baboon heart and the baby's tissue, but because – and this seems quite inconceivable – his team did not bother to perform what is a routine everyday procedure in blood transfusion units around the world: they failed to match the blood groups of donor and recipient. It later transpired that Baby Fae was of blood group O, while the baboon was of blood group AB. Professor Bailey commented: 'The mixing of the blood groups was fatal. We were more afraid of the difference between the species than about the blood. We made a mistake' (*La Repubblica*, 13 May 1987).

As a scientist, I recognize the great scientific interest of the Baby Fae experiment, but as a human being, I maintain that the little girl was used as a guinea-pig and that those responsible should be punished by law. Otherwise, we are all forced to share in the perverse notion that the ends justify the means, a catastrophic maxim that has cast its blight on humankind for millennia.

Let us return to the trial-and-error concept. I prefer to term 'scientific' those methods that others call 'alternative'. They are scientific because they are the most reliable, minimizing the risk of error – that is, the risk of human suffering and death. There are, as already touched on, three basic scientific methods: epidemiology, mathematical models, and cell and tissue culture *in vitro*. These methods may not guarantee sensationally rapid progress, but they are short, safe steps on a straight path. It is often asked why, in that case, they are so little used. The only reason is that universities continue to instruct new generations of students in animal experimentation. They are unable or unwilling to free themselves from a blind and fruitless way of thinking: it is easier to keep to old habits than to innovate.

Some vivisectionists – those blessed, perhaps, with a more critical cast of mind – have begun to have doubts and to look for a compromise. They admit that animal experiments do not provide definitive answers but maintain that they at least give an indication that one is on the right track, making it worthwhile to continue in the same direction. Such an indication can indeed be useful, on one condition – that it is, in fact, correct as far as it goes. I am reminded of the traveller who stops a passer-by to ask the way to St Mary's Church. The passer-by points vaguely in an easterly direction. This is an 'indication', a piece of information that, however incomplete, may help if the direction indicated is the correct one. But if the passer-by, instead of pointing to the east (where the church is in fact situated), indicates the west or south, the indication is not only incomplete but is also wrong and misleading.

The same is true of vivisectionist research methodology. If it gave incomplete but correct indications, it might be of some use. But not only is it of no use, it is also misleading, since only by chance does it provide pointers in the right direction, without the researchers' having any way of predicting whether a fortunate coincidence can be verified or not.

What do the terms 'by chance' and 'by coincidence' really mean? We have no difficulty in admitting that, for example, a substance that is poisonous to a dog can also be so to a human. However, that may be a pure coincidence, obeying the laws of probability, and, in accepting it, we commit an error that could claim victims before we are even aware of the situation. There are plenty of victims of modern medicine – so many that learned papers are written about iatrogenic illnesses, that is, illnesses caused by doctors who seem to have forgotten the basic Hippócratic precept: *Primum non nocere* (First, do not cause harm).

The notion of vivisection experiments on humans is not a macabre fantasy. It is believed to occur widely today. Many vivisectionists themselves are clearly beginning to realize that to experiment on one species of animal in order to extrapolate the results to another species (*inter species* experimentation) constitutes a methodological error. They are therefore turning to *intra speciem* experimentation, which means experimenting on the dog to learn things about the dog, on the cat to learn about the cat, and on human beings to learn things about humans. But this sophisticated variation on vivisection, despite its attraction, does not guarantee results any more reliable than those obtained by experimentation *inter species* (as I shall demonstrate later).

No animal species can be an experimental model for any other species, and only a superficial judgement can be content with morphological similarities, such as: 'The dog, like man, has a head, two eyes, a liver, a heart etc.' Just as crude and misleading is recourse to such behavioural analogies as: 'If I crush the foot of a dog, it howls – if I crush the foot of a man, he cries out; if I remove her newborn baby, the female monkey mourns – if I take away her newborn baby, the human mother mourns.'

These analogies exist, and it would be foolish to deny them – but why do they exist? In having a common root, they are attributes of that unfathomable and indivisible entity we call life. That certain types of behaviour have a common root seems clear when we pause to consider, without scientific bias, any living being. The search for food, flight from danger, reproductive urge and other kinds of behaviour, which we may, for the sake of convenience, term 'instincts', are fundamental attributes of the phenomenon of life.

However, turning to the material components of the tissues of countless animal species, we should pause for a moment to consider the following: can two species of animal be considered analogous, when it is known that the tissues of each species are made up of thousands of proteins (about ten thousand) of which not even one that is common to two species is identical in both, and whose DNA (deoxyribonucleic acid) sequences, which transmit hereditary characteristics, all differ from each

other in the various species?[2] (DNA molecules differ in different animals
in the length of their double helix chains and the number and arrangement of the nucleotides of which they are composed. There are billions
upon billions of possible permutations, since the number of nucleotides
in human DNA, for example, is about three billion.)

A fundamental rule of any scientific experiment is that it must be
reproducible. An experiment is reproducible when it always produces
an identical result, wherever and whenever it is performed and by
whichever researcher. If this is not the case, something is wrong. Either
the hypothesis is wrong,[3] or it is not demonstrable, or the method used
to demonstrate it is flawed. We need to know, therefore, whether experiments on animals (including the human animal) have this intrinsic
property of reproducibility.

One answer comes from research carried out at the University of
Bremen, published in a paper entitled 'Die Problematik der Wirkungs-
schwelle in Pharmakologie und Toxikologie' (Problems of the efficacy
threshold in pharmacology and toxicology).[4] This research shows that:

1. Subjected to ionizing irradiation, young animals react differently
   from older ones.

3. There are major differences in the effects of tranquillizers on young
   versus older animals.

5. In LD-50 tests (LD = lethal dose; the tests are designed to find the
   dose at which 50% of the experimental animals die) carried out on
   rats in the evening, almost all the rats died; in those carried out in
   the morning, all survived. In tests done in winter, survival rates were
   double those recorded in the summer. Where toxic substances were
   administered to mice in crowded cages, nearly all died, whereas all
   the mice given the substance in normal cage conditions survived.

The authors of this research concluded: 'If such minor environmental
differences lead to such divergent and unforeseen results, animal experiments cannot be relied upon in the assessment of chemical substances,
and it is all the more absurd to extrapolate to human medicine results
that are intrinsically false.'

Finally, it should be noted that the above observations were made
not by anti-vivisectionists but by vivisectors themselves, who have shown,
to their credit, the merit of defining the limitations of a methodology
in which they had hitherto firmly believed.

Notes

1. The 'criterion of falsification' expounded by Karl Popper, the Austrian philosopher, asserts that a proposal is not scientific if it cannot also be proved wrong. For example, the proposition 'In a thousand years the sun will be extinguished' is not scientific, because nobody is in a position to demonstrate that the event will not occur.

2. Diversity among proteins and among other components (mainly polysaccharides) of different species (both animals and plants) is basic to all phenomena in immunology, from allergies to organ rejection.

3. A false proposition is of this type: 'Man can fly by waving his arms.' This proposition, however, contains within itself Popper's criterion of falsification (see note 1), because anyone can demonstrate its falsity. On the other hand, a proposition that could never be shown to be false is: 'In a thousand years the sun will be extinguished.'

4. These data were supplied by the medical doctor and surgeon, Dr Werner Hartinger, of Waldshut-Tiengen, Germany.

2. The modern anti-vivisection movement

The movement against vivisection stemmed from an emotional impulse: that of compassion for animals. Marie Françoise Martin, wife of the 'prince of vivisectors', Claude Bernard (1813–78), was an animal lover and founded the French Anti-vivisection Society in 1883 (its first president was Victor Hugo).

Even before this, an anti-vivisection society was founded in England in response to an article by George Hoggan (*Morning Post*, 1 February 1875), a young physiologist who had for four months attended the institute of which Claude Bernard was director. On returning to his own country, he denounced the director's 'mad sadism', asserting, amongst other things, that 'of the experiments which I had witnessed, not one was justified or necessary'. Although this view embodies in embryonic form modern anti-vivisectionist thinking, George Hoggan must still be considered someone who reacted emotionally, unable to tolerate the sight of the suffering inflicted upon animals but probably disposed to accept it as part of an experimentation that was deemed 'justified and necessary' (Ruesch 1976). This is not to take a derogatory view of him – human actions and feelings should, after all, be considered in their historical context. Integrity, together with an intuition ahead of its time, is characteristic of those individuals who, like Victor Hugo, are able to thunder publicly that 'vivisection is a crime'.

How did the general public react to such progressive views? At best, with that benevolent indulgence reserved for eccentrics whose merit was to enliven the humdrum quality of everyday life but who were very far from hindering the 'glorious progress of Science'. A cartoon of the time, illustrating the difference between the two, showed the anti-vivisectionist as a little old woman taking her lap-dog to the park for an airing, and Science as a splendid, crowned noblewoman, holding aloft a flaming torch in the manner of the Statue of Liberty.

Anti-vivisectionists have continued until recently to be labelled 'emotional, irrational people', or 'enemies of progress' – a few well-chosen adjectives being enough to relegate them to the realm of quaint and amusing folklore. At the same time, however, another selection of well-aimed adjectives exalted the work of the vivisectors, who, careful to avoid those uncomfortable terms for themselves, were modest enough to prefer the epithet 'benefactors of humanity'.

There is nothing new under the sun. The motley crew of unwelcome 'benefactors' is a baleful phenomenon that has made human life a misery since the earliest times. The Mayan priests were working diligently for the good of mankind when they extirpated, from selected samples of the human species, one organ after another, managing – with a skill that still amazes today – to keep the victim alive and fully conscious for hours or even days, so that his suffering should not be wasted by the inopportune intervention of death.

Today's 'benefactors of humanity' have exchanged the white vestments of priests for the white coats of a profession, now a symbol rather than a protective garment and a licence to carry out any act of violence against nature, animals and, above all, humankind. These white coats carry the message, perceptible to the mind if not the eye, that 'Everything we do is for your own good' – ergo: 'Allow us to do anything we want'.

But let us continue with the evolution of the movement against vivisection. The 1890s brought a sudden change of course, as powerful as it was unexpected, which momentarily threw off balance even the many anti-vivisection and animal-protection societies. Motivation was overturned, the target changed. The new motivation was (and is) a critical reassessment of medical research, one that makes an unbiased and realistic distinction between its declared aims and its real, often unavowable, ones. The targets are the massed ranks of exploiters, pseudo-scientists and vivisectionists of the poison-producing pharmaceutical and cosmetics industries.

To understand the true nature of the new anti-vivisectionism and to avoid an old cliché, we must be clear on one point: *the new anti-vivisectionists cannot be equated with animal lovers* – although they may indeed love animals. They are for the most part experts who have been sufficiently clear-sighted to ask themselves the fundamental questions: 'For whom are these experiments performed? And what results do they produce?'

George Hoggan, as we have seen, spoke of experiments 'not one [of which] was justified or necessary'; he might have added, 'and many of which are harmful'. This is not a new claim. What is new is the way it is now being used to argue against an unscientific and misleading methodology. That it is not completely new is shown by the following:

Vivisection has caused a great many ills and brought death and suffering to thousands (Wolfgang Bohn, *Ärztliche Mitteilungen*, No. 7/8, 1912).

No experimenter on animals can provide a single useful fact about human disease (D. A. Long, of the British National Institute for Medical Research, in Long 1954).

There really exists no biological basis for transferring to man the results obtained on animals (L. Goldberg, of the Karolinska Institute in Stockholm, in Goldberg 1959).

The idea, as I understand it, is that fundamental truths are revealed in laboratory experimentation on lower animals and then applied to the problems of the sick patient. Having been myself trained as a physiologist, I feel in a way competent to assess such a claim. *It is plain nonsense* (Sir George Pickering, of Oxford University, in Pickering 1964).

Normally, animal experiments not only fail to contribute to the safety of medicines, but they even the opposite effect (Kurt Fickentscher, of the Pharmacological Institute of the University of Bonn, in Fickentscher 1980).

These are unequivocal words, from men firmly established in the academic world, who were honest and courageous enough to denounce its aberrations. Why did they not arouse immediate interest? The answer is simple: it is because they did not reach the ears of the general public. They were never heard outside an environment that was concerned only to stifle them, an environment that clings to repetitive and esoteric rituals in a kind of latter-day paganism and sees in science the golden calf of our times. The statements of Long, Pickering and Fickentscher derive not from a liking for animals but from a critical attitude towards a practice that is useless and dangerous, as well as unprincipled.

Their assertions signal the birth of the new anti-vivisectionism, which we call 'rational' or 'scientific' and which marches alongside 'emotional', 'historical' or 'zoophilic' anti-vivisectionism. There is no contradiction between the two positions: each of them deserves the respect of the other, and in the future each will have to seek to influence the conscience and rational intelligence of both lay people and those who are within the system but who search for a better understanding of this issue. Above all, they should seek to influence the consciences and minds of those young doctors about to enter a profession that is so badly in need of a new Hippocrates.

Perhaps the pioneers of the new anti-vivisectionism did not themselves realize the historical and cultural significance of their ideas. However, it would be too crass to reduce the problem to the two extremes of whether to experiment or not to experiment on animals. The new anti-vivisectionism is part of an immense, as yet ill-defined, worldwide shake-up of numerous false values, of many convictions passively absorbed and of many habits born of laziness.

The increasing influence the new anti-vivisection movement is beginning to exert is indicated by two phenomena in contemporary society.

First, governments are beginning to show signs of apprehension about this new cultural phenomenon. They are beginning to realize that they are alienating a large part of their electorate. They have noticed that people are looking to wider horizons, which extend beyond the problem of the survival of humankind to that of nature and the planet as a whole. From a chaos that we should not deplore, because it is characteristic of emerging new cultures, are arising associations, leagues, movements and even political parties that, significantly, describe themselves by the very colours – green and blue – that evoke nature.

The second symptom revealing the cultural importance of the new anti-vivisection movement is the support, albeit sometimes superficial, that it has gained from a growing number of public figures, including artists, actors and others in the media.

What is the current situation? It can be observed that resorting to animal experimentation has declined substantially. Is this a source of satisfaction to the supporters of the anti-vivisection movement? I can state that it is not. To reduce the number of animals sacrificed on the false altar of vivisection is to forget the real aim of our movement: that animal experimentation – regardless of the numbers involved – is fallacious as long as it is supposed to be useful to humans.

3. The fallacy of vivisection as a biomedical research method

Are there alternatives to vivisection? Of course not. Then what is the point of this book? And why is there widespread disgust at vivisectors? Why do researchers, in increasing numbers, refuse to experiment on animals? And what about the lawsuits brought against vivisectors and the court sentences handed down to them? As with all subjects of debate, semantic definition is required.[1]

There are no 'alternatives' to vivisection, since 'alternative' implies something different but equally valid, but it is hard to find anything in biomedical research that is, and always has been, more deceptive and misleading than vivisection. The methods we propose for medical research should therefore be called 'scientific' rather than 'alternative'.

The vivisectors ask: 'What would you offer scientific research instead of vivisection?' But vivisection is bringing science into disrepute, even with the general public. The vivisectors should therefore ask not 'What are you offering to science?' but, more honestly, 'What are you offering to us vivisectors?' They would, of course, have to give up an easy way of acquiring academic titles, publishing papers, advancing their careers and making money. They would also have to relinquish the chance of ingratiating themselves with the powers-that-be by supporting one thesis one day and, equally smoothly, its opposite the next – all on the basis of 'irrefutable' experiments.

One can produce many examples of 'irrefutable' facts in support of any such arguments, simply by using different kinds of animals: one just has to choose the 'right' kind.

- Do we want to show that the deadly *Amanita phalloides* is an excellent edible mushroom? Then we have only to feed it to the rabbit.
- Do we wish to ruin the trade of citrus-fruit growers? Let us poison

rabbits with the lemon juice we add as a flavouring to our

want to make someone fall asleep? Then let's give them
phine. But do we want to send a cat into a frenzy of excitement?
's give it morphine too. However, morphine has the same effect
on the rat as on a human being – it sends it to sleep.

- If we wish to demonstrate that prussic acid (whose fumes can kill a human) is an excellent aperitif, let us give it to toads, sheep and hedgehogs.
- Do we want to discourage people from eating parsley? Then let's give it to a parrot, which will probably be found lying stone-dead under its perch next morning.
- Should we wish to rule out penicillin as a therapeutic drug, we have only to give it to a guinea-pig or a hamster, which will be dead in a couple of days. (It seems that the lethal action of penicillin on guinea-pigs and hamsters is indirect, in that it is due to a change in the intestinal bacterial flora. However, this does not alter the value of the observation that the same thing does not occur in other animals, including humans.)
- The insipid field pumpkin makes the horse frisky.
- The amount of opium that can be eaten without discomfort by the hedgehog, the pigeon or the turkey would keep the most hardened addict happy for a fortnight.
- If we wish to convince the consumers of tinned food that botulin poison is harmless, let us give it to the cat, and it will lick its lips. Then let's give it instead to the cat's traditional prey, the mouse, and that animal will die as if struck by lightning.
- The tiniest dose of ammonium acetate – used in humans to produce sweating – will finish a rabbit off (Hadwen 1926).
- Bootleggers have caused blindness in thousands of people by adding methyl alcohol (methylated spirits) to their products. But methyl alcohol has no such effect on the most commonly used laboratory animals.
- It is well known to writers of crime fiction that arsenic is poisonous, whereas sheep and hedgehogs demonstrate that this is not so, since they can consume the substance in large quantities.
- The name antimony derives from the French term 'antimoine', that is, 'anti-monk'. In the Middle Ages, a Benedictine monk, Basilius Valentin (born in Erfurt and an alchemist in a French monastery)

noticed that antimony, when added to the mash for pigs, fattened them. So he added it to the soup of his brother monks – and caused a massacre.

- To show that vitamin C is useless, we can withhold it from the diet of the dog, the rat, the mouse and the hamster. They will continue to thrive because their bodies produce vitamin C of their own accord. However, we must certainly not eliminate it from the diets of guinea-pigs, humans or other primates, or they will die of scurvy.
- A hundred milligrams of scopolamine is harmless to dogs and cats, but 5 milligrams would kill a human.[2]
- Strychnine (like arsenic, a favourite weapon of murderers in crime novels) is harmless to guinea-pigs, chickens and monkeys in amounts capable of causing convulsions in an entire human family.
- Sweet almonds – a basic ingredient of marzipan – are poisonous to the dog, fox and turkey.
- Hemlock, well known through the death of Socrates and deceptively similar in appearance to parsley, is relished by goats, sheep, geese, larks, chaffinches, horses, mice and thrushes.
- Amyl nitrite raises the internal pressure in the eyes of dogs to dangerous levels but reduces pressure in the human eye.
- Chloroform, used successfully for decades in human surgery, is poisonous for dogs, cats and rabbits, causing loss of muscular coordination and convulsions.
- Alpha-methyldopa lowers blood pressure in humans, but does not have the same effect on animals.[3]
- Glyceryl trinitrate (and other organic nitrates) lowers arterial pressure in standard laboratory animals, but does so hardly at all in the case of humans.
- Digitalis was considered dangerous because, tried out on dogs, it raised their blood pressure. Thus the application of this drug, so useful in treating some cardiac patients, was delayed, because of animal testing, for at least a decade.[4]
- Metamizol is used as an analgesic for humans but drives cats into a frenzy and causes excessive salivation in them, similar to that found in animals assumed to be suffering from rabies.
- Phenylbutazone (an anti-inflammatory drug) can be given to dogs (and other animals) in strong and frequent doses, as it is rapidly rendered inactive. However, if given to a human being in comparable doses, it would soon cause cumulative poisoning, since in humans

the drug becomes inactive 100 to 150 times more slowly.

- The antibiotic chloramphenicol damages, sometimes badly, the haematopoietic (blood-producing) bone marrow in humans but in no other animal. In Great Britain alone, it was the cause, between 1964 and 1980, of 42 fatal poisonings (Venning 1983).
- Orotic acid has a beneficial effect on the human liver but causes fatty degeneration in the liver of the rat.
- Chlorpromazine (an anti-psychotic drug) can damage the liver in humans but has not been shown to do so in laboratory animals.
- Atropine is not poisonous for rats, pigeons, goats[5] and many strains of rabbit (those possessing the enzyme atropinesterase), but it is toxic for other strains. It is especially poisonous for humans, by whom it can be used only in extremely small doses (0.25–0.5mg). Moreover, it has a negligible effect on horses, donkeys and monkeys – nowadays such popular laboratory animals because they 'so much resemble the human being'.
- Ergotamine is tolerated by the rabbit but is poisonous to dogs and human beings.
- Methyl fluoracetate is poisonous for mammals. However, the mouse can tolerate doses 40 times stronger than those that would kill a dog. Is the human being going to react as the mouse does, or in the same way as the dog?
- Compounds based on organic phosphate (for instance, the disinfectants Mipaphox, Trichlorphon and Dipterex) seriously damage the nervous systems of humans and other animals. But the mouse can tolerate, without apparent harm, enormous doses (up to 1,500 mg per kg of its body weight) of ToCP (Tri-orto-Cresyl-Phosphate), the commonest of these compounds..
- The neurotransmitter serotonin increases arterial pressure in dogs but reduces it in cats (Davis 1979).
- Isoprenaline (an aerosol anti-asthmatic drug) is tolerated by cats in doses 175 times greater than those considered dangerous for human asthma sufferers (Collins 1969).

To sum up: one has only to know how to choose the 'right' animal species to obtain the desired results. This is a version of science that one can shape like bread dough. The trouble comes when one believes that, with this dough, one can produce healthy bread for human beings. It should not be difficult, even for the lay person, to draw a fundamental conclusion from the preceding examples – if animals differ so much from humans in their reactions, how can one test drugs on them that are intended for humans? The truth is that all living organisms, both animal and plant, are at the same time marvellously like, and marvellously unlike, one another. There is no contradiction here, provided that the matter is considered from various angles.

All living organisms are alike because all of them, from bacteria to humans, have certain chemical compounds in common. It is obvious that this should be so, as everything that lives on this earth is derived from it and cannot, therefore, contain more than the 105 elements that are to be found in the world.

All living organisms are different from one another – the diversity is not only between plants and animals, or between different species of each, but individuals of the same species or race are also different from one another. Differences between individual humans have arisen because of the existence of many enzymatic variations,[6] corresponding to different reactions to certain stimuli. Some examples follow.

- About 10% of individuals of Caucasian type, upon reaching their early twenties, are no longer able to tolerate lactose (milk sugar). They are not ill – they are simply a little different from the others.
- Approximately 65% of people find phenyl-thiourea bitter; the rest find it insipid. Why? There is some difference between them, but we do not know whether it lies in the taste buds or elsewhere in the chain that carries the stimulus from the peripheral receptor organ to the brain to be consciously evaluated.
- According to blood group, the population is divided into groups A, B, AB and O. Why should there be this diversity?
- Most people do not eliminate beta-amino-isobutyric acid in their urine, but about 8% do. Why?
- The red corpuscles contain acid phosphatase, an enzyme that is to be found almost everywhere in the organism. But acid phosphatase is not the same in all individuals, who, because of this diversity, are divided into five groups: A, BA, B, CA and CB.
- Red blood corpuscles also contain two kinds of carbonic anhydrase, designated by the symbols CA-Ia and CA-II. But some people have another type, CA-Ib, and others have yet another, CA-Ic.
- Blood contains at least seventeen kinds of transferrin (the protein that carries iron), but the proportions vary in different individuals.

- Albumin comprises 52% of the serum proteins. But some people have two kinds (distinguishable by their different electro-phoretic mobility): albumin A1 and albumin A2.
- The haptoglobins are proteins that bind haemoglobin released by haemolysis, thus avoiding its elimination in urine. There are six normal haptoglobins present in different proportions in different individuals. However, 'abnormal' haptoglobins also exist, greatly increasing the number of individual variants.
- The cholinesterases are enzymes that hydrolyse the esters of choline. Some people have less than the normal amount of these and can be seriously damaged by certain drugs such as suxamethonium, a muscle relaxant.
- Isonicotinic acid hydrazide (INAH), administered to a tuberculous subject, kills mycobacteria, after which it is inactivated and eliminated. But its inactivation does not occur at the same rate in everyone; in 'slow' inactivators, the drug accumulates in the organism until it poisons it.

If one were to go on writing about individual tolerance to drugs, simply to list all of them would require a whole book. A general idea must suffice here. But even if one were to content oneself with the few differences given above, how many variations could there be in their combinations?

A statistician could do the calculations. It suffices to say that possible variations could be numbered in several billions – which is like saying that, among the four or five billion people who live on earth, probably no two of them are identical.

Vivisectors, however, do not wish to know of any differences between individuals or between species. Let us experiment on one species, and we'll know what will happen with another. Obviously, vivisectors do not express these things so explicitly. They do not even believe them. However, they act as if they do. But in fact they, too, know that the results of experimentation on animals cannot be extrapolated to humans and that, strictly speaking, even the results of experimentation on one group of humans cannot be applied to all other groups. The attitude of the vivisector towards animals is clearly contradictory. This contradiction, which forms a convenient screen for the vivisector, has also been denounced by Professor R. Ryder, an English psychologist, in these words: 'On the scientific level, experimentation is founded on the similarities between animals and man; on the moral plane, it is just on the basis of the differences between them and by claiming animals do not feel pain.'

The vivisector claims that:

1. Animals are fundamentally similar to humans.
2. Animals are fundamentally different from humans.

According, then, to whatever is suitable for a particular thesis, it follows that:

1. Animals are similar to humans when it is convenient to claim that one can obtain knowledge of humans from animals.
2. Animals are different from humans when it is convenient to believe that animals do not suffer, are unaware, do not think, and that, therefore, one can do anything one likes with them – morality simply does not come into the matter.

A question naturally arises here. Are the differences between animal species and individuals of the same species, even at the biochemical level, as great as at the macroscopic level? Not at all – to produce conspicuous effects, minimal biochemical differences are enough.

Let us take as an example sickle-cell anaemia (drepanocytosis).[7] The biochemical anomaly that causes sickle-cell anaemia is small and concerns haemoglobin. In this disease, of 572 amino acids that make up the haemoglobin molecules, only one – glutamic acid – is absent, its place being taken by another, rather similar, amino acid – valine.[8] At first this may not seem very significant. However, this 'insignificant' molecular variation can produce the following effects:

1. Some of the red blood corpuscles in these patients do not have the normal discoid shape – instead, they have a sickle shape.
2. If the partial pressure of oxygen is reduced in the blood, the number of sickle-shaped red blood cells (drepanocytes) increases greatly.[9]
3. The presence of sickle cells in large numbers increases the viscosity (or thickness) of the blood, and, in consequence, the circulation of the blood slows down, resulting in a tendency to acidosis (lowering of the pH). The acidosis favours the destruction of the sickle-shaped red blood corpuscles.
4. The increased viscosity increases the resistance to the blood flow in the vessels. This puts a greater strain on the heart. Moreover,

this increased viscosity favours thromboses (especially micro-thromboses).

5. The sickle-shaped red blood corpuscles are more delicate than normal red corpuscles. As a result, intravascular haemolysis (destruction of red blood corpuscles) occurs, and this phenomenon is favoured by acidosis. The haemoglobin, when released, passes into the urine (haemoglobinuria).

6. Due to their fragility, the sickle-shaped red blood corpuscles can be destroyed in great numbers by the spleen and other reticulo-endothelial organs (the liver, lymph nodes, intestinal wall). Extravascular haemolysis therefore occurs in addition to the intravascular haemolysis already mentioned. The spleen, subjected to more work, becomes enlarged (splenomegaly) and, in due course, becomes fibrous (because of repeated micro-thromboses, caused by the increased viscosity of the blood).

7. The micro-thromboses occur for the same reason in the liver, causing enlargement (hepatomegaly) and, in time, hepatic fibrosis.

8. Similar effects occur in the kidneys, resulting in a diminished capacity to concentrate urea. Haematuria (blood in the urine) is frequently found.

9. The heart suffers as much from micro-thromboses as from the increased work required to keep on pumping the hyper-viscous blood. The strain is shown by a widening of all four chambers of the heart, and this can result in a proportionate valvular insufficiency.

10. Similar changes in the central nervous system result in headaches, mental confusion, hemiplegia (paralysis of one side of the body), aphasia (loss of speech), temporary or permanent blindness and paraesthesia (tingling and burning sensations) of the limbs.

11. Chronic destruction of the red blood corpuscles causes anaemia.

12. Anaemia, if chronic and present from birth, slows down body development.

13. Chronic lack of haemoglobin, and the resulting hypoxia (low oxygenation) of the tissues, causes the skin of the legs to ulcerate (due to slowed blood flow). This can result in phlebitis (inflammation of the veins) or generalized infections (septicaemia).

14. For the same reasons, there is often a characteristic swelling of hands and feet, with the possibility of dystrophy (undernourishment) and of ulceration of the skin.

15. The blood-producing marrow, having to provide an increased

number of blood cells, hypertrophies (enlarges). This happens at the expense of the bone tissue containing the marrow. The bone becomes abnormally spongy and loses minerals, and the outer part becomes thin and liable to fracture. The vertebrae tend to become flattened or biconcave (due to the pressure of the pulpy nucleus). Pain can occur in the vertebral column and in all the bones.

This amazing list of consequences derives from the simple substitution, in one single protein, of a molecule of glutamic acid with a molecule of valine.

Now let us consider the following: the various animal species are distinguished from one another (and from humans) by far more than one difference in a single protein, for all (or nearly all) proteins of one animal species differ from those of every other species. Thus, there are millions of proteins, and when one speaks of protein, one automatically includes the enzymes. Yet most vivisectionists claim that animals all behave alike in response to the same stimulus.

Of all animal experiments, drug testing uses the greatest number of animals – many millions in a year and of many different species. This experimentation is also the most handsomely rewarded, not only with honours and titles, but also with cash. Drug testing is carried out principally: (1) to demonstrate that a particular drug is not toxic; and (2) to demonstrate that the drug works.

Toxicity

That a drug may do no good matters little – at worst it could be considered fraudulent. Besides, it does very often have a certain efficacy in that it pleases a lot of people who are anxious to swallow pills and potions. What one should worry about is that it should not be harmful – that is, not poisonous.[10] For this reason, toxicity tests are carried out on animals, but differences between species, as indicated in the preceding pages, are not sufficiently taken into account.

Still less is another factor taken into account: toxicity tests are almost always carried out on healthy animals, whereas the medicine is given to sick humans. But illness, by its very nature, modifies the metabolism of drugs. For instance, fever renders many drugs more toxic, diseases of the liver diminish the capacity of the liver to neutralize dangerous substances, and many kidney diseases slow down the elimination of foreign substances, such as medicines and their by-products, from the body.

Immunopathies (diseases of the immune system) depress reaction to nearly all allergens. A congenital metabolic disorder can render toxic a substance which is normally harmless. None of these conditions exists in the experimental animal, or, if it does, it exists in different forms and has different consequences.

Efficacy

The majority of human diseases do not afflict any of the more well-known animals. Then how, in an animal, can one demonstrate the efficacy of a drug intended for a particular illness in humans? If the illness does not normally afflict the animal, we have to produce it artificially. This is relatively easy in the case of infectious diseases – but it is an ease fraught with pitfalls. The main pitfall lies in the fact that each animal species reacts differently to the same infection. Here are some examples:

- Monkeys (apart from the baboon) are habitual carriers of the simian B virus, which can cause irritation of the mucosa similar to the harmless cold sore in humans. But the same virus (transmitted via the bite of a monkey or by contamination of a wound by saliva) causes a serious, often fatal, human illness.
- The smallpox and yellow-fever viruses do not affect any known animal.
- The rabbit is more susceptible to bovine *Mycobacterium tuberculosis* than to human *Mycobacterium TB*. The guinea-pig reacts in the opposite fashion. But in neither guinea-pig nor rabbit does tuberculosis have any characteristics in common with the disease in humans.
- *Mycobacterium leprae* (which causes leprosy, or Hansen's disease) is able to flourish in only one other animal species apart from humankind – the armadillo, which it does not, however, infect spontaneously.
- The BCG strain of *Mycobacterium tuberculosis* (the bovine variety) is used, thanks to its relative harmlessness, as a vaccine against tuberculosis. Inoculated into golden hamsters, it causes generalized tuberculosis, with death following in 10–14 months.
- *Treponema pallidum* causes syphilis in human beings only. Inoculated into monkeys, it brings about an acute illness quite different from that caused in humans.

• *Actinomyces bovis* causes a fungal skin disease in cattle, whereas in human beings it provokes an often serious disease of the internal organs. In laboratory animals it can be produced only with difficulty and under particular conditions.[11] The majority of other fungi do not give rise to spontaneous diseases in the most common laboratory animals. In order that they should do so, they must first be inoculated into very sensitive areas like the peritoneum, or into hyporeactive ones like the central nervous sytem. *Nocardia, Blastomyces dermatitidis, Blastomyces braziliensis, Coccidioides immitis* (very pathogenic for man), *Histoplasma capsulatum, Cryptococcus neoformans, Geotrichum candidum, Sporotrichum schenkii* and the *Mucoralaes* all behave in this way.

• No animal is known to be susceptible to chromoblastomycosis, which is caused in humans by various species of fungi, among them *Hormodendrum compactum* and *Phialifora verrucosa*.

• Disturbing differences are to be found in the reactions of many mammals to parasitic metazoa. And what is one to make of the way in which these parasites choose a different host for each phase of their development? One example is *Dicrocoelium dendriticum*, the liver fluke, which lives in its adult stage in the intestine of a herbivore, perhaps cattle, and occasionally that of a human. It is common in Eastern Europe and Russia, less so in Africa, Asia and North and South America. The adult worm is 5–15 mm long and 1.5–2.5 mm wide. The eggs pass out with excrement into water and are taken in by a snail, in which, after two metamorphoses, they become larvae (cercariae). The cercariae are deposited on grass, where they are eaten by an ant. In the ant they undergo further development, to become metacercariae. The ant is then eaten, with grass, by a herbivore (again, occasionally by a human). In the herbivore (or in a human) it becomes an adult worm, and the cycle begins again. So *Dicrocoelium* specializes, in its adult form, in living in certain kinds of hosts, while its larvae are adapted to living in other kinds. *Dicrocoelium* thus shows that one animal host is not of comparative value with another, since each animal is host to only one stage of the parasite's development.

• Even fleas are able to distinguish differences between animals. The human flea is *Pulex irritans*, but the cat flea is *Ctenocephalides felis*, and the dog flea is *Ctenocephalides canis*. These last two bite people only occasionally, and then *faute de mieux*.

So far we have considered infectious and parasitic diseases. By inoculating pathogenic agents into animals, the researcher tries to obtain a model of human disease. And so, having created in an animal an infectious disease that is not the same as that in a human being, the experimenter starts trying out drugs to cure it. At this point, the errors multiply in geometric progression.

The error of studying artificially created disease is compounded by treating it with a drug that, in all probability, will be metabolized in the animal in a way that is different from its metabolism in humans. Indeed, it is different to the point that the animal could die before the infection kills it, as occurs with penicillin in guinea-pigs.[12] It is different also because drugs used to combat the infection function not alone but in synergy with the natural defences. For example, the majority of antibiotics not only stop the multiplication of certain bacteria, but also stimulate phagocytosis – that is, the capacity of certain cells (white blood cells (leucocytes) and macrophages, which are found in blood, lymph and connective tissue) to attack and destroy micro-organisms by ingesting them.

However, the capacity for natural defence varies according to species. An indication of this is given by the different proportions in which differing phagocytic cells are to be found in the blood and tissue liquids of different animals, and in the lack of certain cells in some species. For instance, fish and other animals still lower down the evolutionary scale do not possess polymorphonuclear leucocytes, and their defence against infection is undertaken by mononuclear cells analogous with monocytes and macrophages in mammals.

In the struggle against infection, antibodies attach to the leucocytes. There are natural antibodies, which are inherited, and acquired antibodies, which are formed as a result of exposure to micro-organisms or aggressive substances called antigens. The presence of acquired antibodies is shown by a hyperactivity that serves to eliminate or neutralize the foreign substance. Beyond certain limits, however, allergies arise in the form of genuine illnesses, such as bronchial asthma, hay fever, allergic rhinitis and conjunctivitis, nettle rash, erythema nodosum (inflamed swelling of the skin on the legs) and eczemas. In animals, too, contact with antigens causes, as in humans, the development of antibodies. It is even suspected that, in humans, allergic reactions to certain drugs may, in some cases, be due to eating the meat of animals treated with the same drugs. This may explain, for example, an allergic reaction to penicillin in those individuals who claim never to have been treated with penicillin. However, it is not possible, even with the most ingenious methods, to reproduce allergies in animals similar to those that afflict so many people. Why is this? Are not different physical reactions always an expression of more profound biochemical, nervous and psychological differences?

Let us turn now from infections that do not attack animals (or do so in a way different from their behaviour in man) and from immunological phenomena that, in animals, are never similar to allergic illnesses found in man, and focus on another area in which animals differ from man: the collagenopathies.

These comprise a wide range of manifestations, from rare but fatal diseases (such as systemic lupus erythematosus or Wegener's granuloma) to common diseases that affect the quality of life more than its length, such as arteriosclerosis and osteoarthritis. Old age itself is seen by some as a collagen disease, because collagenous tissue in elderly people is always seen to be 'altered' when compared with that of the young.

Collagenous tissue exists virtually everywhere in the organism – it is like the warp in a cloth without which it would be impossible to weave the weft. When it changes, the functional capacity of all the organs and tissues is impaired. If it were possible to avoid the ageing of collagen, we would be able (it is said) to prolong life. So experimental models have to be found.

But how can one construct, for example, the model for arterio-sclerosis? With dogs? – dogs fed on a high-cholesterol diet or on a diet deficient in cholesterol? on a high-lipid diet or a lipid-deficient one? dogs overfed to the point of making the liver burst or underfed to the point of starvation? made into alcoholics or poisoned with tobacco? stuffed with vitamins or deprived of vitamins? And what should one then expect? An arteriosclerotic dog? But such dogs already exist – just let a dog grow old and it will get arteriosclerosis.[13]

Those who believe they can understand arteriosclerosis in humans through animal experiments will feel rather annoyed when they examine the biochemical characteristics of the disease. They look for those factors that cause or favour its development; they blame diet so obstinately that it makes one think of some hypochondriac seeking revenge on a gourmet: 'Eat, eat, and soon you will regret it!' However, when they try to disentangle the confusion by experimenting on animals they will discover the following facts:

1. The main culprit in arteriosclerosis – cholesterol – is esterified principally by oleic and stearic acids in man but mainly by arachidic acid in rats.

2. A diet containing few calories is good for humans but worsens natural arteriosclerosis in rabbits.

3. The atheromas (degenerative fatty deposits on the walls of the arteries) in humans contain high levels of cholesterol and other lipids, whereas the naturally occurring atheromas in the cat and the rat contain relatively low levels. The foam-like cells (cells of the cytoplasm laden with lipids) of human atheromas are 'altered' smooth muscle cells, but the foam-like cells of the guinea-pig's atheromas are monocytes (a kind of white blood cell) that have phagocytized (or ingested) the lipids. Additionally, the atheromas of the dog consist of smooth muscle cells, without (or almost without) lipids. Moreover, the canine arterial wall underlying the atheroma is practically unaltered, while it is severely altered in man. And the small arteries are the first to be affected in the dog, whereas in humans the aorta is the first to suffer. (Incipient atheromas have even been found in seven-year-old children.)

4. A hyperlipidic diet does not cause arteriosclerosis in the rat, but it does so in man, in whom it progresses to arterial hypertension. In the rat, lipids given in excess accumulate mostly in the liver; in humans this happens mainly in the arteries.

5. Compounds that attract particular attention in the study of arteriosclerosis are the lipoproteins, but in humans the VLDLs (very low-density lipids) and the LDLs (low-density lipids) prevail. It is easy to understand how the above-mentioned (and other) differences would frustrate anyone seeking the explanation for human arteriosclerosis in the arteries of animals.

6. Animals also show us up as idiots when, by using certain drugs to treat arteriosclerosis, we seek to prolong our own lives by shortening theirs – and for no good reason. One of these drugs is clofibrate, which in some animals, apart from being completely harmless, reduces the amount of cholesterol in the blood by about 20% – a resounding success, which has enabled the drug to be sold by the ton. But in humans, while very slightly reducing the cholesterol level, it also increases the incidence of heart attacks and damages the liver, the gall bladder and the bile duct, sometimes with fatal results.[14]

Then there is osteoarthritis. Why do joints become so grotesquely and painfully deformed? Vivisectionists attempt to mimic human deformities using dogs, sheep, cats and pigs by beating joints with hammers, injecting them with irritants, dislocating them and irradiating them.[15] It is incomprehensible that the vivisectors should have such a poor understanding of biology, such a crude conception of life, that they do not realize that these tortures cause nothing more than fractures, haemorrhages, thromboses, contusions and inflammation – everything, indeed, except an acceptable model of human osteoarthritis, which is the local manifestation of a generalized collagen disorder.

Nevertheless, the torture continues. And why? Because the number of animals used in the study of arthritis is in direct proportion to the number of drugs labelled anti-arthritic – and to the profits deriving from them. They are many, and they sell very well, but their manufacturers are still not satisfied.

Apoplexy, or stroke, is a disease that threatens humans with sudden death or with severe motor and sensory impairment, especially in old age. This is the consequence of a rupture or blocking (thrombosis or embolism) of a cerebral artery, with consequent ischaemia (lack of blood) and necrosis (tissue death) in that part of the brain. Researchers believe that it is possible to reproduce in an animal an event that in man is spontaneous and usually sudden in occurrence; they do this by surgically closing arteries in the animal's brain. But in this case, too, the results differ profoundly between animal and human – not only in the artificial way by which the change is produced in the animal, but also because the systems of blood vessels in the brains of animals and humans are very different. In most animal species (particularly in the dog), the brain's vascular system has many more collateral and anastomotic (connecting) arteries than are found in humans – that is, neighbouring blood vessels connect with each other, enabling them to take on the work of blocked or injured vessels. Thus the closing of a cerebral artery in animals is compensated for by the collateral circulation far more effectively than it is in humans. Moreover, in many animals embolisms (closures) of cerebral arteries are rendered almost impossible because of the *rete mirabilis arteriosa*, a system of tiny vessels that filter blood-clotting agents and different foreign bodies, solid, liquid and gaseous.

What, then, is the anatomical situation with the primates – that is, those apes that 'so much resemble us'? Here, too, the facts invalidate the comparison – which, from a biological standpoint, is already far too crude. We refer to an anatomical and therefore unambiguous difference: in primates there is an extensive anastomotic (naturally connecting) system of lenticular-striated (lens-shaped, striped) cell nuclei between the lateral and median arteries, which represents the autonomic (or involuntary) nervous system. *There is nothing resembling this in man.*

Notes

1. We use the terms 'vivisection' and 'animal experimentation' synonymously. Vivisectors do not like the term 'vivisection' because of its emotive connotations. On the other hand, it is the historical term handed down to us by the architect of vivisection, Claude Bernard, and even today dictionaries use it as a synonym for 'animal experimentation'. Its Latin roots are *vivi* (living) and *secare* (to cut). *The American Encyclopaedia*: 'Vivisection: Any form of animal experimentation, whether it involves dissection or not.' *Merriam-Webster Dictionary*: 'Broadly, any form of animal experimentation, especially if considered to cause distress to the subject.' *Der Grosse Duden – Fremdworterbuch*: 'Vivisektion: Eingriff am lebenden Tier (zu wissenschaftlischen Zwecken).' (Operation on a living animal for scientific purposes.') Blakiston's *New Gold Medical Dictionary*: 'Vivisectionist: he who practises and defends animal experimentation.' *Petit Larousse*: 'Vivisection ... Opération pratiquée sur un animal vivant, pour l'étude de phénomènes physiologiques.' (Operation practised on a living animal in order to study physiological phenomena.') *Diccionario Manual de la Lengua Espanola*: 'Viviseccion: Disseccion de los animales vivos.' (Dissection of living animals.) *Coalition mondiale contre l'expérimentation sur l'homme et sur l'animal* (Worldwide Coalition against Experimentation on Man and Animal): 'Vivisection: toute opération ou intervention non thérapeutique pour le sujet concerné pratiquée à titre d'expérience sur l'être vivant, homme ou animal, qui porte atteinte à son équilibre physiologique et à l'intégrité de son organisme.' (Any operation or interventionary procedure which is non-therapeutic for the subject concerned, practised for experimentation on a living being, man or animal, which harms the physiological stability and integrity of the organism.')

2. In judging the toxicity of a drug, one must always take account of the relationship between the dose of the drug and the body weight of the animal. Thus the cat (average weight 4 kg) will tolerate, without any evident ill effects, 100 mg of scopolamine, which is equivalent to 25 mg per kg body weight. This is equivalent to a dose of approximately 1,800 mg in a human (average weight 70 kg), which is 360 times the dose human beings can actually tolerate.

3. In arterial hypertension, an important role is played by noradrenalin, a hormone from the adrenal gland which is formed from DOPA, following the sequence DOPA – dopamine – noradrenalin. The alpha-methyldopa blocks this sequence by acting competitively upon the enzyme L-aminodecarboxyase, which prevents the production of the noradrenalin and instead produces

methylnoradrenalin, which is less active than noradrenalin. This mechanism is clearly demonstrated *in vitro*. But when it is transferred to animal experimentation the alpha-methyldopa appears to be ineffective. Dr John J. Oates, however, ignored these results and proceeded directly to clinical trials in humans. Thus was rescued a useful drug for the cure of human hypertension.

4. Digitalis was used for the first time as a diuretic by William Withering in 1785. The observed diuretic effect was, in fact, a side-effect of the improvement in heart function after the drug had been taken. (The effect on atrial fibrillation – heart flutter – was demonstrated by MacKenzie in 1905.) 'We used to believe, as a result of experiments on animals, that digitalis raised blood pressure. Now we know that this is sheer nonsense. Digitalis is a very useful drug in certain cases in which the blood pressure is very high' (Burnett 1942).

5. Goats can graze, without damage to themselves, on the plant *Atropa belladonna*, a common member of the *Solanaceae* family. Its leaves and roots contain hyoscyamine, which, under certain conditions, becomes the isomer atropine.

6. Enzymes are catalysts of organic reactions. They act in extremely small amounts and, while not taking part in them, bring about reactions that would otherwise occur only very slowly or as the result of using large amounts of energy. For example, a common reaction in all animal cells is the oxidation of glucose. To oxidize this glucose outside the organism, a raised temperature or the use of energising oxidants is required, whereas in the cell (thanks to the enzymes) the oxidation of glucose takes place at a low temperature (in mammals at about 37° C, in cold-blooded animals as low as 4–5° C). Enzymes are proteins and become inactive at a temperature of about 60° C. All organic reactions are controlled, guided, accelerated or retarded and coordinated by enzymes.

7. Drepanocytosis (from the Greek *threpanon* = sickle, Latin *cyto* = cell – in English, sickle-cell anaemia) is a hereditary blood disease occurring mostly in sub-tropical Africa but also in Greece, Italy, Turkey, India and the Arabian peninsula. In the American continent, about 9% of the population of African origin are affected.

8. The resemblance between glutamic acid (A) and valine (B) is evident from their respective formulae:

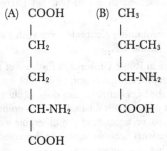

$$\text{(A)} \quad \begin{array}{c} COOH \\ | \\ CH_2 \\ | \\ CH_2 \\ | \\ CH\text{-}NH_2 \\ | \\ COOH \end{array} \qquad \text{(B)} \quad \begin{array}{c} CH_3 \\ | \\ CH\text{-}CH_3 \\ | \\ CH\text{-}NH_2 \\ | \\ COOH \end{array}$$

9. Partial pressure of oxygen in arterial blood is about 100 mm Hg; in

venous blood it is about 40 mm Hg. The tendency to assume the sickle shape of the red blood cells occurs in patients with sickle-cell anaemia when the partial pressure of oxygen in the blood is reduced to about 45mm Hg – which is the situation pertaining even in normal circumstances in the venous blood. The partial pressure of oxygen in the blood can be lowered by breathing in a rarified atmosphere (such as in high mountains), by violent and prolonged physical exertion or as a result of lung diseases that depress the oxygenating function of respiration.

10. 'Toxic/poisonous' may be defined as anything that shortens life or impairs its quality. The concept of toxicity is, however, closely linked with quantity/dose. Many drugs, such as digitalis, strophanthin and atropine, are not toxic: on the contrary, they are beneficial, provided that they are used in very small doses. Oxygen, for example, when breathed in at a pressure of more than 20 atmospheres, kills in a few minutes. Natural foods (proteins, carbo-hydrates, fats) consumed in too great amounts lead to obesity and so are 'toxic' (obesity does, in fact, shorten life). Apart from dosage, toxicity is linked to time. For example, hydrocyanic acid (prussic acid) kills in a few seconds, arsenic in a few hours or months (according to dosage) and tobacco smoke in years. Thus we distinguish between acute toxicity and chronic toxicity.

11. The term 'laboratory animal' is a vague one. Any animal is potentially a laboratory animal, but the selection criteria are cost and convenience rather than scientific validity. If it were to be shown scientifically that the animal whose biochemical reactions were most similar to those of humans was the rhinoceros, would this become the most frequently used laboratory animal? In fact, the commonest animals chosen – for motives far from scientific – are those that are cheap, easy to use, not too heavy to move around, and unlikely to bite.

12. Statement by Sir Howard Florey, joint Nobel Prize winner with Fleming and Chain for the discovery of penicillin: 'It was by good luck that in the initial toxicity tests we used mice, because if we had used guinea-pigs we would have concluded that penicillin is toxic' (Florey 1953).

13. In fact, a true arteriosclerosis is rare in old dogs, and in any case it does not resemble that in man. The only animal that gets anywhere near the human arteriosclerotic condition is the pig. Arteriosclerotic lesions similar to those in humans have been observed in an 80-year-old parrot and a 106-year-old cockatoo.

14. In Italy, drugs containing clofibrate were withdrawn from sale in 1979, but it is still available in the UK.

15. During a lecture at Rome University's Institute of Clinical Orthopaedics and Traumatology, an eminent professor, in front of an audience of horrified students, bent in two the backs of some live dogs to illustrate how the vertebral column snaps when it passes a certain angle. At this point, our indignation may be aroused less, perhaps, on account of the miserable victims of such dreadful sadism than by the students, who were, indeed, horrified but who did nothing whatsoever to stop what was happening.

4. Cancer: a case in point

All vertebrates are susceptible to cancer.[1] To use them as natural experimental models, it would be necessary to maintain, in a natural environment, relays of dogs or several hundred cats or guinea-pigs or mice or rabbits, and wait until the disease developed spontaneously. So what do researchers do? They create a model, inoculating the chosen animal with cancer or causing the disease by various other means, chemical or physical. However, the animal takes its revenge by luring us into a labyrinth of divergent reactions. The same cancer-causing substance gives different results, not only from species to species, but also from one strain to another of the same species. The situation is made more complicated, particularly in some animals, by the spontaneous development of cancer. For example, after 25 months, 20% to 60% of mice (depending on the strain) spontaneously fall ill with cancer.

- In the mouse strain C3HF, urethane gives rise to hepatomas, tumours of the reticuloendothelium and lung tumours (Liebelt, Liebelt and Lane 1954). In the mouse strain C57B1, urethane causes lymphomas of the thymus (Doell and Carnes 1962); in humans, urethane is a good remedy in the treatment of leukaemias.
- Dimethyl-benzo-alpha-anthracene causes lymphomas in mice of the 'Swiss' strain (Pietra, Rappaport and Shubik 1961), but it produces bronchial adenomas (benign tumours) in the 'Strong A' strain of mice (Flaks 1965) and liver tumours in other mouse strains (but only in the males).
- Benzol and arsenic, both carcinogenic in humans, are not so in any of the rodent species commonly used in experimental laboratories.
- 2-naphthyl-amine is carcinogenic for the human bladder but does not cause any type of cancer in mice.
- Benzidine causes bladder cancer in humans; in the mouse it causes a neuroma of the acoustic nerve and intestinal and liver cancer.

- Carbon tetrachloride (CCl_4) produces liver cancer in the mouse, while in the rat it causes cirrhosis of the liver.
- 4-amino-diphenyl causes bladder cancer in humans; in the mouse it produces mammary cancer.
- Chloroform $(CHCl_3)$[2] gives rise to liver cancer in the females of various strains of mice, but not in the males.
- Isonicotine hydrazine (INH), or isoniazid, causes adenomas (benign) and bronchial adenocarcinomas (malignant) in different strains of mice (Biancifiori and Severi 1966), but nothing similar has been observed in humans, despite the enormous use made of this drug in the treatment of tuberculosis over the last four decades.

A particularly tragic example is that of diethylstilboestrol, or stilboestrol (a synthetic oestrogen, commercially known as Cyren or Oestremon), which was first produced in 1938. In 1944 it was announced that this drug checked cancer of the prostate (*The Times*, 24 November). It was subsequently used to prevent miscarriages, resulting in a new chapter in 'negative medical science': transplacental cancer. The drug, when given to pregnant women, causes vaginal or uterine cancer in 95% of their female offspring at anything between 7 and 27 years of age (Greenwald et al. 1971; Herbst and Scully 1970; Herbst, Ulfeloer and Poskanzer 1971). Suspicions were aroused only about twenty years after the drug was put on the market. On 10 October 1965, Senator Edward Kennedy denounced stilboestrol before the US Senate as being responsible for vaginal cancer in 220 daughters of women treated with the drug during pregnancy. By 1977, the number of cases had increased to 333, and in the following years about fifty new cases a year were diagnosed. More recently, further cause for alarm has emerged: in women treated with stilboestrol there has been an increase in cases of breast cancer and benign tumours of the uterus; in male children there has been an increase in the incidence of testicular cancer; in children of both sexes there has been an increase (up to two-fold) in psychiatric disorders (*Medical Tribune* (Italian edn), 7 April 1984). There has also been concern about the effects that food containing the flesh of animals treated with stilboestrol (to promote growth) could have on pregnant women and their children. It is, of course, superfluous to add that diethylstilboestrol/stilboestrol was, before being marketed, 'conscientiously' tested on animals.[3]

To be of any use to humans, research needs safer methods – not an endless accumulation of uncoordinated notions, but a few coherent data. However, 'endless accumulation' provides work for a vast number of those people who make a living out of such a situation, while research on 'a few coherent data' requires only a few, well-chosen, competent and honest people – but then, everyone knows how much easier it is to produce quantity than quality.

There is a whiff of humour in the comment of the English surgeon and medical historian M. Beddow Bayly: 'Research has become big business ... there are clearly a lot of people who regard it as just another way of making a living.' An old story? Not at all – here is the proof, in 1981, from *Corriere Medico*: 'A bye-law issued by Parliament should be enough for 1,500 doctors to be enrolled automatically as researchers. They only have to prove that they have spent a certain period of time at their place of work to be eligible for entrée to a university career, if *only* in the post of researcher' (emphasis added).

If it is true that artificially produced diseases teach us nothing and are misleading, it is also true that, by making careful observation of spontaneously occurring diseases in animals, doctors can realize two objectives:

1. They can widen their own field of experience and improve their ability to observe life in its many forms.
2. They can learn, not only from contrasts but also from analogies.

However, for the doctor to approach the animal in a scientific spirit, it would be necessary to build a bridge between two branches of science – veterinary and human medicine – which are related to each other but which, at the same time, are kept separate by a wall of arrogance and a sense of superiority on the part of doctors. One day I treated a dog whose owner knew me only by sight. 'But,' he said hesitantly when I had finished, 'are you a vet?' 'No,' I replied, 'I'm a medical doctor.' The poor man blushed and asked my pardon again and again. How many people are there who think they have insulted a 'real doctor' by mistaking him for a vet?

The experimenter seeks homogeneous models, but the search remains fruitless, as animals obstinately insist on retaining their individuality. However, the experimenter is not easily discouraged. 'So, they're different are they? Well, we shall make them the same!'

A first step is to breed the purest possible strain. This is achieved through breeding selectively among consanguineous animals. Siblings and their offspring are mated for up to twenty generations. The laboratory strains obtained in this way are designated by names or by symbols: CBA mice, L292 mice, C57B1, C57Br and C3H/He mice, Himalayan rabbits, London-Black rats, Spague-Dawley rats, etc.

But that is still not enough. Animals homogenized from birth cannot remain so after a few weeks of living in different environments and eating different food. So we give them a standard diet. The pharmaceutical and food industries, ever alert to new business opportunities, jump at this market, and soon there is standardized tinned food available for mice, rats, guinea-pigs and the rest. In this way researchers expect to obtain a standard mouse, a standard guinea-pig, and so on – animals that will react in a standard way to various stimuli (drugs, physical agents, etc.).

And what do they achieve? Abnormal, not to say sick, animals are the result, no longer obeying the natural impulses[4] by which the organism would normally regulate its selection of food. They no longer react 'normally' to drugs or to physical or microbiological stimuli. For their part, the various experimental stimuli alter the mechanisms – appetite and thirst, metabolism and excretion – that regulate the ingestion and digestion of food. So the researcher even loses control over the amount of standardized food the animal eats, absorbs and utilizes. In other words, the diet is no longer standard.

In addition, unforeseen circumstances can sometimes, as though playing a joke on us, contribute to upsetting the uniform nature of the animal model. An example of this is the trouble and confusion caused to researchers by C3H-A mice and C3H-AfB mice some years ago. The two strains became ill in almost 100% of cases in laboratories in the USA, with spontaneously occurring liver and breast cancer, whereas this phenomenon very rarely occurred in Australian laboratories. At last the puzzle was thought to have been solved: cedar-wood sawdust was used as litter in the cages in American laboratories, while black pine-wood sawdust was used in Australian laboratories (Sabine, Horton and Wicks 1973).

How, then, can one draw an analogy between these animals and humans, who eat everything, touch everything and are exposed to everything?

However, that is not all. There is also the question of the intestinal flora. These comprise a great number of micro-organisms and it is therefore quite improbable that two individuals, even of the same species, would be identical in this respect. The intestinal flora exert a great influence on an animal's metabolism – indeed, animals (including humans) cannot live without them, as they produce substances that are indispensable for life (such as vitamins of the B group and vitamin K).[5]

So having a standard diet is not enough to produce a standard animal – one needs axenic[6] animals, that is, animals lacking extraneous organisms such as viruses, bacteria, fungi and unicellular or multicellular parasites. One can obtain such strains, but how is it done?

First, animals can be brought into the world by Caesarean section to avoid infection by contact with the mother's vagina. Second, the newborn animal can be put into an aseptic environment[7] and fed with aseptic food.

Thus, the axenic newborn animal grows and becomes an axenic adult (an axenic mouse, rat, guinea-pig, etc.). Deprived of symbiosis with micro-organisms (a phenomenon that was born with the species millions of years ago and conditioned its development); forced to live in steel cages; almost completely isolated from sound; rendered incapable of searching for and choosing their own food in order to balance their own diet day by day; living in artificial light and not having to cope with changes in temperature – what sort of animals can these be? What 'model' do they represent if they no longer represent even their own kind? And what connection do the results obtained from them have with human pathological conditions? The answer to that is 'axenic' results, as sterile as the animals themselves.

Biochemical and anatomical changes can be observed in axenic animals. However, a doubt creeps in here: are these changes due solely to axenicity or to the unnatural environment in which these animals are obliged to live? In this situation, as in others, research seems to create more problems than it solves; it is an activity that spreads out like a fan, with each attempt to deal with one question raising a thousand others.

The anomalies of the axenic animal are anatomical, biochemical and immunological.

The most obvious anatomical anomalies are: substantial enlargement of the caecum (part of the large intestine) (Gordon and Wostmann 1960; Griesemer and Gibson 1963); thinning of the intestinal lamina propria (sheath-like covering); hypoplasia (incomplete development) of the reticuloendothelium (cell-network lining), intestinal lymphatic tissue, mesenteric lymph nodes, thymus, suprarenal glands and spleen.

The biochemical anomalies are: an increase in alkaline phosphatase and a decrease in acid phosphatase in the caecal mucosa (Jervis and Biggers 1964); in the small intestine, a rapid absorption of thymine (found in DNA), glucose, 3-methyl glucose (Gordon 1960) and d-xylose; in the blood, raised cholesterol (Aldridge and Johnson 1977; Ames et al. 1973); in the urine, an absence of urobilinogen (Gustaffson and Lanke 1960), phenyl sulphate and indoxyl sulphate; and in the liver, increased levels of iron and copper. Moreover, the lifespan of the bile acids and the activity of the thyroid gland are reduced, and there is a slowing down of the basal metabolic rate (Desplaces et al. 1963).

The main immunological anomaly of the axenic animal is a considerable diminution in the amount of serum gamma globulins (Gustaffson and Laurell 1960; Sell 1964).

These examples all point towards the concept that is fundamental to all scientific anti-vivisectionism: *the results of animal experimentation cannot be extrapolated to humans.* This statement runs the risk of becoming a monotonous aphorism. But truth can only repeat itself and is, therefore, monotonous, whereas it is incomprehensible that the thousand different and contradictory 'truths' that have accrued through vivisectionist research should not be enough to arouse in the minds of its practitioners the suspicion that, in the elementary but telling phrase: 'There must be something wrong.'

Medical doctors and researchers of every country have expressed, in differing words, the same anti-vivisectionist opinion with regard to cancer:

All our knowledge about the structure, symptoms, diagnosis and treatment of cancer in man comes from those who tackled the problem with clinical methods. This knowledge owes nothing to animal experiments (Professor Hastings Gilford, *The Lancet*, 15 July 1933).

Some researchers believe that, by animal experiments, they will discover the origin of cancer. As an oncologist, I cannot agree. The quantity of carcinogenic substances that it would be necessary to feed to or inject into the experimental animal is so great that it should be obvious that cancer produced in that way is simply the effect of poisoning (Professor Heinz Oeser, *Quick*, March 1979).

Although it is true that the alteration of the genes is the same in all the species, at the same time the alteration of the functions of the genes is different between animal and man. It has been found, for example, that saccharine, which 'facilitates' the development of tumours in the mouse, does not do so in man; and so the panic which had been created burst like a bubble (Renato Dulbecco, Nobel prizewinner 1975, quoted in article by Viviana Kasan, *Corriere della Sera*, 23 June 1981).

Animal experiments do not explain anything concerning the carcinogenic effect of a chemical substance. Research on the chemical cancer risk for man, by experimentation on animals, remains at the stage of hypothesis. We can only trust experiments carried out on man. Experiments carried out on higher mammals should be considered as pure speculation (Professor N. Bruce of California, 1985).

Cancers produced in animals by means of implants or injections can in no way, as regards either cause or effect, be compared with those in man (Professor Purchase, UK).

Leukaemias

There are about twenty common varieties of leukaemia (cancer of the blood), and some rare ones that are difficult to classify. They can be broadly divided into two main groups: myeloid leukaemias and lymphoid leukaemias. The myeloid leukaemias are diseases of the cells produced by the bone marrow (polymorphonuclear leucocytes, red blood cells and megacarocytes), while the lymphoid leukaemias attack the cells produced by the lymphatic organs (essentially, the lymph nodes, spleen and lymphatic tissue of the intestines). How do leukaemias stand in relation to humans and to animals?

1. In humans, leukaemias occur at all ages.
2. Leukaemia has not been found in any known animal species.

However, as one might expect, vivisectors have taken care to even things out by testing on animals a disease typical of humans but absent in all other animals. Experiments in grafting bone marrow and 'spongy' bone[8] are carried out on animals and boasted about as modern experimental therapy. But this method is neither modern, nor does it owe anything to animal experiments: it has been used for various purposes for more than fifty years, particularly in cases of extensive bone damage.

Oncogenic and non-oncogenic viruses

Even the viruses considered – it is not known how accurately – to be 'oncogenic' (tumour-forming) display the differences of the various animal species among themselves and in relation to humans.

Our first question must be: are there actually, in nature, 'oncogenic viruses'? There was a period during the 1970s when it was believed (and hoped) that cancer might be a viral illness. Although there was not then, just as there is not today, a drug capable of 'killing' viruses, we nevertheless lived in the hopes of finding one. With every disease, it is important to discover its cause, since that gives us, if not certainty, then at least a basic hope that we are aiming at a concrete objective. But all hopes have been dashed, and today the viral hypothesis has been almost universally abandoned.

In humans, only one virus is considered oncogenic: the Epstein-Barr virus, which causes Burkitt's lymphoma. But what is puzzling is that this lymphoma occurs only in Africa, whereas in Europe the same virus causes a benign and fairly common disease, infectious mononucleosis (glandular fever). However, the question also arises: is Burkitt's lymphoma really a cancer? And, amid all this uncertainty, what have animals to tell us?

As usual, they provide us with information that seems to have been shaped on purpose to confuse our ideas. Here are the well-proved facts: all the most familiar animals are subject to the illness of cancer. But how much of this is attributable to viruses? We have no reliable data, and the few we have are experimental, with all the attendant incertitudes of experimental methods – that is, methods created artificially by humans.

Using viruses, we have succeeded in producing a melanoma in *Drosophila melanogaster*, the fruit-fly; we have induced virally a sort of cancer in a variety of frog, *Rana pipiens*, and in another amphibian, this time of the newt family (urodele), *Trichurus viridescens*; a lymphasarcoma has been produced by viral means in a variety of African toad, *Xenopus laevis*; we have virally caused, in the chicken, one of the best-known experimental sarcomas, Rous sarcoma; and, with the herpes virus, mammary tumours have been obtained in the arboreal ape, *Oustiti*.

To state that these results, as far as humankind is concerned, are disconcerting would be an understatement. Worse still, it is not clear that the viruses used to induce 'cancer' in fruit-flies, frogs, chickens and toads are, in fact, responsible for the disease and are not merely opportunists, taking advantage of the depression brought about (by experimental manipulation) in the animal tissues to instal themselves effortlessly therein. But there is more: it is not at all certain that we are dealing with true cancers, given that they have been shown to lack one of the fundamental characteristics of cancer and one that makes it a malignant disease: the capacity to spread metastatically (that is, from one part of the body to another).

The importance of early diagnosis: a myth?

There are sound reasons for doubting that early diagnosis is the main tool in preventing metastases (which make the prognosis so unfavourable – or is this only a myth?) What is one hundred per cent true is that a missed early diagnosis gives the doctor a chance to reproach the unfortunate patient – 'Why didn't you come to me earlier?' – thus forcing him or her to share the responsibility for this most unwelcome of diseases.

But let us come to the crucial point: is early diagnosis a major contributor to, not to say the main condition for, successful therapy? Let us look beyond the type of therapy used for specific cancers and specific organs (chemotherapy, radiotherapy, cobalt therapy, gamma radiation, surgery), to the issue of whether an early diagnosis really makes the final outcome of cancer any less grave. The various therapies available are, indeed, often followed by a favourable survival time, but the question remains: is that outcome really due to the therapy, or is it only *apparently* so? Early diagnosis has indisputably meant that the reckoning of the survival time starts earlier, thus making it appear longer – a view endorsed by eminent scientists.

Dr John A. McDougall states that 'in most cases [of cancer] early detection does not increase a person's lifespan but only the length of time a person is aware he or she has cancer' (*Vegetarian Times*, September 1986). One might ask the question: is it, therefore, psychologically positive to be aware of such a dramatic situation?

Dr Linus Pauling (twice a Nobel Prize winner) is even more disparaging: 'Everyone should know that most cancer research is largely a fraud and that the major cancer research organisations are derelict in their duties to the people who support them' (Page 1996).

Notes

1. In trout, a frequently occurring kind of cancer is caused by aflatoxin, the toxin of *Apergillus flavus*, a fungus that attacks some foodstuffs, such as peanuts. Aflatoxin seems to be responsible for the frequent occurrence of liver cancer in the populations of Africa and South-East Asia.

2. Chloroform was used for the first time as a narcotic by the English physician John Snow (1813–58), in Edinburgh in 1848.

3. As if drugs were not enough, even cosmetics can cause cancer. According to Bruce N. Ames of the University of California, about 90% of all hair dyes with oxidizing properties are carcinogenic (Colin Tudge, *World Medicine*, Autumn 1975).

4. An egg-laying hen eats grit. The cat, an exclusively carnivorous animal, sometimes seeks out grass to eat. They are obeying orders from their myriad cells.

5. All vitamins and provitamins (e.g. carotene) are synthesized by plants and micro-organisms. Animals eat the plants, thus taking in vitamins and storing them in their tissues. These tissues (the flesh) become a source of vitamins for carnivores and omnivores. Apart from their food, animals obtain some vitamins (of the B group and vitamin K) from their intestinal flora.

6. Axenic is derived from the Greek *a* = without + *xenos* = foreign, extraneous. The synonyms SPF (specific pathogen free), disease-free and gnotobiotic are also used. The possibility of obtaining axenic animals was postulated by Louis Pasteur in 1885. Nuttal and Therfelder obtained the first axenic guineapig in 1885, but the animal lived for only thirteen days. At the beginning of 1928, major studies on axenic animals were carried out at the LOBUND Institute (Laboratory of Bacteriology, University of Notre-Dame) in the USA. During their life in the womb, animals are, in general, axenic, because the placenta does not allow most of the micro-organisms that may be present in the mother's blood to pass through to them. There are, however, exceptions: in the cat, the protozoon *Toxoplasma gondii* ((Griesemer 1963); in the dog, the larval stage of the helminth *Toxacara canis*; in humans, *Treponema pallidum* (the organism that causes syphilis), and among viruses, the German measles virus, the cytomegaloviruses and herpes zoster, which causes chicken pox and shingles.

7. Aseptic environments are obtained by the use of 'isolation units' (sterilizable containers of metal and plastic, such as Reynier's isolation unit, Gustafsson's, Trexler's and Lev's isolation units). These apparatuses are provided with filters for air decontamination, windows for observation of the interior, and apertures with sterile rubber gloves fixed to them for the arms and hands of the operators.

8. The spongy part of the bone contains the haemopoietic marrow (which produces most of the blood cells). For that reason, bone marrow and spongy-bone transplants are roughly comparable.

5. Birth defects: can animal experimentation help to avoid them?

Nowadays, almost everyone has heard of chromosomes, and many even have a vague idea of how they work and the strange tricks they can play. People are more knowledgeable than before, but, as always happens in human affairs, as soon as a spiteful Fate puts a weight on one side of the scales, she immediately puts an equal or heavier weight on the other.

In the past, malformations were caused mainly by genetic factors, which tended to disappear automatically, since in most cases those affected were unfit for survival and reproduction. Today, environmental[1] causes predominate – produced by the very section of humanity that proclaims itself to be working 'for the benefit of mankind'. The list of teratogenic drugs, or those suspected of being so, grows day by day.[2] Likewise, the list grows of newborn babies with their hands growing out of their shoulders; with their spinal cords exposed; or with their hearts functioning like traffic lights gone crazy, letting the blood flow in the most bizarre directions.

But luckily there are animals to fall back on – let's test a drug on an animal, and we will then discover its teratogenicity and so rule it out. This sounds simple and convincing. Unfortunately, however, things are not quite so simple. We test on animals and subsequently discover that we have been fooled – that is what happened with thalidomide.[3] Not one of the laboratory animals treated with thalidomide exhibited, in the tests required by drug-licensing laws, the neurotoxicity that this drug produced in substantial numbers of humans. Thus, in 1957, Chemie-Grunenthal triumphantly put it on the market, claiming that it was 'a harmless tranquillizer particularly suitable for the pregnant woman'.[4]

In 1961, in order not to be left behind in the race for profits, British Distillers, *after repeated and rigorous animal tests*, distributed the drug, changing its name to Distaval. As a result, thousands of phocomelic children[5] were born around the world (Lenz 1966). However, thanks to Professor S. T. Aygün, virologist at the University of Ankara, who prevented the drug from being imported into his country, Turkey was not affected. The USA was also spared because Dr Kelsey, of the Federal Food and Drug Administration (FDA), held that the drug had not been sufficiently tested on animals, and that some studies had indicated the possibility that thalidomide might cause, *in humans*, peripheral neuropathy (nerve disease) (Sjöstrom and Nilsson 1972).

Moreover, it should not be thought that Contergan is the only teratogenic drug that has been concocted by the pharmaceutical industry for the benefit of humanity. Drugs found to be teratogenic in humans include all the alkylating compounds (Schardein 1976): busulfan, chlorambucil, cyclophosphamide, nitrogen mustards; many antibiotics effective against cancer, such as actinomycin C, actinomycin D, chromomycin A3, daunomycin, azastreptonigrin, puromycin, sarcomycin and streptonegrin; the anti-metabolic aminopterin (used to counteract folic acid); methotrexate (Milunsky, Graef and Gaynor 1968); 6-azauridin (Vojta and Jirasek 1966); many general anaesthetics (Corbett et al. 1974; Pharaoh et al. 1977); codeine, probably aspirin (Nelson and Forfar 1971; Richards 1972); and the anti-emetic meclozine.

Most anticonvulsants are teratogenic (Elsehove and Van Eck 1971; Loughnan, Gold and Vance 1973; Meadow 1968; Millar and Nevin 1973; Niswander and Wertelecki 1973; Smithells 1976; South 1972; Speidel and Meadow 1972), specifically phenobarbitone, phenytoin (Barry and Danks 1974; Fedrick 1973; Starrveld-Zimmermann et al. 1975), primidone, troxidone, pheneturide, methylphenobarbitone, ethosuximide and trimethadione.

The anticoagulants of the coumarin group, such as warfarin (Pettifor and Benson 1975; Warkany 1975), are also considered teratogenic. Under suspicion are the tranquillizers derived from phenothiazine, lithium carbonate (Schou et al. 1973), meprobamate (Milkovich and Van Den Berg 1974), diazepam (Safra and Oakley 1975; Saxen and Saxen 1975) and the anti-malarial drugs quinine and quinidine (Sullivan 1979) (also used as abortifacients). Slightly teratogenic are the glycaemia-reducing drugs of the sulphonylurea group.

Progestogen hormones are teratogenic, especially ethisterone and norethisterone (which masculinize female foetuses), as are the oestrogen–progestogen compounds, which can cause not only masculinization but also more serious malformations such as anencephaly and spina bifida. Contraceptive drugs taken at the beginning of pregnancy (when a woman is still unaware that she is pregnant) can cause heart defects and malformations of the spinal column, trachea, oesophagus, kidneys and joints (Harlap, Prywes and Davies 1975; Heinonen et al. 1977; Janerisch, Piper and Glebatis 1974; Nora and Nora 1975). The thyroid-inhibiting drugs thiourea and carbimazole, the perchlorates and the iodides can, when taken by the mother, enlarge the thyroid gland of the foetus to the point of causing asphyxia at birth by compression of the trachea (McCarrol et al. 1976; Milham and Elledge 1972; Schardein 1976).

The above list of drugs that are capable of harming the foetus teaches us three things:

1. All these drugs, before being approved for the market, were conscientiously tested on animals. As a consequence of the 'optimal' results obtained, they were offered to the public – or, to put it more realistically, were imposed on the public, by intensive advertising.
2. According to the toxicologists Dr Klaus and Dr Lwoff (*Münchener Medizinsche Wochenschrift* 1976), 61% of malformations in newborn children and 88% of all stillbirths are attributable to the damage caused by drugs taken by the mother during pregnancy.
3. Finally, it is worth considering the following statistics: in the Federal Republic of Germany during the 1950s, out of every 100,000 babies born three were malformed – by 1967, that number had increased to 500 out of 100,000. In the USA, in 1977, 200,000 malformed

TABLE 5.1 Teratogenic effect of some substances in different species

Substance	Teratogenic	Non-teratogenic
Aspirin	Rat, mouse, guinea-pig, monkey, cat, dog	Human
Azathioprine	Rabbit	Rat
Caffeine	Rat, mouse	Rabbit
Cortisone	Mouse, Rabbit	Human
Insulin	Chicken, rabbit, mouse	Human
Triamcinolone	Mouse	Human

babies were born. No spontaneously occurring biological phenomenon has ever had such a dramatic upsurge.

How, then, does one establish whether a drug is teratogenic or not for humans? Animals will always give a misleading answer, or a correct one only by fortunate coincidence. This concept is illustrated in Table 5.1. The table does not need a commentary, but it does raise the question of what one should do to find out whether a drug is teratogenic for human beings. Obviously, a drug cannot be tested for teratogenicity by the same clinical methods used for other drug effects.

There is one method, however, and that is the use of human cell cultures – not those of other animal species, since the methodological error of vivisection would thus be transferred from the whole animal to its cells.

To return to the case of thalidomide: this is a subject of constant debate between vivisectionists and anti-vivisectionists. Curiously, however, the same event is used to support two opposing theses. Anti-vivisectionists hold the view that the thalidomide catastrophe came about *despite the experiments that were done on animals*. Vivisectionists, on the other hand, maintain that it came about because *not enough animal experiments were done*. According to vivisectionists, therefore, it is not enough to experiment on a few species of animal – experiments should be done on very large numbers of species.

However, if drugs generally were tried on a large number of animal species, sooner or later all those drugs would be discarded. We would, for example, discard aspirin, which is teratogenic for mice, rats, guinea-pigs and some apes, and toxic and teratogenic for cats. Caffeine, which is teratogenic for rats and mice, would also be discarded, as would cortisone, which is teratogenic for mice and rabbits. Thus we would need only to extend the number of species on which we experimented for any particular drug to find at least one species in which damage would be produced.

Just for the sake of argument, let us accept the hypothesis that, if it had been tested beforehand on pregnant animals, thalidomide would not have been put on the market. But then, it is equally valid to hypothesize that, in order not to spend time and money on research, industry could have adopted our thesis: What occurs in some animal species does not necessarily occur in humans. We could go on hypothesizing endlessly, so let us return to concrete facts.

It is an incontestable fact that thalidomide not only causes foetal malformations in humans and some other species, but also causes damage to nervous and other systems. In the nervous system it causes a multiple neuritis, sometimes irreversibly, which manifests itself in restlessness, general discomfort, limb tremors and weakness, dizziness, memory loss, cramps, muscular aches, disordered reflexes, loss of co-ordination, ataxia (loss of movement control) and lack of balance. In the most severe cases there is partial paralysis as well as arterial hypotension, itching, haemorrhages and constipation. *Nothing like this was demonstrated by animal experimentation before the drug was licensed.* And we cannot assume that experimentation was not performed extensively, as required by German law.

However, teratogenicity is the most well-known side-effect of thalidomide. Vivisectionists, in that sad and solemn tone of one who recognizes his or her own faults, say: 'We are guilty of negligence for not having tested pregnant animals. If we had done so, disaster would have been averted.' Certain facts could make this appear to be correct. *After* the disaster, thalidomide caused malformations in the newborn of some animal species: one rabbit species out of 150 (the white New Zealand rabbit), the ape *Macacarius philippinensis,* the mouse, the rat and the dog. So the argument at first sight appears to hold water. However:

1. If it is true that, before the catastrophe, the drug had not been tested on pregnant animals, how do they explain the fact that it was advertised as 'harmless for the pregnant woman and the foetus'? On what did they base such a reassuring statement?

2. Why did they not also mention the animal species in which such malformations did not occur?

3. What dosages of thalidomide were administered by those who wanted to demonstrate, at any price, that experiments on pregnant animals could have prevented the catastrophe? There is one example only, quoted in a book by expert witnesses at the Alsdorf[6] trial: mice were given half a gram of thalidomide per kilo of body weight – a dose nearly 600 times greater than that usually given to humans. Any so-called harmless substance becomes toxic when introduced invasively, into whatever organism, in such ludicrously enormous and completely unrealistic doses.

Thalidomide is still on the market. It appears to be effective in the treatment of systemic lupus erythematosus and severe forms of acne.

How were these unexpected effects identified? It cannot have been by animal experimentation, since animals do not suffer from either condition.

Notes

1. An environmental cause is one that transforms a genetically normal embryo into a malformed one, either by altering the chromosomal sequence or by disorganizing its phenotypical (physical with environmental) development. 'Natural' environmental causes are certain bacterial infections, such as syphilis, or viral ones, such as German measles and herpes zoster.

2. 'Teratogenic' is from the Greek *teras*, monster + *genes*, born.

3. Thalidomide – N-phthalimidoglutarimide. Its best-known brand name is Contergan, but there are about forty more, of varying dominance in different countries: Distaval, Kevadon, Neurosedin, Softenon, Talimol, Calmorex, Imidalab, Imidan, Imidene, Pantosediv, Sedimide, Sedoval, and so on.

4. *Time*, 23 February 1962: 'Contergan ... after three years' testing on animals, has been declared harmless, so that it may be sold freely, without medical prescription, in the Federal Republic of Germany.' The campaign to promote Contergan was launched on 1 October 1957. The winning slogan was 'As Harmless as a Lump of Sugar'. Thousands of letters to doctors and pharmacists and repeated guarantees of the product's absolute safety suddenly made it a huge commercial success. Soon, four out of every ten people wanting tranquillizers turned to Contergan (*Corriere della Sera*, 18 April 1987).

5. Phocomelia is a congenital deformity characterized by short, stubby hands or feet attached close to the body (from Greek *phoke*, seal, + *melos*, limb).

6. The trial of Chemie-Grünenthal, the manufacturers of Contergan (thalidomide), opened in the small town of Alsdorf on 12 April 1967 with the indictment by the magistrate Josef Havertz. It was, after the Nuremberg trials, the longest trial ever held in Europe. Twelve hundred witnesses gave evidence. On 18 December 1970, with the consent of the prosecution counsel, the court, under Dr Dietz, decided to close the trial. The parties reached an out-of-court settlement whereby Chemie-Grünenthal paid DM114 million to the thalidomide victims. The Swedish company Astra, which had marketed the drug, paid an agreed sum of 68 million crowns (at the time, $13,850,000) to 100 babies on 12 March 1963. Distillers, the company that produced thalidomide under licence in England, withdrew the drug on 27 November 1961.

6. Medical advances and public disillusion

Everything that has a beginning returns to its point of departure, even ideas and the greater and lesser schools of thought. New ideas disturb the establishment, so newcomers are attacked in order to preserve the old beliefs. People pretend not to realize that an old system of philosophy is dead long before the decline of its practical applications. Ideas have a natural impetus at the beginning of each new cycle, but become fixed and stale.

Over thirty years ago Professor Pierre Lépine[1] stated: 'We are sorcerers' apprentices, especially in the scientific field. We boast of discoveries which poison us. I think that future generations will need much time and commitment to get rid of the disastrous consequences of our research' (Lépine 1967). But extricating ourselves from this quagmire is prevented by those who have a vested interest. Is this a scientific, an intellectual or a spiritual interest? No – it is, of course, a banking interest.

All (or nearly all) new ideas start out as idealistic and spiritual but end up as concrete and materialistic. It is difficult to doubt the idealistic spirit of the Renaissance anatomists Vesalius and Malpighi, but the narrow-minded materialism of their heirs is also not in doubt. Scientific research has become a money-eating machine, like the pinball machines of Las Vegas.

In many countries, national research councils hand out enormous sums of public money to this or that university clique for 'serious research'. This sounds fine, but how is 'serious' to be defined? Its definition is a matter of precedent: make sure you don't rock the boat; honour the 'great achievements' of your predecessors; don't tread on certain toes.

These indispensable conditions for 'serious' research are impeccably fulfilled by those repositories of a musty and debased pseudo-culture, the universities. There is no point in an independent-minded researcher, an unbiased scholar or a philosopher without financial resources attempting to publish an innovative book, or a 'non-aligned' sociologist asking for a grant of a few cents. There is plenty of money available, and it is generously awarded – but always to the same people.

According to an ancient but still relevant observation, lay people have a capacity (wrongly considered instinctive, but actually an accumulation of subliminal messages expressed through ideas and in defensive behaviour) to perceive impending danger and to put up adequate defences against it. This can be seen in the way that people are turning away from orthodox medicine in favour of such therapies as acupuncture, homoeopathy, chiropractic, osteopathy, hypnotherapy, hydrotherapy, reflexology, iridology, herbalism, dieting and 'touch' healing.

The media have become aware of this phenomenon and are trying to evaluate it statistically. The following extract is from *Il Medico d'Italia* of 3 January 1985.[2] 'France: 46% of French people have already turned to alternative medicine. Homoeopathy is the most popular (37%), followed by acupuncture (21%), herbalism (10%), and hydrotherapy (7%). The reasons given for preferring "alternative" medicine include: its more natural character (51%); "orthodox medicine is useless" (40%); and "more attention is given to the patient", that is to say, the holistic approach (21%).' Even more significant was the response of the people of Milan: questioned by CENSIS poll, 58% replied, 'because alternative therapies are less damaging' (ibid.).

Another straw in the wind, but symptomatic of the trend, is this quotation from the *Corriere Medico* of 20 November 1984: 'Anita Davies, homoeopath, interviewed about the rate of cure among her patients, described homeopathy as "just like orthodox medicine – a third get cured, a third derive some benefit from it, a third remain unchanged by the treatment".'

In Taiwan, the population of about 17 million turn in almost equal proportions to Western medicine, to Chinese medicine and to shamanistic ritual. A group of American doctors examined the results statistically and found that there were the same numbers of successes and failures in all three groups.

As can be seen, the situation is hardly encouraging for orthodox medicine. I should like, however, to clarify a possible misunderstanding: it is not my intention to attach undue significance to this item of news, nor, for that matter, to use it to support my thesis. It should be taken only as the ringing of an alarm bell, signalling a shift that is taking place in the minds and choices of ordinary people. The phenomenon exists and is, moreover, observable by all. Today, herbalists' shops are springing up like mushrooms in every quarter of every city.[3] Not only that, but many chemists' shops are no longer filling their shelves with medicines 'obtainable only on prescription' – they are, instead, making room for ceramic jars of dried herbs and powdered roots. And people buy them, preferring to spend their money on packets of herbs mixed on the spot, perhaps to the herbalist's own recipe, rather than to take home beautifully packaged tablets and suppositories guaranteed by 'science'.

One should remember that alternative medicine is gaining ground purely on its own merits, taking no part in the publicity campaigns that invade our homes and consciousnesses with the dogmas of orthodox science. Moreover, the phenomenon is not only spreading amongst the public: many doctors also now send their patients to herbalists or recommend acupuncture, osteopathy or chiropractic. Other doctors actually practise these disciplines themselves – and with success, they claim. One might ask cynically: 'You mean financial success, don't you?' But that is not so – or rather, not always so. On the other hand, to investigate too closely the economic aspect of certain decisions taken by many science-oriented doctors would do no good to those who, disdaining 'quack' remedies, hold faithfully to the dogmas promulgated by the universities and quoted in the leaflets that accompany their medicines.

It should be made clear at this point that I am not attempting to promote alternative medicine, nor do I wish to compare it with orthodox medicine. I am, however, interested in the incontrovertible historical fact that a large part of the population is turning its back on orthodox medicine, and I regard this as a very significant (some would say worrying) phenomenon, which we should neither keep quiet about nor unduly emphasize. One thing at any rate is certain: public opinion is divided, and that throws suspicion on the credibility of orthodox medicine – which is, as our adversaries themselves proclaim, essentially vivisectionist medicine.

How do the 'scientists' react to these challenges? They do so in the way most convenient – that is, by refusing to admit any reasoning other than their own. Being unable to deny the evidence – of surgical operations rendered painless to patients by acupuncture or hypnosis, peptic ulcers cured by reflexology, and so on – they adopt a superior attitude to such 'absurdities', finally accepting them only condescendingly, after subjecting them to their own scheme of thinking and after providing mechanistic explanations (which often result in a clumsy attempt to plagiarize what they have failed to understand). For example, attempts to explain the analgesic effect of acupuncture resulted in the 'gate theory',[4] while hypnosis is explained in chemical terms, attributing to the brain the capacity to produce, at will, a type of morphine. Any explanation will do, provided it upholds the mechanistic outlook that forms the basis of the tottering scientistic edifice that claims to explain everything.

But time runs on, and the anxieties of our adversaries increase correspondingly. They begin to realize that something is changing. Dismayed and worried, they see that their supposedly impregnable fortress is made of cardboard. News is leaked – perhaps unintentionally – by certain newspapers. One such item of news comes from a strictly orthodox medical journal: 'One should remember that the so-called anti-vivisectionists are becoming so much a mass movement in the United States that they constitute a real political problem' (*Tempo Medico*, 4, 15 March 1987).[5] I confess that I fail to understand why anti-vivisectionists should be referred to as 'so-called'. A harmless adjective used disparagingly? The arrogance of someone convinced that they know better? It hardly matters. What is interesting – and amusing – is the incredulity of the writer of the article in stating that anti-vivisectionism is becoming 'a mass movement', even in the USA – a country in the vanguard of the most obtuse faith in 'science'. It is the reaction of someone ambling happily along who suddenly gets a kick up the backside.

Another event further dismayed many incredulous 'benefactors of humanity'. This time, politicians had been moved to legislate against vivisection:

Provincial law of 8 July 1986, No 16, Province of Bolzano, approved by the Provincial Council (vom Landtag genehmigt) on 21 July 1986.

REGULATIONS FOR THE PROTECTION OF ANIMALS

The Provincial Council has approved
and the President of the Provincial Council has promulgated
the following law:

Article 1

Decree

The autonomous province of Bolzano has decreed that, within its own sphere of competence, animals of all kinds should be protected.

Article 7 (c) states: 'The same penalty *applies to anyone who carries out experiments on living animals, even if solely for scientific or teaching purposes'* [emphasis added].

Notes

1. Professor Pierre Lépine, member of the French Academy of Sciences and National Academy of Medicine, was at the time director of the Department of Bacteriology at the Pasteur Institute in Paris.

2. The news was later given further coverage by the *Corriere Medico* of 6 February 1985. The original source was an investigation undertaken by the Globalpress Agency.

3. In Milan alone, from 1986 to 1988, the number of herbalists rose from 166 to 221, an increase of 33% (*Il Medico d'Italia*, 3 (January): 3).

4. Gate theory: this states that pain goes through a 'gateway' to reach consciousness. But if another pain is added (caused artificially by acupuncture), the gap left by the open 'gate' lets only one pain go through. (This is a very simplified form of a much more fanciful and confused theory.)

5. The article, strictly toeing the vivisectionist line as behoves a periodical that owes its existence to pharmaceutical advertising, expounds the ideas that Carl Cohen of the Philosophy Faculty of Michigan University published in the *New England Journal of Medicine*. The philosopher's opening words are: 'What are the rights of animals? None.' The rest is easy to imagine – and it is also easy to imagine that we are living back in the Middle Ages.

7. Biomedical research: aiming at an 'exact' science

No objective science is absolutely exact, not even the so-called 'exact' sciences. Only mathematics is exact. But mathematics is a subjective science, a creation of the mind to bring order to the perception of objectivity.

In science, only that which can be verified or reproduced at will counts as exact, the data being sufficiently constant in time and space. Something is exact, then, only within the limits of time and space. It is, in fact, 'exact' to say that the acceleration of gravity ('g') has the value of 980.665 cm/sec^2, but it is necessary to specify 'on the earth's surface, at latitude 41°'.[1] Were the measurement to be taken on the moon or on Jupiter, it would no longer have that value. It is also 'exact' to say that mercury solidifies at -39°C and that water freezes at 0°C, and it is true that ethyl ether boils at 37°C. But these are true only at the atmospheric pressure on the earth's surface.

Of all the sciences, biology is the least exact. However, we should try to achieve the greatest possible precision in it. If we cannot reach the unattainable mathematical ideal, we can at least approach the relative precision of physics, chemistry and mechanics. If we do not attempt to bring biology on to this straight and narrow path, its progress will continue to be uncertain and contradictory – white today, black tomorrow; high today, low tomorrow; useful today, harmful tomorrow. For example, in Italy, spaghetti was long considered lethal for a diabetic. By the 1980s diabetics, to stay healthy, were being advised to obtain 60% of their calories from a plateful of spaghetti (Simpson et al. 1981).

It is a commonplace that to live long you must eat sparingly and keep slim. But according to Professor Keys of the Epidemiology Department of the University of Minnesota, thirty years of statistics have demonstrated that fat people live longer than thin ones (*Il Giorno*, 16 October 1988, p. 5). The food industry is close to collapse one day and enjoying a boom the next, depending on the ups and downs of prevailing views on cholesterol. And there is plenty more conflicting advice: 'People with stomach problems should eat boiled rice.' 'Boiled rice causes heartburn.' 'To combat arteriosclerosis, eat a low-fat diet.' 'To combat arteriosclerosis, eat a well-balanced diet.' 'Butter is deadly for your arteries.' 'Butter may be used without fear but, as with all fats, should be used sparingly.'[2]

Why all these contradictions? Because:

a) There is something wrong with the methodology.
b) There is something wrong with research targets.
c) There is something wrong with the organization of research.

Methods

Research using animals turns its back on the human being and creates a tangle of ideas that, in turn, require further research. It is like a problem factory in which thousands of researchers, working with a useless machine, are clever enough at thinking up solutions but not intelligent enough to grasp the fact that they are going round in circles. That may seem an arrogant judgement on the intellect of people who are considered by the general public to be 'intelligent' by definition. But ours is not an isolated view. Here is what Dr James Watson,[3] Nobel Prizewinner for Medicine and Physiology, said in 1962: 'Contrary to the commonly held view, which is supported by the newspapers and by scientists' own mothers, many scientists are not merely mentally ill-equipped but are also just plain stupid' (quoted in Coleman 1977).

As regards those particular scientists who are vivisectors, here is the resigned comment of Dr James Burnet, director of *Medical Times*: 'We should leave the vivisector to wander like a lost soul in the desert which he himself has created' (Burnet 1954). On the contrary, we can no longer afford to let this situation continue. The desert is becoming too expensive, costing us both money and public health, which in turn costs us more money. It is also a waste of brains, because those who 'wander in the desert' include some talented people.

Targets

Researchers have clear ideas about their targets: career and money. To make a career one has to become known, and to become known one has to publish papers. But the daily avalanche of publications disappears into archives that no one consults. Progress needs little, but lucid, information. Sensational results, soon denied, hamper science. Progress needs the cautious, small steps of a few honest researchers. Nevertheless, publications are valued like fruit and vegetables, according to weight, in both the European and North American systems of appointments to research posts.

The second aim of researchers is to earn money, and this comes from public funds (national research councils) and the pharmaceutical industry, the latter requiring, though not at its own instigation, that animal experiments be performed. In the nineteenth century, politicians – bowing to orthodox science – passed laws prescribing tests on animals and the way they should be done.

One of the main prescribed methods in the testing of a drug for toxicity is the evaluation of the LD-50 (50% lethal dose) test. The experimenter ordains that the greater the number of animals used, the more reproducible the experiment. As with all reasoning based on statistics, this seems impeccable. However, using the same substance, the LD-50 test finding in one laboratory can, in the same animal species, be up to four times lower than in another laboratory and up to ten times lower than that indicated by the manufacturer.[4]

At this point, the nimble-minded experimenter may object that it is

TABLE 7.1 LD-50 testing of methyl-fluoracetate

Species	mg/kg (*per os*)[5]
Dog	0.15
Cat	0.3
Guinea-pig	0.4
Rat	3.5
Rabbit	4.0
Mouse	6.7
Monkey	11.0

Source: Mitruka, Rawnsley and Vadehra 1976.

not enough to experiment on only one animal species. Many species must be used, and the more numerous the species, the more reliable the results. This seems like cast-iron logic. However, Table 7.1 shows what happens with, for example, methyl-fluoracetate.

The monkey is 73 times, and the mouse 44 times, more resistant than the dog. Moreover, let us note what happens in 'related' animals, such as guinea-pigs, mice, rats and rabbits (all rodents): the guinea-pig is ten times more susceptible than the rabbit, its near relative, which shares the same feeding habits and so on, whereas the cat shows a result similar to the guinea-pig's, with which it has no close links. Clearly, we cannot rely on results that prove erratic in members of closely related species, let alone results extrapolated from one species to another.

But that is not all. The LD-50 test demonstrates the capacity to kill one or more species of animal but tells us nothing about the non-lethal damage it can cause. It seems that death is often not the worst of evils, as witness the victims of clioquinol,[6] a drug which, when used to cure diarrhoea, caused subacute myelo-optic neuropathy (SMON) in about 30,000 Japanese and other people around the world – obviously not without first having been conscientiously tested on animals according to the procedures prescribed by law, including the LD-50 test. Nevertheless, bureaucracy and the law still impose the LD-50 test 'to safeguard public health'. Are the researchers unaware of all this? Of course not, but industry provides their salaries, and politicians do not want to rock the boat. After all, industry does not pay researchers only.

However, apart from researchers in industry and in the universities, there are still honest doctors. Why don't they protest? First of all, because they are not well enough informed; then, because it is dangerous. They could end up like the ex-president of Chile, Dr Salvador Allende, and his doctor colleagues, who plotted to eliminate all useless drugs (in effect, all but a few dozen) from the pharmacopoeia. But the conspiracy was discovered, the doctors were eliminated, and the drugs remained.[7]

Few people, even doctors, know about SMON. Let us, then, allow Mrs Tamako Suzuki to describe it. At the age of forty-two, she preferred to commit suicide rather than endure the pain and disability caused by Oxyquinol (a brand name of clioquinol).

Testament of Tamako Suzuki

Oxyquinol – ban it! It should be outlawed! Nobody, not even my nurse, can understand how much I have suffered these last three years, during which my body has been racked with pain. I am aware of becoming weaker day by day. I have pain in my back, my chest, my shoulders, my head, my eyes, my nose, my teeth, my ears. I cannot describe the pain I suffer, all over my body – only those who have been afflicted by SMON can know what the pains are like.

Organization

Proper biomedical research would require a network of connections and the rapid exchange of information. As the most fruitful research is that based on the observation of spontaneously occurring phenomena in man, it would be necessary – at least for those illnesses that throw up the greatest problems – to transmit the observations made at any one place as rapidly as possible to a central collecting point, equipped to analyse the data electronically. (We can surely now achieve this via computers – see Chapter 14.)

Notes

1. At the poles, the acceleration of gravity has the value of about $9.83\text{m}/\text{sec}^2$, while at the equator, the value is $7.79\ \text{m}/\text{sec}^2$.

2. The harmfulness of butter (and other animal fats) was thought to be due to its lack of polyunsaturated fatty acids – which, for decades, were promoted as a defence against cholesterol, the arch-enemy of our arteries. This is an absurd exaggeration (though a welcome one to the producers of soya, maize, sunflower-seed oils and the like). Indeed, if one were to lend credence to the statistics, butter itself would be considered the defender of our arteries. In the UK, between 1930 and 1960, its consumption went down considerably in favour of vegetable oils, but during the same period there was a *sixfold* increase in mortality due to heart attacks. (From an article by Emanuele Djalmi Vitali in *Recenti Progressi in Medicina*, 73 (4), also published in *L'Espresso*, 26 (5 July 1987): 193.)

3. The zoologist James Watson, in collaboration with Francis Crick, identified the double helix structure of DNA (deoxyribonucleic acid) and became director of the Cold Spring Harbour Laboratory of Quantitative Biology at Long Island, New York, in 1968.

4. The LD-50 is the dose capable of killing 50% of the animals to which it is administered. The LD-50 test was used for the first time in 1927 by the industrial pharmacologist J. W. Trevan (see Trevan 1927) to determine the safety doses of digitalis and insulin.

5. *Per os* = Latin 'by mouth'.

6. Clioquinol (iodochlorhydroxyquin) – brand names: Oxyquinol, Vioform, Nioform – was produced by Ciba-Geigy in Basle, by its subsidiary in Japan and by the Japanese firms Takeda and Takabe Seijaku. Clioquinol was a constituent of various medicines: Enterovioform, Intestopan and Sterosan. At the time of the first lawsuit, in Tokyo in 1976, 186 drugs containing clioquinol were in circulation. SMON is the result of poisoning of the spinal cord and the optic nerve, leading to paralysis of the lower limbs and serious disturbances of vision, even blindness. The most serious cases are fatal. In Japan, in 1977, 3,268 people demanded compensation for damages sustained following the use of clioquinol, but it is estimated that between 20,000 and 30,000 had been poisoned (*The Lancet*, editorial, 1977). In August 1978, a Tokyo court ordered the Japanese subsidiary of Ciba-Geigy to pay compensation of 3,250 million yen (about $12 million) to 133 victims who had sued the manufacturers. According to the deposition of Dr Olle Hansson of Göteborg, Sweden, who was called as an expert witness by the Tokyo tribunal, clioquinol had been tested on cats (Hansson 1979). Cases of clioquinol poisoning have also been recorded in Austria, Germany, Norway, the USA and Great Britain. The connection between SMON and the consumption of clioquinol was discovered by Tsubaki and colleagues in 1971.

7. The violence with which the doctors who had collaborated with Dr Allende were persecuted is described by Albert Jonsen and his colleagues in 'Doctors in politics: a lesson from Chile', *New England Journal of Medicine*, 291 (1974): 471–2. The military coup struck its victims down on 11 September 1973. The names of the thirteen doctors who were assassinated are: Jorge Klein, Jorge Avila, Enrique Paris, Hector Garay, Bruno Garcia, Juan Carlos Cerda, Hernan Jenriquez, Jean Guichard, Arturo Hillers, Absalon Wegner, Claudio Tognola, Jorge Jordan Domic and Eduardo González (Jonathan Kandell, *New York Times*, 8 April 1974, p. 3).

8. The argument for vivisection

The vivisectors keep as their trump card a malicious question with which they hope to drive their opponents into a corner: 'Will you not admit that, in the past at least, vivisection has helped bring about progress in medicine?' The key to its answer lies in the phrase 'in the past at least'. We see the past through the prism of what came after, whereas we cannot do that with the present. In short, we have the eternal ambiguity of *post hoc, ergo propter hoc* ('following this, therefore because of this'), or justification by hindsight.

Vivisectors can quote hundreds of ideas concerning human medicine obtained with the help of animal experiments. They omit, however, to tell us that these ideas proved useful in understanding human illness only *after* they had been confirmed by clinical observation: at the time of their formulation, they told us nothing useful whatsoever about humans.

In that case, how were they used? They were either held to be valid *a priori*, as an act of faith, or they had to await confirmation by clinical observation. This 'trust-through-faith' attitude is the cause of the worst catastrophes of modern medicine, and, even when it is not provoking headline-making disasters, it misleads and, moreover, delays progress. It would be interesting to know how many of the ideas contained in textbooks of human physiology are in fact valid for human beings, and how many experiments are being done now (especially on the nervous system) that follow the tortuous path of tests performed on cats, dogs, mice and monkeys.

Have there never been animal experiments that have been worthwhile for the study of humans? Of course there have been, but they became significant for humans only in retrospect, years later, even many years later. As Professor Herbert Hensel, physiologist at the University of Marburg, has said: 'The probability of experimental results in animals and in man coinciding is so slight that it is comparable to a game of chance. Nevertheless, on this improbable game of roulette we bet millions of dollars each year' (quoted in Hartinger 1995).

One example of this upside-down thinking is that of the discovery of the Rh (rhesus) antigen (or Rh factor).[1] There are those who claim that, without the studies on monkeys and rabbits performed by Land-steiner and Wiener (1940; 1941), the Rh factor would never have been discovered, and many people would have died as a result of blood transfusions. This claim is false: if the studies on monkeys and rabbits had not been undertaken, the Rh factor, *which had already been discovered in humans*, would simply have been given a different name.

It was, in fact, about a year before the publication of the results from Landsteiner and Wiener that Levine and Stetson described a new agglutinin (that is, an antibody that causes the red blood corpuscles to adhere together) in the serum of a woman called Mary Seno, who had given birth to a stillborn child (Levine and Stetson 1939). After the delivery, the woman received a blood transfusion from her husband (who had group O blood – that of a 'universal' donor), and this caused a serious allergic reaction. Levine and Stetson thought (correctly) that the husband's blood contained a 'factor' that was responsible for the reaction, and they thus discovered the new agglutinin, but did not give it a name. Had they done so, the name or symbol of their choice, *and not the Rh symbol*, would have been used (Sacchi, Reali and Rossi 1975).

A short time afterwards (not before), Landsteiner and Wiener dis-covered that, by injecting the blood from the *Macacus rhesus* monkey into the abdominal cavity of the rabbit, an agglutinin appeared in the latter's blood – similar (but not identical) to that found by Levine and Stetson – to which they then gave the symbol 'Rh'.[2]

Sensational news serves splendidly to fill newspapers and to feed hopes, only to be followed by disillusion worse than the original evil. Such news serves also to prop up the pharmaceutical industry. The direction taken by medicine in recent decades follows a typical pattern: sensational headlines followed by the suppression of subsequent denials.

Optimists continue to claim that, despite its ups and downs, medical science has made progress. That, too, is a *post hoc, ergo propter hoc* piece of reasoning. One thing is certain: without vivisection, there would have been other methods. These are precisely those that are being proposed ever more insistently today. We call them 'scientific' methods; others call them 'alternative'. (See Chapter 3 for further discussion of these terms.) And without vivisection, would we have had better medicine, fewer thalidomide-type tragedies, fewer victims of diethylstilboestrol and clioquinol?

We are not attempting here to guess whether there would have been more or fewer such tragedies. But history shows beyond any doubt that tragedies took place, and that is enough for us. Moreover, they are still happening – and will go on happening unless experimenters face up to making a decisive change of direction. Mistakes are unavoidable in all the sciences, but it is unacceptable that medicine should arrogate to itself the role played, in the past, by cholera, the plague, tuberculosis, syphilis and smallpox.

Among the evils caused by vivisection there is one whose consequences are difficult to calculate: the delay in the development of scientific (that is, non-animal) experimental methods.

Perhaps we have now reached that turning-point.

Notes

1. About 85% of people are Rh-positive – that is, their red blood cells contain the Rh factor (or Rh antigen). If the blood of an Rh-positive person is transfused to an Rh-negative person, Rh antibodies form in the blood of the latter. If the same individual then receives another transfusion of Rh-positive blood, a potentially fatal reaction occurs.

2. Because the agglutinin obtainable from a rabbit immunized with the blood of a *Macacus rhesus* monkey is not identical to that of a human and can give misleading results, anti-Rh serum, for use in blood typing, is taken from volunteer Rh-negative blood donors, who agree to be immunized with a transfusion of blood from Rh-positive donors. The risk run by these volunteers – should they themselves one day need a blood transfusion – is handsomely recompensed by the industries that produce diagnostic serums. To emphasize the fact that human anti-Rh agglutinin is not the same as *Macacus rhesus*–rabbit agglutinin, it was proposed to give the latter the symbol LW (Landsteiner–Wiener). So, with due respect to these two great researchers, their studies on *Macacus rhesus* and rabbits have been of no more use than to give the wrong name to a discovery made by others.

9. Surgical training and the practice of vivisection

There are surgeons who are quick to assert that, if they did not practise on animals, they would lack dexterity, steadiness and precision. It is true that surgery is a physical activity that constantly improves through repetition. However, some surgeons, just as categorically, assert the opposite opinion: practising on animals, they say, *corrupts* manual skill. Here are the opinions of some eminent surgeons:

> The wounds of an animal behave so differently from those of man that the conclusions drawn from them by the vivisectors are completely valueless and have caused far more damage than benefit ... Vivisection as a method of research has constantly led those who have employed it into altogether erroneous conclusions, and the records teem with instances in which not only have animals been fruitlessly sacrificed but human lives have also been added to the list of victims, by reason of its false light (Sir Robert Lawson Tait;[1] see Ruesch 1977). [He was speaking at the end of the nineteenth century – that is, during the peak of enthusiasm for vivisection.]

> Many years ago I carried out sundry operations upon the intestines of dogs, but such are the differences between the human and canine bowel, that when I came to operate on man, I found I was much hampered by my new experience; that I had everything to unlearn; and that my experience had done little but unfit me to deal with the human intestine (Sir Frederick Treves, director of the London Hospital and physician to King Edward VII; see Ruesch 1977).

> I challenge any member of my profession to demonstrate that vivisection has been of the slightest use for the progress of medical science and in healing (Dr Charles Clay, president of the Manchester Medical Society and founder member of the Obstetrics Society of London, *The Times*, 31 July 1880).

I have never known a good surgeon who learnt anything from animal experiments (Abel Desjardins, president of the Society of Surgeons of Paris; Desjardins 1925).

The aim should be to train the surgeon using human patients by moving gradually from stage to stage of difficulty and explicitly *rejecting the acquisition of skill by practising on animals ... which is useless and dangerous in the training of a thoracic surgeon* (Professor R. J. Belcher, paper presented at Symposium on Thoracic Surgery, Sorrento, 14–16 February 1980; emphasis added).

Biomedical research does not need animals. It is foolish and even dangerous to continue to follow this traditional way. The difference between man and animal is so great that it usually leads us into error. We know increasingly that artificial organs can be used in man without first testing them on animals. Whether they are artificial valves or pacemakers, they have been tried out directly on man without first having been tried on animals (Professor Luigi Sprovieri,[2] paper presented at Symposium on Thoracic Surgery, Sorrento, 14–16 February 1980).

Practice on dogs probably does make you a good veterinarian, if that's the kind of practitioner you want for your family (Professor W. Held, Chicago).

So the arguments against practising on animals are at least as authoritative as those in favour. How, then, should a surgeon be trained, and how can a trained surgeon become more proficient? There are two traditional and irreplaceable ways: pathological anatomy and learning from other surgeons.

Pathological anatomy

Pathalogical anatomy involves practising on cadavers (in which the author had long professional experience). Above all, it is the cadaver that teaches the surgeon to proceed with ease around the human body and to know, millimetre by millimetre, what lies beneath the next cut.

However, people are not all made exactly alike – anatomical variations are innumerable and often misleading in the living body. These constitute one of the most insidious pitfalls for the surgeon, who must never be caught unawares when making instantaneous decisions. But this is only possible if he or she has seen the same thing many times, regardless of whether it is on the operating table or on the dissection slab.

Nevertheless, the surgeon approaches the cadaver reluctantly. The pathologist usually carries out autopsies alone in the anatomy theatre, where a doctor could learn immeasurably more than from any book and where the surgeon could learn how to recognize his or her own mistakes and how to avoid them in the future. (Insufficient familiarity on the part of doctors and surgeons with the anatomy theatre is an educational and organizational problem.)

If anatomical variations in humans form one of the most insidious pitfalls for the surgeons, even for the most expert, is it superfluous to add that such anatomical variations *cannot be learned from animals?*

The cadaver is, by definition, a body with altered organs. Even when death can be attributed clinically to the breakdown of a single organ, one is surprised at the number and variety of changes that appear in different organs at autopsy. The surgeon should have a visual perception of these changes at least as clear as that of the pathologist, who is accustomed to seeing them every day. For this reason, an apprenticeship of two or three years in pathological anatomy should be obligatory for all trainee surgeons. Instead, a lot of time is wasted rummaging around in the entrails of animals, which are almost always healthy and can teach nothing about human anatomical pathology.

Learning from other surgeons

This second method is indispensable in the training of surgeons. These instructors need not be eminent surgeons. Surgery is an art, or rather a skill, which is learned 'on the job'. It may be that a modest provincial surgeon has actually improved a surgical procedure and can teach it to others, provided that they are humble enough to learn from him or her – unfortunately, this rarely happens.

Experimenting with new methods

Experimenting with new surgical methods on animals brings us back to my earlier point about the different reactions of animals to different stimuli and hence the uselessness and irrationality of the vivisectionist type of surgical experimentation. Even the most obvious differences between animal and man are frequently disregarded, as in the following example.

In 1979, Professor A. Pizzoferrato, of the Rizzoli Institute of Bologna, appeared in court.[3] He had carried out the following experiment: in two beagle dogs, the head of the femur was removed and replaced with a prosthesis. Three medical doctors (one an orthopaedic specialist) called as expert witnesses submitted various reasons to show the absurdity of this procedure. But the most obvious criticism makes it astounding that the experiment was thought up at all: dogs are quadrupeds. And that entails taking into account several peculiarities of body geometry and equilibrium:

1. In the quadruped, the axis of the femur is almost perpendicular to the axis of the vertebral column, whereas the human femoral axis and vertebral axis are nearly parallel.
2. As a result, the weight on the hip joint in the quadruped is very low (about one-sixth of the whole body weight), whereas in humans it is much greater (about three-quarters of the whole body weight). Another fact not taken into account is that, in the case of a small dog, the total weight of the animal is far less than that of a human, while the structure (and hence the weight-bearing capacity) of the bones remains about the same.

For these reasons, it is obvious that the femoral prosthesis might work well in the dog, but it is just as obvious that it would function badly in a human.

The experiment described above is not an exception. It was not carefully singled out from thousands of valid experiments to illustrate a preconceived idea. On the contrary, it would be difficult to find, in all the literature on human surgery, a single valid animal experiment. Obviously, not all experiments are as clumsy as the one just cited, but all are valueless for one or more reasons. This shows that their purpose is not to achieve progress in surgery but to increase the avalanche of publications by the researchers who perform them.

Teaching[4]

At university, medical students studying surgery and other specialities are obliged to kill frogs in order to repeat, as has probably been done millions of times since the time of Galvani,[5] the phenomenon of nerve excitation and conduction. They may also be obliged to bleed dogs to death in order to observe the collapse of the circulatory system, and to open the chest cavity to observe the beating heart, or to see the beating stopped through the effect of certain drugs, or to see it start beating again by the use of certain other drugs.

These experiments teach the students nothing. For instance, they teach nothing useful about the resuscitation of the *human* heart, first because of the anatomical differences between the thorax in humans and in other animals, and second because the circumstances in which cardiac arrest occurs in humans are almost never comparable with those induced experimentally in animals. The fact that such 'experimental demonstrations' continue to take place demonstrates only the stupidity and cultural backwardness of a teaching concept that serves much more to gain grants and prestige for the teachers than to impart knowledge to the students.

Modern audio-visual methods, computer and film techniques, which are being constantly improved, provide us with teaching aids that are far more detailed and instructive than such absurd exercises as those described above. These aids put us in direct contact, so to speak, with the operating theatres of the greatest surgeons as they are in the very act of operating directly on humans, with all the science and care required by such a responsibility – and not with the technical and instrumental clumsiness that might derive from the knowledge that they are working on a dumb animal, which, moreover, will be killed soon after. Thus, students can only 'unlearn' such procedures as the latter – unless the aim is to school them in torture, to make them indifferent to blood and suffering and to acquire contempt for life. But these sentiments are the opposite of what we all ask (since we are all potential patients) of the very people to whom, one day, we may have to entrust ourselves.

Students seem to be far more aware than their teachers of the outdated nature of the schools in which they are obliged to learn. Protests by students and young doctors are heard all over the world against methods that are not only cruel but also stupid and corrupting, both morally and technically.

Microsurgery

Microsurgery is a fairly new method. The surgical site is enlarged through an optical device, which enables the surgeon to perceive structures hardly, if at all, visible to the naked eye. He or she then has to become accustomed to the new dimensions and learn to adjust his or her hand movements to them. This fact is used as an argument in support of those who maintain that training is more easily done on animals than on humans. But this assertion is denied by other experts, particularly in the USA and Britain, who advise practising not on animals, but on human placentas or on artificial vascular models.

In microsurgery too, the concept remains valid that the only proper way to train the hand (and the eye) is to learn from an expert and then become independent, beginning with small operations on humans and selecting cases in which the risk of damage is minimal.

Computer imaging

High-performance computers allow visualization of two-dimensional images to be rebuilt as three-dimensional, thus enabling the surgeon to simulate a surgical procedure before performing it on the patient.

Organ transplants

With regard to this type of surgical intervention, we limit ourselves in this chapter to technical questions. The technical problem is soluble for any surgeon who has acquired proficiency in traditional techniques. A greater problem is that of organization: there has to be a greater number of assistants and a spacious and adequately equipped operating theatre. However, with transplants, the major problem is immunological – that is, the problem of rejection.

But this cannot be resolved by using animals, whose immune systems differ radically from those of human beings. Therefore, to study the problem of rejection in animals means wasting energy, brains and money, with very slight chances of gaining any useful information at all from such research, let alone any conclusive results. We even run the risk of acquiring information which is apparently useful but which, on closer examination, turns out to take us further from our goal and to complicate the existing problems.

And this, indeed, is a characteristic of the pseudo-science that is modern medicine: it continually makes for new problems that remove us further from reality. However, this situation creates new jobs (and new incomes) for a host of 'specialists'. This is, or seems to be, the only positive aspect of that ludicrous and wasteful process dressed up as 'science' but based upon the shaky foundation of animal experimentation.

Has animal experimentation ever contributed to the success, if only technical, of transplant surgery? Has it smoothed the way to the next step – transplants on humans? Has the sacrifice of human victims been thereby avoided? Some answers follow.

Surgeons who set about trying out any new technique make their first attempts on animals, above all to cover themselves in the event of failure on humans. We have good reason to believe that this concern prevails over all others, including the technical and scientific.

Chairs of experimental transplant surgery have been founded. The new professors are often former assistant surgeons, who accept such posts as a means of staying on at the university. Obviously, these secondary figures in the medical-surgical profession will never admit to the uselessness or fallaciousness of their work. Moreover, the prestige of the university chair still carries weight with the public, the politicians and the public administrators and fosters the (false) idea that a (false) methodology is indispensable.

The first heart transplants were performed just over thirty years ago in Cape Town, South Africa, by the surgeon Christian Barnard.[6] He had practised for a long time on sheep (and perhaps on other animals), presumably with good results, since he decided to go on to humans. But what have been the true consequences of his practices on animals? All these first patients died in the space of a few weeks or months. So it is thanks to their sacrifice, rather than to the previous experiments on animals, that a technique has evolved that today makes it possible for a growing number of surgeons to carry out heart transplants. This is confirmed by data from the University of California, where heart transplantation technique was studied in 400 dogs, in a nine-year period of research. When the technique was eventually applied to humans, the first two patients died from complications that had never occurred in the dogs, and only in 1980 did as many as 65% of the patients who had undergone the operation survive for one year.

As for the recipients of transplants, we certainly know the immediate effects on them, but we know little or nothing about the long-term results. For these facts we have to look to the media, which display the successes on their front pages, while deaths are relegated to the inner or back pages. The public's ears ring with the triumphant cries of rival 'transplanters', as these rush to the nearest telephone to give the happy tidings to the waiting media. But has a serious survey ever been made of the actual outcome for these patients? Have enquiries been made of the families to ascertain their quality of life and not merely how long these 'beneficiaries of science' survive?

Christian Barnard's second transplant recipient, Phillip Blaiberg, at death's door from impending rejection (and after a donor for the second transplant had already been found), was fully aware of the real situation and, preferring death, refused his written consent to the new intervention. Why? We know of one risk – only one for the moment – hanging over those who accept transplantation: the transplant patient, because of the immunosuppressive drugs administered to prevent rejection, is subject to a cancer risk 100 times greater than the average.[7] In particular, reticuloendothelial tumours (of tissues lining blood and lymph cells, etc.) have an incidence 350 times greater than the average in patients administered immunosuppresive drugs for kidney transplantation. So rejection is not the only problem. Cancer, too, lies in wait. But on this point the media are silent.

Notes

1. Robert Lawson Tait, eminent British surgeon and gynaecologist (1845–99), originator of a method of repairing the perineum called 'Tait's operation'. His aversion to animal experiments is clear from the title of a paper read to the Birmingham Philosophical Society on 20 April 1882: 'On the uselessness of vivisection upon animals as a method of scientific inquiry'.

2. Luigi Sprovieri is considered to be the father of extracorporeal circulation.

3. The charges were brought by L. Macoschi, president of LAN (Lega Antivivisezionista Nazionale – National Anti-vivisection League) in Florence.

4. For this section and the two following on microsurgery and organ transplants, I am indebted to Werner Hartinger, MD.

5. Luigi Galvani, physicist and doctor (Bologna, 1737–98) caused a tetanic (abnormally spasmodic) jerk of the gastrocnemius (calf muscle) in a frog he was dissecting, having accidentally touched the animal's sciatic nerve with calipers, one end of which was of copper and the other of zinc. However, the phenomenon was, in fact, due to the electrostatic current produced by the two metals being connected to a conductor, which in this case was the nerve.

6. The cardiologist Christian Barnard of the Groote Schuur Hospital in Cape Town, on 2 December 1967 removed the diseased heart of Louis Washkansky, a 53-year-old man, and replaced it with the heart of Denise Darvall, a young European woman killed in a road accident. Washkansky died on 21 December, from viral bronchopneumonia. Barnard made his second attempt on 2 January 1969, on Phillip Blaiberg, a 50-year-old dentist, using the heart of a boy. Blaiberg survived for 20 months. In 1974, Barnard tried to transplant a

'secondary' heart without removing that of the patient, but he failed. In 1977, he transplanted into a man the heart of a baboon – again, an all too easily foreseeable failure. In Italy, the first heart transplant was performed on 13 November 1985 by Professor Vincenzo Galluci in Padua Hospital. The donor, an 18-year-old boy, had died in a road accident. The recipient later died of AIDS.

7. *British Medical Journal*, 3 March 1984: 659–60; see also Speciani 1984.

10. Human volunteers: the ethical question

In seeking to clarify the moral implications of human actions, one is invariably confronted by a smoke-screen, behind which sits a sophist who shuffles the cards and pulls out the one most to their own advantage. Some actions, however, can never be hidden by a smoke-screen, since they advertise their stupidity and iniquity in neon lights. Let us leave judgement on the cruelties perpetrated on animals to the 'animal-lovers' and pose the following question: does vivisection constitute a threat to humanity only through the errors by which it misleads science, or does it threaten us more directly? And, if so, how? People are indeed threatened in a direct way, because the same experiments are carried out on them as are carried out on the animals. Such experiments are performed on volunteers and non-volunteers alike.

There is a great deal of talk about experiments carried out on volunteers, especially in the USA, but there is very little documentation concerning them. So where and how are volunteers recruited? This is done above all in prisons, and the typical proposal runs roughly as follows: 'Would you prefer to be roasted at once in the electric chair or be injected tomorrow with cancer cells?'

This 'freedom of choice' seems to salve the conscience of the experimenters, but there is worse to come. There are experiments on non-volunteers. Dr S. Krugman provides us with an example. However, the deeds of this doctor need an introduction: experiments on human beings are at the peak of an 'escalation'. This escalation begins with Galvani's frog ('galvanized' into involuntary movement although dead) and progresses along a series of vertebrates from mice, rats and rabbits to cats, dogs, monkeys and primates. Nevertheless, even the most obtuse 'scientists' have to admit, sooner or later, that results obtained on primates cannot be extrapolated to man. So the last hurdle has to be overcome. And this is where Dr Krugman comes in.

Dr Krugman was convinced that he had found a vaccine against the hepatitis B virus by boiling infected serum (Krugman, Giles and Hammond 1971). The results seemed to justify his optimism – partially, at any rate. But how did things really turn out? It is not, in fact, enough to boil infected serum and call it a 'vaccine'. One also has to demonstrate that it affords protection against the illness. There is no point in testing it on animals; one has to see what happens in humans. At this point one would need to vaccinate several thousand volunteers and then check how many of them *spontaneously* contracted viral hepatitis compared with the same number of unvaccinated people. But that would be a long and expensive procedure – a short cut is needed, and Dr Krugman found one.

The doctor was in charge of a paediatric department at the New York School of Medicine.[1] In 1971 he selected 39 children aged from 3 to 10 years, 'vaccinated' fourteen of them and inoculated all of them with the hepatitis B virus. All 25 'unvaccinated' children became ill, as did five of the 'vaccinated' children. The vaccine was, then, successful, even if only partially. But what about the children? The outcome for them is less clear. It is true that none of them died during the observation period of 140 days. But what may have happened to them afterwards? (Viral hepatitis can result in progressive chronic hepatitis, an almost always fatal condition.)

Dr Krugman is merely the wretched victim of a mentality – the vivisectionist mentality – with which he was inculcated as a student. This mentality, having found in Dr Krugman a susceptible subject, evolved in him so far as to reach the heights of research achievement, or the depths of depravity, depending on your point of view.

He has some illustrious predecessors – for example, his fellow countryman, Dr Zollinger, who, in order to study the correlation between the thymus gland and transplant rejection, removed the thymus (a fundamental organ in the immune system) from 18 children hospitalized for surgical correction of heart defects. Many of them died of immune deficiency, a present from Dr Zollinger (see Macoschi 1987). We have spoken of 'escalation'. Once such a perverse mechanism has been set in motion, it is difficult to stop and almost impossible to reverse.

In 1978, seven years after Dr Krugman's experiment, a powerful chemical and pharmaceutical firm decided to test, on humans, an agricultural insecticide. The test was carried out in an agricultural area of Egypt: six boys, aged between 10 and 18, were paid to walk about in a cotton field leading a dairy cow by the halter with one hand and holding a filter-paper with the other. Shortly afterwards a crop-spraying aircraft arrived, covering cotton, cattle and children with a cloud of white dust.[2]

What happened to those children? Perhaps nothing unpleasant for the time being, but what may have happened to them in a few, or many, years' time? And if, for example, the substance causes cancer or foetal abnormality, or both, who will realize the connection? Who will, perhaps 20 or 30 years later, connect that fleeting experimental moment with the illness and possible death of people who, in the meantime, have gone their separate ways after leaving their home village and carrying with them an illness contracted while innocently playing in a cotton field?

In 1984 the following headline appeared in the Italian press: 'Incredible trade in foetuses for the cosmetics industry ...' (*Corriere della Sera*, 20 August 1984). Please note the word 'incredible', which created an initial impact – only to be followed, in another headline some forty days later, by the first signs that people had already got used to the idea: 'Inquiry into whether foetuses are being used in Italy – a circular from Under-Secretary Costa to the Italian Prefecture' (*Giornale di Vicenza*, 7 October 1984). Note how the bureaucratic mind begins to 'normalize' things, sinking to the level of the pharisaical 'inquiry into whether it is *also* happening in Italy'. And hear how the under-secretary addressed the Prefecture on the matter: 'Without wishing to underestimate moral sensibilities in this matter, we would bring to your attention the provisions of the Presidential Decree of 21 October 1973, No. 803, which includes reference to "the removal and preservation of cadavers and anatomical parts" etc.' Steeped and indeed drowned as he must be in a society imbued with scientific fetishism, how could he have expressed himself otherwise? How could he have avoided reducing the problem, which threatens to destroy the basis of human society, to a simple 'circular ... to the Italian Prefecture'?

However, let us continue on the downward path to 'normalization'. A newspaper linked by its very nature – and perhaps by its need to survive – with the prevailing academicism, somewhat pathetically announces: 'Call for unambiguous laws concerning experimentation on foetuses' (*Corriere Medico*, 21 November 1984). So, after three months, we are at the stage of accepting the 'incredible'. There is, of course much more to it than mere acceptance, because regulation means not merely accepting such a method but also even protecting it by law.

While I was preparing the third Italian edition of this book, there occurred a further development. *Medico d'Italia*, No. 85 of 1986, printed the following:

Research and experimentation using human foetuses

Mr Ferri, MP (Christian Democratic Party), in a question to the Minister of Health, emphasized that, in Europe, many pharmaceutical and cosmetic companies are using human embryos and foetuses which are not necessarily dead in medical and scientific research and experimentation. ...

The President of the Social and Health Commission of the Council of Europe has condemned the strong pressure exerted by industrial lobbies, operating in the medical and scientific sectors, for an unrestricted use of human embryos and foetuses for industrial and commercial purposes without specifying whether these are to be living or dead, the only stipulation being the consent of the mother ... The Ministry of Health is asked whether or not it intends to regulate this highly delicate sector by law.

Here politicians are seen to be taking measures that admit and regulate the use not only of dead embryos and foetuses, but also of live ones.

Let us take a closer look at the statement: 'The President of the Social and Health Commission ... has condemned the strong pressure exerted by industrial lobbies.' What are these lobbies actually demanding? They want total control in the use of human embryos and foetuses, *'without specifying whether they are to be living or dead'*. In other words, they want interference from nobody. They want to use those foetuses (dead or alive) just as they please, *the sole limitation on their activities 'being the consent of the mother'*, who would presumably be suitably compensated as an incentive.

We mentioned earlier Dr Krugman and his dual personality: on the one hand a standard-bearer of the vivisectionist mentality; on the other, an articulate defender of the view that true experimentation is that conducted *intra speciem* (that is, on human beings) in the study of human medicine. But Dr Krugman is not the first to have experimented with a vaccine on humans. He has an illustrious predecesssor, the 'inventor' of vaccination, the English physician Edward Jenner (1749–1823).

In 1796 Jenner injected a peasant boy, James Phipps, with pus taken from a cowpox swelling that had developed on the hand of Sarah Nelmes, a milkmaid. Up to that point little harm had been done, as it was well known that cowpox was not dangerous for humans. But matters took on the hue of dangerous experimentation when, two months later, Jenner inoculated his 'guinea-pig' boy with smallpox.[3]

All went well. The boy proved to be immune, thanks to the vaccination – or at least, that was the conclusion drawn by Jenner. This
conclusion, however, today appears premature, to say the least, and a
typically mistaken case of *post hoc, ergo propter hoc*. In fact, in the eighteenth
century about 65% of the British population contracted smallpox, but
only 8.5% died of it, and only 20% of cases developed a serious, though
not fatal, illness.

There therefore remains a 70% chance that the boy used by Jenner
as a guinea-pig belonged to the 35% who are naturally resistant, and it
is open to question whether the vaccination carried out on him by
Jenner altered his previous condition in any way. At any rate, the moral
of the story lies in the undeniable fact that Jenner used the boy as an
experimental animal, perpetrating on him a true act of 'vivisection'
(see note 1, Chapter 3). Jenner published the results of his studies under
the title 'Inquiry into the Causes and Effects of the Variola [smallpox]
Vaccine' in 1798.

Experimentation on adults and children is now routine. I am about
to denounce not just the activities of individuals, which might be excused
by a plea of some sort of mental illness, but rather those of whole teams
of people active in an institution – that is, the whole complex of imposing
buildings, sophisticated scientific apparatus and staff drawn from various
professional disciplines, such as doctors, biologists, chemists, physicists,
administrators and subsidiary personnel. All of these are to be found in
the National Institute for Cancer in the USA. I quote below a report in
Il Giorno of 19 April 1982, based on an article by Giuliano Dego in the
Washington Post:

> *Treatment for cancer in the USA worse than the disease itself*
> In a scandal that is spreading like an oil slick, the National Institute for
> Cancer has admitted having carried out experimental treatments for
> cancer which are more deadly than the disease itself. In the last two
> years the Institute has been responsible for giving treatments to tens of
> thousands of patients, including many children, using more than one
> hundred and fifty experimental drugs.

Note the recurrence of the word 'children', and the increase in the
numbers used – no longer the 39 victims of Dr Krugman, nor the six
Egyptian children, but reference is now made to tens of thousands of
patients. The article continues:

Many of these drugs have caused a more painful death than the illness itself would have done.

This is a typical and brutal feature of vivisection: the infliction of harm, allied to contempt for life, regardless of whether the victim is an animal or a human being.

The *Washington Post* [demonstrated that] the number of deaths attributable not to cancer, but to the experimental drugs which were intended to cure it, amounts to six hundred and twenty.

Robert Young, administrator at the Food and Drug Administration, admitted: 'There is, at times, little regard for human life.' In Boston, a hospital used a new drug from the National Institute for Cancer on some children. In the space of a few days their kidneys failed. No wonder – the use of these medicines has now become purely and simply a matter of routine, without sparing a thought for the people we administer them to.

The article continues:

How do these deadly drugs act? They cause hundreds of deaths due to liver, kidney and heart failure, respiratory diseases, destruction of the bone marrow, brain damage, paralysis, strokes and coma.

Given that these are supposedly anti-cancer drugs, the following sentence is almost comical:

Some of these drugs actually stimulate the development of tumours and cancers.

Up to now we had probably all assumed that the experimentation was carried out only on those suffering from cancer. But the sentence quoted above seems to refute this: if, in fact, some patients developed cancer, *they didn't have it before*. Thus, the claim that everything humanly possible was being done for patients *incurable by other means* is unmasked as a deception. This, then, is experimentation pure and simple.

There is further evidence, published in the Journal of the American Medical Association on 1 January 1982, that these medicines are cancer-causing:

Some chemotherapies have been shown to be carcinogenic by their effect on the fingers of the nurses (who, by definition, are presumably healthy).

Wearing gloves is no protection. Their fingertips become fluorescent and remain so, despite washing.

Finally, I would like to thank, in particular, the anonymous official at the National Institute for Cancer for his explanation in seeking to justify experimentation on human guinea-pigs:

> Our theory is that there really must be a chemical that cures cancer. We decided that the only way of discovering it is to keep pumping millions of these substances into the veins of human beings.

Assuming that each product has to be 'pumped' into the veins of a hundred subjects (the indispensable minimum for the effect of a drug to be calculated statistically), the human subjects would have to number hundreds of millions. People are to be treated just like mice.

However, I should like to reassure readers that my attitude to such reports is a critical one. It should not be thought that I take too seriously the assertions of a foolish official at the National Institute for Cancer. Nevertheless, one incontrovertible fact remains: foolish they may be, but it cannot be denied that people of this kind exist, and not just as isolated examples but in great numbers, in vivisection laboratories everywhere.

The vivisectionist world is firmly entrenched and rests on solid material foundations. It does not lack money (from the pharmaceutical industry, plus state and private subsidies), it has the support of academics and universities, and it has the law on its side – a law that can codify established ideas but is incapable of producing new ones. Moreover, vivisection is supported by structures such as hospitals and clinics: with their staff in white or blue-green gowns, face masks, sterile caps and gloves, they exert a firm grip on the minds of a public that is hopeful of an existence with fewer aches and pains or a life that at least lasts a little longer. One may despair of struggling against such an establishment or of ever undermining its dogmas.

The most unexpected help rendered to anti-vivisectionists came from vivisectionists themselves, when the latter decided to cross the threshold from animal to human experimentation. This amounted to confessing that experimenting on animals is useless and provides precisely the affirmation that underpins all anti-vivisectionist thinking.

In addition to the active experiments (deliberately causing wounds, administering potentially harmful substances and so on), there are also passive experiments, which consist of withholding interventions useful to the life or welfare of their subjects:

- In 1905, William Fletcher divided the inmates of an asylum for the insane (in Kuala Lumpur, the capital of Malaysia) into two groups of 120 persons each. Those in the first group were fed on polished rice and those in the second on unpolished rice. Forty-three patients in the first group became ill with beri-beri, and 18 of them died.[4]
- In 1932, the Venereal Diseases Division of the Public Health Service of the USA approved the Tuskegee project (named after a small town not far from Montgomery, the capital of Alabama). This involved over four hundred black people afflicted with syphilis, who were left completely untreated in order to study the natural course of the disease until the central nervous system became affected (tabes dorsalis) and death occurred.[5] This experiment continued until 1969 – that is, 30 years after the discovery of penicillin, which could have protected the victims against the most serious consequences of the disease.
- The following experiment was carried out in the USA, in a Navajo reserve, from 1970 to 1975. Constrained to live in the reserve, deprived of the ample space that had, for centuries, guaranteed them a healthy life, the Navajo – so that they might maintain their own ethnic and cultural identity – had rejected technological civilization and had been reduced to living in cramped huts made of wood and mud, in dirty conditions and on a gravely deficient diet. The experiment consisted in introducing into the reserve the most sophisticated modern medical treatment, with consulting rooms and scientific equipment, famous specialists, technical personnel and first-class nursing help. At the same time, the Navajos were allowed to go on living in their usual environmental conditions. After five years, the result was a slight reduction in the cases of tuberculosis and of otitis media (inflammation of the middle ear) in the children. Otherwise, mortality and morbidity were unchanged. What did this experiment demonstrate? It showed that the health of human beings depends on their environment, and that modern technological medicine fails to cure those diseases caused by conditions favourable to their development. The researchers, of course, expected a completely different result, which explains why they took good care not to repeat and extend the scope of an experiment that threatened to destroy trust

and confidence in an establishment that is as well entrenched as it is profitable – the health industry.

The above examples show how well-founded are the concerns of anti-vivisectionists faced with a medical practice increasingly dehumanized by the vivisectionist method and mentality. Those who should be most worried, however, are the doctors themselves, as it is they who are obliged to carry out the precepts of a teaching that reduces them to agents of the health industry. And in fact the number of doctors who rebel against the vivisectionist mentality is growing.

The vivisectionists, emboldened by the power they wield, at once react with arguments aimed at frightening their opponents, who are not so much those medical doctors who have already taken up definite positions as those who are turning tentatively towards a medicine with a humane and anti-vivisectionist outlook. Orthodox science, arrogating to itself all claims for progress in modern medicine, accuses doctors who show signs of wavering of being inconsistent: 'I notice you don't mind using diagnostic and therapeutic methods *that have already been tested on animals.*' To this challenge, which smacks of blackmail, Werner Hartinger responds:

1. The fact that animal experiments have been, and continue to be, carried out does not prove that they are indispensable to human medicine.
2. The fact that a doctor may use allopathic drugs *does not mean that he or she agrees with animal experimentation or admits that it is rational.*[6]
3. The fact that (apart from undesirable side-effects) more or less useful results can be obtained *does not prove that analogous or better results would not have been obtainable using other methods.*
4. A judgement on whether the results of animal experiments can be extrapolated to humans can be made only *after the results obtained on animals have been compared with corresponding experiments carried out on humans.* Until that is done, it is not possible to make any valid assessments.
5. Consequently, the diagnosis and treatment of illness in humans is based not on animal experiments but on *clinical trials carried out on humans.*[7]

The moral problem for vivisectionists

However, it seems that vivisectors may not be the cynical monsters that anti-vivisectionists would perhaps like to believe. Vivisectionists, too, face a problem, a moral problem, but they face it in a directly contrasted manner – and, incredible as it may seem, they march shoulder to shoulder with a great many animal-lovers concerned with the same issues. Thus, while scientific anti-vivisectionists, fighting vivisection because of the damage it causes to human medicine, have been grouped together in the public's mind with old ladies who feed stray cats, the vivisectors themselves are beginning to grow tender-hearted at the thought of the fate of the poor cats that are tortured. But it is impossible to stop torturing cats (according to them), because this would almost mean 'the end of medical science'. They could, however, reduce the numbers used in experiments – in other words, retain the quality of torture but reduce the quantity.

Vivisectionists of this school and some animal welfare campaigners are in the same boat and so support each other. I am reminded of the words of Hans Ruesch, the father of anti-vivisectionism: 'The animal welfarists are our worst enemies' – a statement that sounds like the well-known adage, 'With friends like these, who needs enemies?' The reductionists propose reducing the number of animals by avoiding repetitive experiments and by other minor expedients. It therefore seems more than likely that, having sniffed out an ill wind, they may try to offer the anti-vivisectionists this sort of cold comfort: 'Due to our great efforts, the number of animals sacrificed has dropped this year from 200 million to 180 million.'

There are also those high-minded people who advocate the prohibition of vivisection for 'frivolous' purposes such as cosmetics but who want to keep it for 'serious' ones such as medicine. This amounts to classifying vivisection as a 'serious' activity, which should be reserved for 'serious' things like physiology, pathology, therapy, surgery – in short, for that system of human medicine that, precisely because of its vivisectionist methodology, is becoming increasingly hard to take seriously.

The moral condemnation of vivisection by scientific anti-vivisectionists is based on human moral grounds, leaving the moral arguments in favour of animals to animal rights campaigners, to animal-lovers and to the defenders of the laws regarding animal rights. Our moral concern, in defence of human beings, finds support and confirmation in two observations, the one historical and the other of our own time.

First, it is a historical fact that, after a couple of centuries of vivisectionism and billions of experiments on animals, neither the number of people who have fallen sick nor the number of fatal illnesses has decreased. It is only for bacterial and parasitic diseases (but not for viral ones) that medicines have been found capable of acting on causes, by killing the micro-organisms that produce such diseases. All other serious or fatal illnesses are constantly on the increase, and all that we have available against them are certain drugs which, in some cases, seem to have an effect on certain symptoms – an effect that, however, is not always amenable to evaluation and is all too often not pro-

TABLE 10.1 Deaths from various causes, Switzerland, 1930 and 1978, showing percentage increase

Cause of death	1930	1978	% increase
Cancer	5,994	13,802	132
Diabetes	445	1,207	171
Leukaemia	95	340	257
Cardiovascular disease	5,074	18,071	260
Liver diseases	382	839	108
Population	4,066,000	6,298,000	50

TABLE 10.2 Cancer statistics from the USA and Italy, showing percentage increase

USA	1971	1981	% increase
Cancer: cases	330,000	420,000	21

Italy	1940	1969	% increase
Cancer: mortality per 1,000	80	184	130

Source: Speciani 1984.

portionate to the damage (euphemistically called side-effects) that some medicines are capable of causing. Furthermore, the placebo effect is never taken sufficiently into account.

Second, what is happening in our own times is obvious to all. Human experimentation is growing at an amazing rate. And it is not a question of simple, legitimate, clinical experimentation but of genuine *vivisectionist* experimentation. Tables 10.1 and 10.2 show some statistics on the increasing death rates for the more common diseases.

The three Rs: a gift to vivisectors

Reduce – Refine – Replace: the originators of this idea in support of vivisection, published in The Principles of Human Experimental Technique, were zoologist William M. S. Russell and microbiologist Rex L. Burch (Russell and Burch 1959).

The first R: Reduce the number of animals used in experiments. Vivisectors are frequently heard to say: 'We are working for the welfare of humans, for the welfare of us all. And for this noble purpose we need to experiment on animals. Nevertheless, in our enormous love for nature and animals, we have devised optimal methods for the practice of our unwilling cruelty on a reduced number of animals.'

The second R: Refine the methodology. We know very well that vivisectionist methods of torture are very 'refined'. However, vivisectionists doubtless still have the potential to refine their cruelty still further (although their defence would be that they mean to refine the cruelty out of a system which should not, we argue, exist on any terms, since it is scientifically invalid, as is the first R, since 'zero' is the only valid answer).

The third R: Replace animal experimentation with other methods. Of all the three Rs, this is perhaps the smartest. The reasoning runs thus: 'We can no longer confront the increasing public opposition to vivisection. Nor can we face up to the scientific arguments proving that vivisection is even more of a crime against humanity than against animals. So, let us play for time. The safest way to do this is to show people that we are studying methods to replace animal experimentation. People know that this will take time – the very time we need to continue our dirty work.' (One is, of course, supposed to assume that 'valid' animal experiments *can* be replaced by other, equally valid, experiments, thus vindicating the present system, scientifically at least – which is the very point that anti-vivisectionists are contesting.)

The ultimate abomination: experimenting with the human foetus

We are now at the top of a mountain. The ascent, begun with Galvani using a frog and progressing through a series of experiments on mammals, monkeys and apes, has taken us to the summit – experimentation on humans. Before commenting on this, however, let us eliminate a possible misunderstanding.

I am not talking here of clinical trials, the final and indispensable testing of any drug. Clinical trialling is an obligatory step and is both logical and legitimate, provided it is entrusted to competent doctors in a well-equipped environment, where observation of clinical symptoms is followed up by laboratory analyses capable of showing rapidly any changes a drug, still imperfectly known, can bring about in various organs. In this way, those side-effects that give doctors cause for concern, and remind them constantly of the need for caution, can also be discovered.

However, the level of experimentation reached by vivisectionists has gone far beyond this. I acknowledge a certain reluctance to discuss something so shocking, but experiments have been carried out on human foetuses, and I believe that this is still happening secretly, in different circumstances and for different purposes. Dramatic evidence of such experiments emerged in Europe and the USA in the early 1980s.

In March 1981, at the French–Swiss border, French customs officials examined a refrigerator lorry. The exporting countries were Hungary and Yugoslavia, the importers of the merchandise French cosmetics firms. The suspicions of the French officials were aroused by the high freight charges of whatever goods the vehicle was carrying; the truck was opened up, and the refrigeration compartments were found to contain many hundres of deep-frozen foetuses.

In fact, the first evidence of this trade had emerged even earlier. In 1977 the Japanese newspaper *Asahi Shimbun* exposed a trade in foetuses between South Korea and the USA via Japan. The price was a modest $25 per foetus. It later became known that the traffic had been going on for six years and that about four thousand foetuses a year were being transported. The carrier used was Japan Airlines. Nobel Prizewinner George Wald declared that between 1970 and 1978 approximately 1,200 kidneys from human foetuses were imported into Western countries from South Korea. In the same period, the number of induced abortions in South Korea increased considerably: in 1970 the number was slightly lower than the number of births; in 1977 the number of abortions was three times that of births.[8]

Another question arises. Is it not likely that buyers, in order to save overseas shipping costs, would seek (and find) the 'raw material' in their own countries, that is, in France, Italy, Great Britain and the USA? There is indeed a well-documented news item on this point from the USA, reported in the French newspaper *Libération* on 8 February 1982. In Santa Monica, California, a container in the vicinity of a disused clinic that had formerly belonged to one Mel Weisberg aroused suspicion. It was later found that he had paid the suppliers of the contents with a cheque that had bounced. The firm that had hired out the container came to reclaim it, opened it and found 'more than 500 human foetuses preserved in formalin in plastic containers and labelled with the names of the donors' (that is, mothers).

The accounts here are journalistic items of a rather sporadic and fragmentary kind. It seems that a veil of discretion has been drawn over them by relegating them to the inside pages. Why?

I seem to see on the reader's face a quizzical look, perhaps also expressive of a plaintive hope – these are, after all, only *dead* foetuses, or, better still, embryos, that is, products of conception that have not yet reached their eighth week of life in the womb. The fact is, however, that the foetuses involved in this trade seem to have been obtained in the following way. There are clinics specalizing in abortion. The women who go to them are convinced by skilled persuaders that they should continue the pregnancy for as long as possible. (The more mature the foetus, the higher the price it will fetch.) At the agreed time, the foetus is removed by Caesarian section. Since in many cases this takes place at the twenty-eighth week (that is, between six and seven months), one is talking no longer of a foetus but of a moving, crying infant.

Here is an account by two journalists, M. Lichtfield and Susan Kentish, of an interview with an English gynaecologist who was a procurer of foetuses. They were introduced to him as representatives of a potential buyer. 'One morning four of them were born, one after another. They cried but I didn't have time to kill them at once, because I had too much to do that morning. I am not a hard man, but a realist. You need to be a *man of science* and unemotional, if you want to avoid having your judgement clouded by sentiment' (Lichtfield and Kentish 1974; emphasis added).

From what I have said so far, one might assume that the desire to perform vivisection on human beings is a recent phenomenon, arising from the realization that experimentation on animals serves no useful purpose. But this is not the case. Even in the nineteenth century, vivisection of human beings was lamented as 'a coveted but unattainable goal'. Claude Bernard advocated 'vivisection of human beings as the ultimate goal of experimental medicine'. Later E. E. Slosson, a professor at the University of Wyoming,[9] declared: 'A human life is nothing compared with a new discovery. The principal aim of Science is the advancement of human knowledge *at any sacrifice of human life*' (*The Independent*, New York, 12 December 1985; emphasis added).

We come to two final questions: what are these foetuses being used for, and is the practice continuing in some countries? The answer is a disappointing one: we hardly know. This is because everything happens behind the closed doors of research institutes, pharmaceutical and cosmetics companies and 'science' laboratories whose watchword is 'Silence'. To the uncritical science-worshipper, the justification for experimentation on human foetuses is found in the myth of the advancement of knowledge. But is this excuse valid when one of the intentions is merely the development of cosmetics?

What is more, it seems that foetuses used in biomedical and cosmetics research are not obtained from spontaneous abortions. Gonzalo Herranz,[10] professor of histology and human embryology at the University of Navarre, Spain, made this clear when explaining the use of embryo tissues for cell cultures *in vitro*:

To obtain embryo cells, embryos from spontaneous abortions cannot be used, nor can those obtained by means of abortions performed via the vagina: in both cases, the embryo will be contaminated by micro-organisms. The correct way consists in having recourse to Caesarian section or to the removal of the uterus. Only in this way can bacteriological sterility be guaranteed. In either case, then, to obtain embryo cells for culture a programmed abortion must be adopted, choosing the age of the embryo and dissecting it *while still alive*, in order to remove tissues to be placed in culture media.

Given these premises, we face the dilemma of whether the deliberate, systematic destruction of a human creature to obtain cell material can be justified, when it is recognized that this is of great interest to fundamental research and for the diagnosis of some human diseases. Are research and diagnosis of such great value that they justify the destruction of human beings?

A declaration of the Permanent Committee of Medical Doctors of the European Community and of the World Medical Association, published in 1985, states: 'A human embryo cannot be considered as laboratory material but rather as a potential human being. The respect which is due to it implies, in consequence, that any research should be subject to the Helsinki and Tokyo Declarations, adopted in 1975 by the World Medical Association.' Here is an extract from those declarations: 'Concern for the individual should always prevail over the interests of science and society ... the medical doctor has the duty to protect the life and health of persons undergoing biomedical research.'

It does not seem to me that these principles are compatible with programmed abortions carried out to obtain cell cultures. I cannot think otherwise, even if the women themselves want a termination and despite the fact that scientific, diagnostic and commercial interests have combined to create a climate of opinion which makes it seem desirable. The Geneva Declaration [see Appendix] affirms that the doctor has the duty to take the greatest care to safeguard the life of a human being from its conception and will not, even under threat, use his knowledge to infringe humanitarian laws. Human embryos are the weakest members of the human family. They are the object of unjust discrimination in the case of abortion. In contrast with what happens to other minorities that are discriminated against, human embryos have hardly anyone to defend them.

My overall conclusion, therefore, is that since animal experimentation is fallacious and misleading, and it is unethical to use human foetuses obtained by elective rather than spontaneous abortion, we are obliged to conclude that all *in vitro* cultures of human embryo tissues should be abandoned, recognizing nevertheless that this kind of research procedure is scientifically valid.[11]

At this point a logical objection may be raised: is it legitimate to deprive science of a research method that even some anti-vivisectionists consider to be not merely very valuable at the present time but also even more promising for the future? Considered objectively, the situation does not appear as dire as that presented by Professor Herranz. To obtain a cell culture (or cell strain), only a small quantity of tissue is required. Thus a single organ (liver, connective tissue, epidermis, etc.) can yield many cultures. A single foetus, then, can provide abundant material *if it is used in a rational way*.

However, two problems remain unsolved:

1. the vitality of the embryo organs; and

2. their bacteriological sterility.

Concerning the first point: if it has been established that the death of the embryo has already occurred naturally, a new logic comes into play and is the same as that which allows us to perform an autopsy. If we find this idea unacceptable, we should also renounce the practice of performing autopsies, and that takes us into entirely new realms.

The second problem – bacteriological contamination of the embryo – does not seem to me to be insoluble either, because:

1. Bacteriological contamination that occurs during the passage of the embryo through the vagina affects only the outer tissues (skin, mucous membranes of the body's orifices), not the internal organs.
2. When seeding the cell culture with tissue samples, we can easily seed bacteriological media with the same samples to find out whether or not bacterial contamination has occurred. If it has occurred, it is an easy matter to discard the contaminated cultures and await an occasion to prepare fresh ones.

Allow me, however, to bring this chapter to a close on a disturbing note, which illustrates the degree to which absurd habits inherited from vivisection have become embedded in our culture and scientific practice. Due, perhaps, to the difficulties I have outlined in obtaining human embryo cells, it is in fact the case that cells from embryos of other animal species are cultured in the laboratories of institutes or specialist companies. These are then used in experiments intended to provide anwers to human health problems. Thus the methodological error that lies at the root of all vivisectionist thinking is perpetuated and extended. The error remains, the focus merely being shifted from the whole animal to its cells – with the same misleading results that some researchers are apparently unwilling to renounce.

Notes

1. Willow Brook Hospital, Staten Island, New York.

2. This episode occurred at Abu Hemus on 16 June 1976, at nine o'clock in the morning. The firm responsible for it was Ciba-Geigy of Basle, and the pesticide used was Galecron. The names and ages of those boys were: Mohammed Ali, 12, Said Hassan, 14, Hawad Esmaiel, 12, Mabrok Moustafa, 10, Zakaria Abdou, 18, and Ragab El Aziz, 14. The results of the experiments are described in a reprot dated 10 September 1976, entitled 'Medical Surveillance Programme', and edited by the Agrichemical Division of Ciba-Geigy.

The same pesticide was produced under the name of Fundal by the German firm Schering. The toxicity of the product was known before the experiment in Egypt was undertaken, as is confirmed by the fact that in the same year (1976) it was withdrawn from sale (from *L'Unità*, 24 April 1983, in an article by Pier Luigi Bellon, professor of chemistry at the University of Milan). Another pesticide, Leptophos, produced in the USA, is not deadly for insects only – it also causes serious neurologicalchanges in the workers producing it. Its factory has been closed and the pesticide banned from use. However, the unsold supplies were sent to Egypt; the number of human victims has never been established, but one can count the number of cattle Leptophos killed – about one thousand (from an article by Giorgio Celli, *L'Espresso*, 14 (April 1987): 192).

3. The cowpox virus, which causes a skin disease in cattle mainly detectable in the eruption of vesicles or pustules on the udders, also affects humans by infeetion through direct contact ('milkmaid's disease'). The virus is very similar to the smallpox virus, which is harmless to cattle but causes serious illness in humans. The two viruses have some antigens in common; therefore the antibodies stimulated by one virus are similar to those stimulated by the other, with a reciprocal protective effect ('cross-immunity'). Smallpox vaccination was practised in India from ancient times and in China from AD 1063, the inoculate being taken from the pustules of those suffering from a mild form of the disease. In 1718 Lady Wortley Montague, wife of the British ambassador to Turkey, introduced the method to that country.

4. Beri-beri (from the Sinhalese *beri*, weakness) is a vitamin B_1 deficiency disease, characterized by weakness, polyneuritis and a decline in mental faculties. It ends in heart failure.

5. Tabes dorsalis (locomotor ataxia) appears in the third stage of syphilis and is a result of sclerosis (hardening) of the dorsal columns of the spinal cord. It produces shooting pains, uncoordinated movements of the limbs, skin anaesthesia, pains in the stomach, larynx and rectum, changes in the joints, disturbances of vision and, in the final stages, incontinence of the sphincters.

6. Allopathy (Greek *allos*, other + *pathos*, suffering). Modern Western medications aim at producing an 'opposite' effect, i.e. cure, to the disease being treated. (Compare homoeopathy (Greek *homo*, same), or 'like cures like'.)

7. Werner Hartinger, *Mensch und Tier: Geschwister der Evolution*, Klosters: CIVIS.

8. Statement by George Wald, reported in Rolande Girard, *Le Fruit de vos entrailles.*

9. C. Bernard, *Principes de Médicine Expérimentale* (published posthumously).

10. Professor Gonzalo Herranz was at the time president of the Committee of Medical Ethics of Spanish Doctors and vice-president of the Permanent Committee of Medical Ethics of the European Community.

11. From an article by Professor Herranz in *Il Sabato* (no. 15, 26 April 1986) in reply to a previous article in the same journal by Paolo Cucchiarelli and Marina Ricci.

11. Genetic engineering: the new frontier

Ours may be the age of genetic engineering, but history teaches us that this, like all ages, will come to an end. Some forty years ago, axenic (specific pathogen-free) animals had their day (see Chapter 4). This gave rise to many hopes but resulted in a total failure, which went unremarked – except by the experts, who kept the fact to themselves. With genetic engineering, however, the stakes are much higher, for it promises to cure such life-threatening or severely disabling diseases as cancer and arthritis, as well as various hereditary enzyme disorders.

The genome

Each of the cells that, in their billions, comprise the human and animal organism owes the transmission of its somatic characters to genes. Chromosomes are made up of genes, and the chromosomes themselves are contained within the cell nucleus. Each cell of the individual organism, whatever its function (renal, hepatic, intestinal, muscular, cerebral), contains the same genes, which together comprise the genome.

The gene

The gene is a section of DNA (deoxyribonucleic acid), composed of nucleotides containing the four bases (adenine, cytosine, thymine and guanine). Each gene relates to only one somatic character. As the genes number between 70,000 and 100,000, each individual expresses that number of characters, which they transmit to their offspring. Each of the 46 human chromosomes is about 3 microns (3000ths of a millimeter) in length and contains nearly 2,000 genes. From this one can calculate, or rather imagine, the size of a single gene, which can be 'photographed' only by an electron microscope.

Types and targets of human genetic engineering

Let us focus on two types of genetic engineering: indirect (performed on the animal genome), and direct (performed on the genome of the human embryo). The indirect type aims to provide an animal (as distinct from a human) with characteristics compatible with the human immune system, so that its organs may be used for a human recipient without risk of rejection. The animals most commonly used for this purpose are pigs, calves, chimpanzees and baboons.

The direct form of human genome manipulation aims to remove from the human embryo those genes that are carriers of hereditary (or suspected hereditary) diseases. These include cancer, arthritis, diabetes, cystic fibrosis, some forms of epilepsy, Alzheimer's disease and a hundred or more other 'genetic' diseases, some of which (for example, depression and suicidal tendencies) have traditionally been regarded as behavioural.

Gene sites

The gene is too small to be seen under the optical microscope. The first step in the genetic engineering process, therefore, is to draft a genetic 'map', on which are plotted the sites of individual genes on the chromosome, together with their functions. This forms the basis for all further processes, from genetic tests on drugs to genetic modification of somatic and sex cells. So far, over 16,000 gene sites (20%) have been located and fed into the USA databank, On-line Mendelian Inheritance in Man. I must stress, however, that their clinical functions have not yet been assessed with any certainty; this is likely to take at least another 20 years.

There are other difficulties, too. For one thing, the potential interactions between the transplanted gene (possibly taken from an animal) and the genes of the host genome are still unknown. For another, many hereditary diseases are linked to more than one gene, and the consequences of engineering performed on a series of interacting genes are unpredictable. It will be many years before the solution (if any) to this problem is found.

Techniques

To insert or remove a gene, genetically modified viruses are used, many of which are destroyed by the host immune system. This in itself creates a difficult technical problem, but the greater concern is whether we can be sure that the modified viruses are and *will remain* harmless. Viruses have been shown to be very prone to spontaneous mutation, the best-known examples being influenza and HIV. Should we not therefore be concerned about viruses allegedly rendered 'harmless' by genetic modification?

Successes

Genetic diagnostics have demonstrated that approximately 750 genes are linked to hereditary diseases. Common diseases that are linked to a single gene are cystic fibrosis, Huntington's chorea and muscular dystrophy. Together, these represent 2–3% of known diseases. But genetic engineering will cure neither these three nor countless other diseases. At best, it will prevent human embryos contracting them. It is highly improbable that the present sufferers of a particular disease will derive any comfort from the fact that the responsible gene has been identified. In more general terms, who will be interested in knowing that their chance of being personally afflicted by a given illness is 'x' rather than 'y' times the average?

Unpredictable effects

Practitioners and supporters of genetic engineering should be considering facts, rather than opinions and prejudices, and carefully weighing up actual risks versus promised benefits. Hartinger (1995) provides a few examples:

- Genetic manipulation of certain bacteria has produced very unexpected results, which, moreover, differ from laboratory to laboratory. No one can guarantee that the same may not occur in humans – with catastrophic consequences. For example, the bacterium *Escherichia coli* gave rise in one laboratory to a dyestuff, while in another this normally harmless micro-organism was converted into a pathogen.
- Australian researchers modified the TGF-alpha gene (which affects

cancer growth) in mice. Instead of the severe malformations expected, the mice developed curly hair.

* In vegetables, too, gene modification can have odd results. Bean plants were modified to increase their resistance to herbicides and produced an animal hormone.

* The consequences of producing, by bacterial gene modification, a synthetic insulin, analytically identical to natural insulin, were more serious. The amino acid L-tryptophan, a so-called harmless by-product, caused 30 deaths and 1,000 cases of illness.

Nevertheless, the researchers proceed undaunted with their manipulation of humans, animals and vegetables.

Apparent victories, actual benefits

Genetic science is performing miracles, which we watch with the willing suspension of disbelief of spectators at a conjuring show.

Identification of criminal tendencies Not so long ago, the Italian criminologist Cesare Lombroso (1836–1909) marked out as criminals people with 'ugly faces'. In his day, he was taken seriously by a society imbued with a blind faith in science. We shall never know how many people paid the price for that strange philosophy. But more sophisticated (and therefore more dangerous) are the modern genetic engineers and their supporters. For example, according to Daniel Koshland, editor-in-chief of *Science*, genetic engineering will help to solve such problems as drug abuse, sexual violence and criminal tendencies – all of them, he claims, social ills written into the genes of certain individuals. In February 1995, the Ciba Foundation held a symposium in London with the unequivocal title 'The genetics of criminal and antisocial behaviour'. In view of this, we may well ask if free will has any future.

Psychological damage Is it, in fact, useful for anyone to know that their destiny is written in their genes? Is it going to help anybody to know that they are destined (or at least have a predisposition) to contract cancer, diabetes or arthritis? On the contrary, it can only arouse anxiety in the individual (if he or she believes it), with potentially devastating psychological effects. And if people care nothing for the predictions of genetic science, why does it still go on?

Social implications There are industrial and commercial concerns that are already using genetic forecasting to select employees. They are even honest enough to say, 'Prevention is better than dismissal'.

Assured profits Some organizations (mainly life insurance companies) are interested in promoting gene technology. Their professional persuaders promise prevention of cancer, arterial hypertension and arthritis, but their real purpose is to increase insurance premiums for those who run the risk of contracting diseases identified by genetic forecasting. Will genetic labelling of individuals reach the point where only the healthiest will be insurable?

There also exists a market that gets richer with every gene discovered and is already offering commercial do-it-yourself genetic diagnosis of ovarian and intestinal cancer. In the USA they are marketing the Brca-1 test, which detects the gene responsible for breast cancer. This market is likely to expand.

But will the same market offer cures for the diseases so readily diagnosed? Francis Collins, director of the Human Genome Project in the USA, warns: 'While waiting for diagnoses and ethical positions, I advise no one to undergo genetic tests. At present they do not help; they only cause anxiety.'

12. Clinical trials: the moral maze

There are two approaches to experimentation on humans: the vivisectionist method, which has been used in the past, though less widely than today, and the clinical experiments carried out in hospitals and universities.

The two kinds of experimentation should not be confused with one another. The first – vivisectionist experimentation – is similar to that performed on animals and is to be rejected on both ethical and scientific grounds. The second – clinical experimentation – is permissible on legal grounds, is ethically justified and is necessary from a scientific point of view. Most progress in medicine, especially in pharmacology and therapy, arises from this method. But within what limits and according to what rules is clinical experimentation permissible? I shall discuss this later.

Vivisectionist experimentation

The fundamental concept of scientific anti-vivisectionism is expressed in the following proposition: *No experimentation carried out on one species can be extrapolated to another species.* This basic concept has been accepted not only by the majority of anti-vivisectionists but also by those vivisectionists who, having realized the unreliability of experimentation on animals, have taken the human being as the experimental model for the human being. We should consider them as the allies of anti-vivisectionists, since they agree that experimentation *inter species* (between species) must be rejected. However, they maintain the notion of experimentation *intra speciem* (within a species) as being valid, a method on which anti-vivisectionists place serious limits, and not on ethical grounds alone.

Experimentation *intra speciem* – which means making the human the experimental model for the species 'human', the dog the experimental model for the species 'dog' and the cat the experimental model for the species 'cat' – does indeed seem to offer an attractive choice that seems unimpeachable on logical and scientific grounds. But such is not the case. On the contrary, experimentation *intra speciem* is in many cases almost as misleading as experimentation *inter species*. This is because it rests on the fundamental positivistic error of applying analytical methods to the biological and natural sciences, whereby the living organism is sub-divided into its component parts, analysed and then reassembled like a jigsaw puzzle, in the belief that the original likeness can be reconstructed and indeed enriched through the analytical process – in other words, that the sum of the knowledge of the parts is equal to the knowledge of the whole.

However, this approach overlooks that imponderable element to which each of us gives a different name, according to our own cultural, national and religious background. It may be called the soul, psyche, intelligence or spirit. I have chosen the term *Life* – an attribute immanent in anything that moves, grows, suffers, reproduces itself and dies: an attribute that cannot be analysed and quantified in physical, chemical or mathematical terms but that nevertheless exists.

A pure scientist might at this point object: 'I don't believe in your attribute that cannot be analysed, precisely because it cannot be analysed. I don't believe in anything I can neither touch nor see.' How does one respond to this? Using the same language one might reply: 'For millions of years people lived without touching or seeing radio waves, cosmic waves, infra-red light, ultra-violet light … but they still existed.'

The systematic application of the analytical method to the biological and natural sciences has neglected that element called Life and has led medical science down a blind alley, to get out of which 'future generations will need all their time and commitment' (Lépine 1967). But the light is beginning to shine through a few chinks – which are expanding more rapidly than one might expect.

This process of neo-civilization owes much to an ever-more frequent and easy contact with Oriental scholars, mystics, philosophers and poets. This does not mean that the West should adopt Oriental ways of thinking and living, but it does mean admitting that the Western way of living, thinking and learning (that is, pursuing science) is not the only possible one; it possesses neither the sanctity of infallibility, nor is it the key to the universe. Many people, even though they may not have had a scientific training (or perhaps for that very reason), have grasped this truth intuitively. This is shown by the growing number of people with different social and religious outlooks who are moving in directions other than the majority, freely and courageously choosing new ways of living.

Let us return now to vivisectionist experiments on humans. As already argued, experimentation *intra speciem* is often as misleading as experimentation *inter species*, especially when it is a matter of experimentation on humans.

Human experimentation was widely practised in Nazi concentration camps. The following is a typical example and took place in a barracks for Jewish deportees. They were given, by a doctor, 24 hours to decide whether to volunteer for an experiment. The next day many 'volunteers' reported for duty. Ten of them were selected, all men aged between 20 and 30. They were transferred to clean, comfortable quarters equipped with good beds and decent toilets. The food was plentiful and good. But the prisoners also knew what lay at the end of this well-paved road, and in due course the inevitable day of the experiment arrived.

The subject of the experiment? 'For how many hours can a human body withstand immersion in water at temperatures of 10–12° centigrade?' This was the situation in which *Luftwaffe* pilots found themselves when forced to bale out over the North Sea: from that moment, how many hours would the German air and naval forces have in which to rescue them? The experiment took place in a swimming pool. The agony was timed with a stop-watch.

This was only one of the experiments performed on prisoners. The Nuremberg archives contain records of many other atrocities committed for experimental purposes, but for our thesis one is enough. We have used it not to provoke criticism on ethical grounds of facts that *preclude* any possibility of being judged on those grounds, but to evaluate objectively the *scientific* validity of the experiment.

In fact, the experiment is scientifically invalid. The doctors who performed it knew it would have been pointless to use animals and that this 'clinical' method showed that their approach was worthy of the instruction they had received at their excellent German universities. They were mistaken, greatly mistaken, as were their universities. The error is explained by the following proposition: 'In many cases humans are not appropriate experimental models for humans.' Why not? Because, at the very moment when the person ceases to be such and becomes an experimental model, the union between body and soul, soma and psyche, matter and Life is destroyed. The researcher then has nothing but a piece of empty matter that has little in common with the matter that, not long before, contained and acted as a vehicle for Life.

Let us try to answer the following question: can we compare one of these tragic victims – torn from their families, transported in cattle trucks for days on end without food and water, thrown starving into a foul shed and, in the final, most tragic and terrifying stages, fattened like pigs for the slaughter before final death – with a young pilot, in fine physical and mental condition, trained to physical and technical perfection, exultant in the aftermath of battle, determined to survive and aware that his comrades will try to rescue him? Can there be any comparison between the Jewish guinea-pig and the pilot hero, and is there any doubt as to which of them will survive longer in the cold water? The answer seems clear. 'Of course!' comes the reply. 'The Jewish guinea-pig will die first, it's quite obvious.' But in fact that is not so. Viewing the question from a different angle brings us to the opposite conclusion. Let us compare again the physical and psychological condition of the two subjects, this time from a different standpoint:

1. The Jewish victim (the 'experimental model'), now deprived of all hope, retreats within himself and prepares himself for his impending release in death. This state of introversion and resignation depresses vital forces, relaxes muscle tone and reduces production of reactive hormones (adrenalin, steroid hormones). The metabolism slows down, the tissues produce less heat, less heat is lost in the water, so death by hypothermia is delayed.
2. By contrast, the fighter pilot calls on all his physical and mental energies, keeping himself alert and active: there is increased production of reactive hormones, muscle tone is raised and heat production increases. More heat is lost in the water – and chilling rapidly occurs.

Herein lies the paradox: both hypotheses are scientifically valid, although antithetical. The hypothesis with the plus sign is cancelled out by the hypothesis with the minus sign. The arithmetical mean is zero. The experiment taught nothing, meant nothing.

And indeed, recent history shows that not one of the experiments carried out in Nazi concentration camps has been of any value to medical science. Nevertheless, such experiments were *intra speciem*, the ideal aimed at by present-day scientists, who, more than fifty years later, persist in performing them, violating not only every moral precept but also all scientific logic.

Making a jump in time of 40 years, and in distance of 1,000 kilo-metres, let us move from Auschwitz to Pavia. Here the atmosphere is pleasant and relaxed. On the grassy banks of the River Ticino, sports clubs are engaged in strengthening the minds and bodies of young people. But not all the young people.

Corriere Medico, 10–12 November 1980: 'Human guinea-pigs enrolled for 50,000 Lira a day.' This took place in the Clinic of Industrial Medi-cine at the University, but the journalist (Luca Ciferri) claimed that the same thing happens in other Italian cities as well. Numbers of young people undergo voluntary experimentation to check the absorption rate of certain drugs. The rest is reported in an anodyne way, in a newspaper that on the same page carries an advertisement depicting a bottle, on which the words '——— SOLUTION is the answer to liver failure, stomach pains, dysmenorrhoea, etc.' appear in large letters. In other words, it is a newspaper heavily dependent for its income on the pharma-ceutical industry. The human guinea-pig interviewed is an engineering student. The article begins: 'One chilly autumn morning ... I walked through the entrance gate of the Clinic of Industrial Medicine in Pavia. That was to be the beginning of my experience as a legally sanctioned human guinea-pig.' Let us keep in mind that last point – 'legally sanc-tioned'.

The student is happy about his undertaking and expresses his appreciation of the director of clinical research at Lepetit, Dr Giuseppe Buniva, who 'has always been very frank and open with me in response to my questions about the risks I might run', and so on. It sounds an altogether idyllic situation: everything is in order, everybody is happy, including the guinea-pig. Then, on being questioned, he replies: 'You want an exact list of the medicines I tried out as part of the experi-ments? A hypotensive, chloramphenicol, and rifampicin.'

But here an alarm bell sounds: chloramphenicol and rifampicin? Here is a list of the side-effects of chloramphenicol from the book *Bittere Pillen*[1] (Langbein et al. 1983):

Harmful effects –

In skin creams: serious allergic reactions.
In eye drops: serious blood reactions, allergic reactions.

In general use: serious blood reactions, kidney reactions.

Warning: No more than 30 grammes of chloramphenicol in total should be taken in the course of an entire adult life, and a single course of treatment should not last more than 14 days, due to the possibility of serious damage to the kidneys from this medicament.

An article entitled 'Iatrogenic diseases' (doctor/medicine-induced diseases) also tells us that chloramphenicol can, if administered for a long time, cause inflammation of the optic nerve, impairment of hearing and aplasia (abnormality) of the haematopoietic (blood-cell producing) marrow (D'Arcy and Griffin 1979). That should suffice as far as chloramphenicol is concerned. Now let us turn to rifampicin, about which *Bittere Pillen* tells us: 'Side-effects: serious liver reactions, gastro-intestinal disturbances, severe headaches.' And 'Iatrogenic diseases' adds: 'Impairment of vision, colour blindness.'

But for now we are less interested in the victim, who, however voluntary and well-informed he may be concerning the potential risks, is still not capable of making a judgement concerning a reality that could end tragically. More to the point is the fact that he defines himself as a legally sanctioned guinea-pig. Sanctioned by what law? Does a law exist in Italy that permits experimentation on healthy people, possibly transforming them into sick or even dead ones? And if either of these two possibilities were found to be true, who is responsible? Is a piece of paper signed by the experimental subject enough to absolve the researcher from legal responsibility? And if death results, would this not be a case of homicide? We shall leave these questions to the lawyers. Let us content ourselves with the observation that the cases outlined above contravene the Hippocratic oath.

What happens in Germany is described by the German journalist Günter Wallraff (1985). He wanted a personal record of the large-scale ill-treatment and exploitation of Turkish immigrants working in the Federal Republic of Germany. To that end, he disguised himself as a Turk, dyed his hair black, wore brown contact lenses in his blue eyes, obtained Turkish identity papers and learned to speak German with a Turkish accent. This enabled him to uncover not only the facts he had anticipated but other, rather surprising ones as well.

A number of Turks, driven almost to suicide by the inhuman way in which they are treated in some industries, find less tiring but more deadly work in certain pharmaceutical companies. As porters? As cleaners? No – as human guinea-pigs in drug trials. Graffiti on a wall in Duisburg urged: 'Stop experiments on animals – use Turks!' Our pseudo-Turk decided to take this exhortation literally, and so, as the Levantine Ali Sigirlioglu, he presented himself at LAB in Neu Ulm, a company that had already assembled 2,800 'collaborators', that is, human guinea-pigs of all races, but mostly Turks, Indonesians, Latin Americans and Pakistanis. He signed a consent form and received his first dose of phenobarbital combined with phenytoin.

The product information for phenytoin given in large doses over a long period of time states: 'There is a risk of motor disturbances, hyperplasia and bleeding of the gums, hyperglycaemia, hyperlipidaemia, megaloblastic anaemia, porphyria and necrosis of the liver.' The combination of phenytoin with phenobarbital is particularly dangerous, with a risk of asphyxia and circulatory shock, sometimes fatal.

Our bogus Turk took the first dose and was at once afflicted by visual disturbances and the next day by deafness, headaches, sensory numbness and bleeding of the gums. All the other trial participants who had undergone the same treatment complained of the same symptoms. He decided to stop participating. But then he was able to do so – he did not need the money so badly. The rest of them, however, had to continue, even though they knew the symptoms would worsen appreciably in the eleven weeks of the trial. They knew, too, that if they withdrew, they would not receive the 2,000 Deutschmarks they had been promised. They therefore continued, despite enormous suffering, so as not to lose the wages they had earned so far. The contract is a noose that tightens round the neck of anyone who enters into it.

Günter Wallraff, alias Ali Sigirlioglu, did well to flee. But how many others have died after months or years of chronic poisoning, disregarded and perhaps despised because they were mistaken for drug addicts or alcoholics? How many have been left with their health impaired for the rest of their lives?

With a touch of cynicism one might ask: 'But don't these experiments serve any useful purpose at all?' Norbert Rielbrock replies: 'About two-thirds of these trials are absolutely useless. They are experiments done for commercial motives.'[2]

Günter Wallraff tried again with another firm, Bio-Design of Freiburg in Breisgau, at a wage of 2,500 Deutschmarks for fifteen days. The drug to be tested was Masperinon, an aldosterone antagonist with diuretic activity. Its harmful side-effects (as listed in *Bittere Pillen*) are:

hormonal disorders, impotence, irreversible breast development in males, voice changes, loss of strength, electrolyte imbalance; also headaches, mental confusion, gastric colic and skin changes. The contract to be signed by the experimental subject states: 'In the event of withdrawal, Bio-Design may require the volunteer to repay the costs incurred during the trials.' This time Günter Wallraff gave up before even embarking on the trial, not wishing to have to pay for the hospitality offered by Bio-Design.

The facts described above, whether they concern the University of Pavia or the Turkish guinea-pigs in Germany, teach us that any kind of crime may go unpunished in the guise of scientific research. What is it, then, that protects the scientist from prosecution and the opprobrium of public opinion? One returns inevitably to the claim, 'We are working for the good of humanity'; or the cynical 'Sacrifice of the few for the benefit of all'; or the perverse 'The end justifies the means'. Thus the aim is always very noble and the means indispensable, given that they are used for such noble ends.

So what is the final verdict on vivisection? From the ethical standpoint, vivisection on humans is no longer extolled as meritorious, even by the most convinced and unbiased vivisectionists. From the scientific standpoint, vivisection on humans is hardly less misleading than that performed on animals. The only possible conclusion, then, and the one that should be presented as such to legislators, is as follows: it is both essential and a matter of urgency that laws should be passed to make vivisectionist experimentation a crime against the safety and life of the person, and provision made for adequate compensation to those damaged by it.

The experiments carried out on student volunteers in Pavia and Turks in Germany are only the tip of a gigantic iceberg in the sea of misinformation in which the public is fraudulently immersed. And what of the submerged portion of the iceberg – the huge volume of trials of which we hear nothing? These take place every day under our noses, in hospitals and, above all, in teaching hospitals. This kind of activity is on the borderline between genuine vivisection and clinical experimentation, taking advantage of human 'material' readily available in hospitals and clinics in order to turn trusting, unsuspecting people into experimental animals. It involves mainly drug trials but also the misapplication of diagnostic measures, often because doctors – perhaps newly graduated from universities – want to try their hand at various procedures: pointless gastroscopy or oesophagoscopy; bronchoscopies that are too often redundant because diagnosis has already been made by other methods; urography, descending or ascending, the former dangerous because of the risk of intolerance to radiological contrast media, the latter risking the transfer to the renal pelvis or the kidney itself of infections that would otherwise be limited to the lower urinary tract – etc., etc.

Even skilled doctors, consultants or professors – 'authority figures' – often feel the need to prove to their administrators that some sophisticated and very expensive piece of equipment, claimed by them as indispensable but in reality superfluous, is being sufficiently used (never mind whether rightly or wrongly) to justify its purchase.

The most widespread experiments are, however, the trials carried out on drugs, mainly to determine the toxicity of new drugs. These arose from a need to establish standards, that is, from laws that impose this kind of testing on humans ('clinical trials') as a prerequisite to the licensing for sale of drugs, cosmetics, or any substances that can come into contact with humans and are potentially harmful. Again, this demonstrates that we are dealing with problems of a commercial nature, whose solution requires political intervention.

Clinical trials

Clinical trials are indispensable, indeed inescapable. Paradoxically, one could say that if they were not performed one would end up doing them anyway. What does this mean? It means that, if trials were not carried out in a systematic, well-directed way, in institutes equipped for the purpose, and if a new drug were launched without having first been tested in hospitals, the first involuntary experimental subjects would be the first people to use it, with all the possible consequences, many of them disastrous, that might ensue. A new drug or diagnostic procedure must, therefore, be tried out for the first time on people. So what is the problem? The problem arises precisely in the selection of those people. Let us analyse the criteria that should guide our selection.

Trials on healthy volunteers This method is unacceptable, for both technical and ethical reasons.

The basic *technical objection* is that drugs are usually given to sick persons, while the volunteers are, by definition, healthy people. One does not have to be an expert to realize that a sick organism is not the same as a healthy one. Even the simplest illness changes many (if not all) biochemical parameters, in ways that can be quantified and even in ways beyond our ability to quantify. As a result, the majority of reactions in a sick person are different from those in a healthy one. They may give pointers, but, as has already been stated (see Chapter 1), these are too vague to be valid in scientific terms, especially when a vague and imprecise concept risks being transformed, in practice, into a real and concrete danger.

The *ethical objection* is the following. The trials are performed on volunteers, that is, on people who accept responsibility for what happens to them. But what sort of volunteers are they? They may be paid volunteers, and this is an obvious contradiction in terms. It is not justifiable for people to run such risks, even when necessity obliges them to sell their bodies to become 'patients'. The concept of necessity may embrace situations ranging from the worst kind of poverty and starvation to simply wanting to buy a motor-scooter. Therefore, it should not be a question of the volunteer demonstrating the voluntary nature of his or her participation; rather, it is up to the researchers to decide on the ethical legitimacy of putting the health of others at risk. When can they be sure they are within the limits of such legitimacy? 'Never,' is the simple and absolute answer, even in relation to that category of volunteers who are 'prepared to sacrifice themselves for the sake of Science'. Human society rests on certain norms or conventions accepted by the majority; such a sacrificial motive clearly deviates from these norms, therefore such deviant behaviour can only be a sign of mental instability. This nullifies the concept of 'voluntary' participation.

The researchers assure us that 'When we engage volunteers we explain precisely and objectively to them the aim of the trial, how it is to be carried out, the controls which will be applied, the risks [always 'insignificant'] that they may run – hypothetically speaking.' But the reality is rather less reassuring. As a rule, the transaction between the would-be guinea-pig and those with an interest in the outcome of the trial is entrusted to 'hidden persuaders', envoys of the pharmaceutical company concerned. They know how to gain the confidence and sympathy of the individuals they are dealing with in order to convince them that the choice depends exclusively on their own free will, that no one would ever try to coerce them, and that they, the 'persuaders', are their friends and counsellors, more inclined to dissuade than to urge them on.

But what kind of conviction can be formed in the mind of a lay person (as, for instance, the engineering student cited previously) who hears talk of transaminases, alkaline phosphatases, haematopoietic function – words that are intelligible to the persuader, while for the victim they have only the mesmerizing effect of a promise made by the oracle at Delphi?

Blackmail and persuasion by deception Blackmail can be exerted in many ways, ranging from the brutality of offering two alternatives – both of them terrifying but one being less imminent and seeming to offer some hope – to the hypocrisy of the blackmailer, who, with the smile of a friend and benefactor, seeks to convince by claiming, 'It's for your own good!'

A different but equally reprehensible approach takes place in some prisons in the USA, where bartering by inmates for a reduction in sentence by risking their physical well-being is common practice. This fundamentally confuses striking a bargain with genuine freedom of choice.

No less repellent than blackmail is the deception perpetrated on a patient suffering from a particular illness, by persuading him or her to accept a therapy or a diagnostic procedure that is thought to be useful for a *different* illness, which is done by arousing in the victim the illusory hope of a possible beneficial side-effect; for example, trying out an anti-rheumatic therapy on someone who is ill with cancer with a 'You never know ...' or 'It has been observed that ...' or some other vague or muttered hints, which are sufficient to exploit the unfortunate sufferer, who needs very little persuasion to breach his or her fragile psychological defences in the name of a fragile hope.

Homologous trials These clinical trials are legitimate on the technical level and acceptable on the moral one. They are homologous (related) to the patient, because it is understood that research is done for the benefit of that particular patient, and not for others or for the whole community; and they are homologous to the illness, that is, they relate to the illness for which the trials are performed and to that illness alone. Homologous trials are subject to strict regulations:

1. The trial participant must be afflicted with an illness. Volunteers should therefore be excluded, whether they are healthy or are affected by a different disease.

2. The drug or diagnostic procedure should possess qualities considered reasonably suitable for acting beneficially in relation to that particular illness.
3. The patient must give consent. If he or she is considered incapable of giving meaningful consent, someone else, capable of giving it in the interests of the patient only, should be asked to undertake this responsibility.
4. The treatment or diagnostic procedure should be applied only when no other methods exist that are considered to be of benefit to the patient.

As we can see, the patient is the focus of all therapeutic endeavour: everything should be aimed at benefiting him or her. The concept is implicit that no trial may be carried out as a sacrifice of the one for the benefit of the many – an aberration that has caused incalculable damage and suffering to just those 'many' who collectively constitute all mankind, the victim for thousands of years of unwelcome 'benefactors'.

Conclusions

These are conclusions relevant to the present chapter, but they summarize anti-vivisectionist thinking in general, as dealt with in this book:

1. Experiments on animals are misleading and therefore harmful to human medicine.
2. Experiments on humans have strictly observable technical and ethical limitations.

At this point, a scientist in the habit of reasoning exclusively in terms of experimentation will object: 'But what methods are we left with on which to base medical progress?' The answer is that in no field of science is progress entrusted exclusively to the experimental method, and this applies even less where medical progress is concerned. In every science, experimentation goes hand in hand with observation of natural phenomena. This is particularly true for medicine. Indeed, one might say that medicine is, roughly speaking, two-thirds a science based on observations and one-third an experimental science. But unfortunately the experimental part fell prey from the start to a gross methodological error, that of vivisection.

Vivisection, therefore, has been a global error and must be ended.

Freed from this error, future researchers will be able to base medical research on a genuinely scientific foundation (as we shall see from Part II of this book). That will require a total, difficult and painful revision of those concepts that have been taught, to the detriment of both ourselves and the medical profession. Future researchers must in time restore to medicine that scientific integrity that has been usurped by the vivisectionist aberration.

Notes

1. *Bittere Pillen* (Bitter Pills): its 864 pages list about 2,300 medicaments, for each of which the side-effects (that is, toxic effects) are reported. Moreover, for each medicine the book provides separate 'recommendations' such as the following: '(1) effective therapeutically, (2) effective only in some cases, (3) not very effective, (4) not to be recommended.' Medicines 'not to be recommended' amount to 846, that is, 32.4%, and those characterized as being 'not very effective' total 223, that is, 12% of all those listed.

2. Norbert Rielbrock, Professor at the University of Frankfurt am Main, in a ZDF television programme on 28 August 1985.

II. Scientific methods of biomedical research

Introduction

Let us call them scientific, not alternative, methods. 'Alternative' implies the notion of choice: 'For this particular research should I choose vivisection, or this or that other method?' Such would be the reasoning of a researcher if vivisection were simply one scientific method among others.

Which are the scientific methods, and how many of them are there? This question, which is very often asked, actually has no basis. Every piece of research (or working hypothesis) requires the definition of the most suitable method for that particular research. The skill of the researcher consists not so much in conceiving a new hypothesis, as in being able to find, each time, the best method to demonstrate or invalidate it.

Medical science was born at the same time as philosophy in the Western world, at the time of Thales (5th century BC) in Greece. However, it has run two irreconcilable courses, one being to observe humankind and the other being the attempt to use the animal as a model for humans. The second method has overwhelmed the first and led it astray. Its influence has been powerful, because it gives the illusion of being a short-cut to clinical and anatomical–pathological observation.

11. Scientific methods of historical research

Introduction

13. The epidemiological method

Pathology is the study of the diseases of individuals. Epidemiology is the study of the diseases of whole populations. Epidemiology is therefore the extension of pathology from the individual to the collective, from small-scale to large-scale observation. But it would be wrong to consider it a mere collection of data and observations. Properly used, it can be a valuable tool of experimental science.

Experimental science postulates that a phenomenon can be repeated an indefinite number of times by using 'models'. When Galileo dropped a lead weight from the leaning tower of Pisa, establishing that it always hit the ground on the same spot slightly to the east of the perpendicular, he showed not only that the earth rotates, but also the possibility of obtaining the same result an indefinite number of times.

The successes of experimental science applied to inanimate bodies (physics and mechanics) suggested that, in medical–biological research also, by using 'living' experimental models one might obtain the same result an indefinite number of times. As the human being was the main object of interest among living creatures, a search was made for an experimental model. But this search, proceeding perhaps a little too hastily, stepped on a dangerous if predictable banana skin, namely, the illusion of using the animal as a model, thereby introducing into biology the mechanistic outlook prevailing in the study of inanimate bodies.

The very use of the generic term 'animal' represents a rather crude conceptual error to those whose thinking is not exclusively mechanistic. In fact, the word 'animal' is a collective term that, referring to *all species of animals*, expresses an abstraction. The misunderstanding consists in seeing in this pure abstraction a concrete experimental model – that is, an object or complex of objects that we can touch, manipulate, modify, take to pieces, put together again and destroy.

Right from the start, biology, seen in such a mechanistic light, resulted in a series of distortions, because it did not take into account a real if unfathomable element, *Life*, which permeates all beings capable of autonomous development and reproduction. But the biologists of the Age of Enlightenment freed themselves from that uncomfortable element by devising one of the most strident deceptions in the history of human thought. 'If the reality called *Life* disturbs us, let's get it out of the way,' went their argument. 'It suffices to affirm that the "beasts" do not possess the essential attributes of life – the ability to think, observe, express themselves, love, hate or suffer – and immediately they are transformed into mechanical models which we can manipulate at will. As for the ability to move, feed, reproduce – we can explain that as a complex mechanism of nervous reflexes and of inherited impulses, which we will lump together under the heading "instinct". In this way, animals (except, of course, for humans) can become models that are as useful as cog wheels, wires, pulleys, alembics.' Today, the errors of this line of reasoning, a burdensome inheritance from the anthropocentric Age of Enlightenment, are beginning to be recognized.

The question now arises: if we give up the illusion of experimental models, how can we study humans? The answer is: by *observing* humans. One of the most natural and immediate methods is the observation of spontaneously occurring phenomena, in as great a number as possible of human 'models' throughout the world. The concept of epidemiology includes this kind of observation and permits the multiplication of individual observations on a scale sufficient to draw conclusions analagous to those that in the mechanical and physical sciences are called 'laws'.

In epidemiological methodology, the multiplication of observations made on spontaneously occurring phenomena substitutes for that 'capacity to be repeated *ad libitum*' which is obtained in the mechanical and physical sciences by means of experimental models. The main difference lies in the fact that the models used in the sciences of 'inanimate bodies' can be studied behind the closed doors and in the comfort of a laboratory, while facts that may become available from an epidemiological study are scattered over an area of 149,107,000 square kilometres – i.e. the area of the earth above sea level. This will give some idea of the complexity of the means needed to exploit the enormous potential of the epidemiological method, which requires a powerful international effort of organization, new technical tools and, above all, a new mentality, which can develop only when the erroneousness of today's methods is clearly recognized.

Epidemiology[1] developed from spontaneous observation. Primitive humans avoided swamps that 'caused fevers', and the seafarers and merchants of antiquity knew that in certain countries they could fall ill with diseases that were unknown in their own lands. In Rome, laws imposing quarantine on those returning from Africa and the Orient implied the concept of an epidemiological map of infections and contagions many centuries before the discovery of bacteria.

An example of an epidemiological study in the pre-bacteriological era is that made by Dr John Snow,[2] who in 1849, by using a map of London to define the areas of cholera infection, pinpointed an infected waterpipe as the source. At the beginning of the bacteriological era an epidemiological study was conducted by Robert Koch, who, in Egypt in 1883 and a little later in India, discovered *Vibrio comma*, the cholera bacillus. An example of epidemiological observation not involving bacteriology is one that noted a greater incidence of skin cancer in Europeans living in the tropics and linked the illness to the excessive amounts of ultra-violet light to which they had been exposed (dark skins are protected by the pigment melanin).

With regard to heart disease, results of fundamental importance were obtained in the 1960s, thanks to an epidemiological study undertaken in the town of Framingham in Massachusetts, USA. Five thousand volunteers agreed to undergo a series of clinical and laboratory examinations and to reply to a questionnaire concerning their general lifestyles, their eating habits, their use of tobacco, the amount of exercise they took daily, and so on. The investigation was repeated in the same way every couple of years, and in 1969 the following conclusions were reached: those individuals most at risk from heart disease were the smokers, those who included too much animal fat in their diet, those who did not take much physical exercise, those who were obese and those who suffered from high blood pressure.

These risk factors are today so well known that it seems almost superfluous to mention them. However, at the time the investigation was being conducted, laboratory researchers were squandering time and money in the attempt to reproduce heart diseases in animals, overlooking the elementary fact that human beings themselves and their habits offered reliable experimental models: they had only to give recognition to this and to devote their attention to its investigation. But the lack of will to undertake research in this way is proved by the fact that, even today, whole armies of laboratory researchers persist, like their predecessors, in conducting absurd studies on animals.

Why is this? It is because epidemiology is an uncomfortable method of research, requiring perseverance and seriousness of purpose, and it does not lend itself to the production of the piles of 'scientific' publications upon which researchers build their careers and fortunes. Epidemiology, the science based on the observation of humans and the spontaneously occurring events that afflict them, could have a decisive role to play in research on cancer, on certain acquired metabolic dysfunctions and on degenerative diseases – all 'mysteries' of medicine in our time. Yet the epidemiological method is used little and inappropriately. The cost of efficient organization is, of course, high, but it could be cost effective if money were not wasted on useless research carried out in the laboratories of hospitals and universities and by pharmaceutical companies, which seem more interested in creating new diseases than in fighting old ones.

Today, some people believe that epidemiology consists of collecting the data freely available from the health institutions of various countries. This is an inexpensive method but ducks responsibility and provides hardly even a semblance of reality. Actually, the most interesting facts, especially those concerning certain diseases such as cancer and vascular disease, would be those that could be supplied by underdeveloped countries, in areas where the populations are only minimally exposed to industrial pollution or adulterated food. However, such countries have neither the ability nor the will to supply accurate information: that supplied by some missions and hospitals run by Westerners is only partial or limited to their respective areas of influence and is hence misleading. Moreover, many governments, perhaps due to a mistaken sense of national prestige, conceal certain truths. In India, leprosy is regarded as a sad memory from the past, yet the enormous suburbs of Bombay swarm with sore-ridden shadows of human beings.

The epidemiological method, applied competently and extensively to all diseases, can yield very significant results. This holds true, above all, for those illnesses of unknown cause that will probably never be conquered without the adoption of this method. Cancer is one such disease.

Epidemiology of cancer

The first step in the study of a disease is to look for its cause (aetiology). If the cause is found, the following measures are necessary: one must find out how the disease behaves or functions (pathogenesis) and how it may be avoided or neutralized (prevention and therapy). However difficult these steps may be, they are nevertheless moving in the right direction.

In cancer research, attention is directly mainly at the cause, and the number of conditions that seem to cause the disease is surprising. However, as none of these conditions gives rise to cancer in everyone exposed to it, one is forced to conclude that they may not be the cause of it but simply favour its emergence. As this is a puzzling and as yet unresolved problem, let us take cancer as an example of how much has already been learned about a disease in very poorly organized and resourced epidemiological studies, and how much more could be achieved with better facilities.

Reading the reports of researches already carried out, however fragmentary and disjointed they may be, we sense at every step that something very near the mark is passing us by, that numerous contradictions may only appear to be such, and that it is precisely in those contradictions that that one might find the key to unlock the secret of the disease. The huge number of substances and environmental factors that seem to trigger cancer suggest that there is a *single cause*. In fact it is quite improbable that a large number of very disparate causes should bring about a single effect. Rather, it is more logical to suppose that different factors may 'weaken' the entire organism or one of its parts, thus allowing that same cancer-causing 'something' to take root, or inhibiting the action of another 'something' that blocks and destroys an incipient cancer.[3]

Epidemiological cancer research aims at distinguishing quantitative and qualitative differences in its geographical distribution. Answers are sought to the following questions:

1. If, in one population, there is a high (or low) incidence of cancer, what are the lifestyles that can cause such a deviation from the average?
2. What conditions could be responsible for the higher or lower incidence of a particular *type* of cancer?
3. How influential are environmental factors versus genetic or racial factors? (When faced with conspicuous differences between two or three countries, we must always be able to exclude differences in research methodology and accuracy.)
4. Is a certain type of cancer actually rare in a given population, or is it simply not being researched by adequate means?

5. Is the incidence of a cancer being calculated from the results of autopsy or from clinical observation? For example, latent cancer of the prostate – demonstrable by biopsy or autopsy – is relatively frequent. Is prostate biopsy used with equal frequency in Sweden and Japan, which appear to have a widely divergent incidence of prostate cancer? And what is the percentage of autopsies carried out in these two countries in relation to the total number of deaths? In other words, were the statistics compiled in the same way?

One must clarify the respective roles of race and environment as causative factors. For example, the incidence of primitive cancer of the liver (hepatoma) is high in Africans but only average in American blacks. This leads to the hypothesis that the former may be exposed to an environmental factor to which the latter are not, and that race has nothing to do with the matter. On the other hand, racial differences cannot be excluded when considering certain tumours. For instance, testicular cancer is rare in black people all over the world (Tulinius 1970). Only the epidemiological method could have provided that information, and this in turn prompts the question: what is it that protects black people from testicular cancer?

Geographical distribution worldwide The most interesting observations made on the geographical distribution of cancer are the following:

- Cancer of the lip in South Africa occurs about fifty times more frequently in white than in black people; worldwide, it occurs more frequently in peasants and fishermen who are more exposed to sunlight. So, do the sun's rays give rise to cancer? And if so, how and why?

- Cancer of the mouth and the oesophagus have a high incidence in India (Jussawalla and Deshpande 1971) – apparently in connection with the habit of chewing the nuts of *Areca catechou* and the leaves of the betel plant (*Piper betle*), together with tobacco and lime (calcium) – and in New Guinea, where tobacco is chewed on its own. Is there a relationship between these facts and lung cancer induced by cigarette smoke?

- Cancer of the nose and throat occurs frequently in South China and the Mongol populations of Indochina, Indonesia, Malaysia and the Philippines, as well as in North and East Africa (Clifford 1970;

Muir 1971). Genetic predisposition is suggested as the cause. But might there not be an environmental factor common to the various countries mentioned? And might not a more accurate statistical investigation throw light on the matter?

- Cancer of the oesophagus is frequent in Central Asia, Northern Iran and in the Transkei. There are no plausible explanations for this geographical distribution, but a more thorough investigation would probably give us one.
- Stomach cancer is frequent in Latin America and in Japan. It is decreasing in Europe and the United States (Muoz and Connelly 1971).
- Cancer of the colon and of the rectum is frequent in Europe and North America. It is rare in Japan but occurs as commonly in Japanese immigrants in the USA as in the rest of the US population, which suggests an environmental cause (Hill et al. 1971).
- Cancer of the liver is frequent in South America and in South-East Asia. In those areas the mould *Aspergillus flavus* is a common contaminant of food. Does aflatoxin, produced by *Aspergillus flavus,* cause cancer of the liver? If so, how does one explain the fact that in India, where contamination by *Aspergillus flavus* is common, liver cancer is rare? It is clear that the problem has not been thoroughly investigated: aflatoxin could be harmless and the carcinogenic factor something else. Or it could be that aflatoxin is carcinogenic only in association with another, unknown factor that does not exist in India.
- Cancer of the gall-bladder has a high incidence in one of the Native American populations (the Pana tribe) of the south-western United States and seems to be associated with the frequent occurrence of gallstones (Rudolph et al. 1970). But in Europe and the USA, despite frequently occurring gallstones, cancer of the gall-bladder is rare. Why?
- Cancer of the paranasal sinuses is frequent in Japan and amongst the Bantu of South Africa, who smoke tobacco mixed with aloe, which contains high levels of nickel and chrome. This is in line with the incidence of this cancer in the USA and Europe among workers in industries using these metals (Acheson et al. 1970). So it is very likely that chrome and nickel are carcinogenic, and this is a piece of information that we could perhaps never have obtained experimentally.
- Lung cancer is common among the Maori of New Zealand, in

Finland and in the United Kingdom. It is also frequently found in Chinese women in Hong Kong (Segi and Kurihara 1963), in 30% of whom, however, it takes the form of adenocarcinoma, which is quite rare in the other groups.

- Pleural mesothelioma occurs frequently in asbestos workers all over the world (Wagner 1971), so asbestos can certainly be considered a cancer-causing agent for the pleura. Why, then, do not *all* those who are habitually exposed to asbestos fall ill?
- Breast cancer is frequent in North America and Europe, rare in China, Japan and some African communities. The rarity of breast cancer in Japanese women may be attributable to a racial factor, as seems to be indicated by its low incidence in Japanese women born in the USA, even among those of the second generation.
- Cancer of the bladder is common in Connecticut (USA). In New Zealand it is 13 times more frequent in those inhabitants of European origin than among the Maori. What habits do the Maori have that differ from those of European stock? Or is the difference racial? The epidermoid type is frequent in Africa, where it seems to be associated with infestations of *Schistosoma haematobium*, but it is also frequent in the Birmingham area in England, where this association does not exist.
- The highest frequency of malignant melanoma in the world is in Queensland, Australia. Why? The Australians are immigrants from all over Europe. Is there, then, a local factor that specifically favours this type of tumour? And why in Queensland, and not the whole of Australia?
- Squamous skin epithelioma is prevalent in white-skinned populations. Skin cancer of the basal type is extremely rare in very dark-skinned races.
- Cervical cancer is common in countries with low standards of living. Early sexual relations and a large number of partners seem to favour the disease. It has been observed that the risk for women rises as their husbands are unfaithful. Is it possible that there is transmission by contact?
- Cancer of the uterus, in contrast to cancer of the cervix, is more common in countries with a high standard of living.
- Cancer of the prostate is frequent in Norway, Sweden and Canada (Doll et al. 1970) but is rare in Japan.
- Cancer of the penis is common in Asia and Latin America. It is rare

among Jews, and it has been thought that circumcision is a protective factor, especially when performed in infancy.

- Cancer of the kidney occurs frequently in Sweden and New Zealand (Doll et al. 1970). A predisposing factor could be the high consumption of analgesics containing phenacetin (Angervall et al. 1969).
- Kaposi's sarcoma is rare in Europe and in North America but frequent among Jews from Eastern Europe. It is also common in Central Africa. Why such a haphazard distribution?
- Tumours of the central nervous system have the highest incidence in Israel, while they are rare in Asia and Africa.
- The lowest incidence of cancer of the thyroid is in Natal, South Africa, and the highest in Hawaii and Colombia.
- There is a low incidence of malignant lymphomas in rural areas of Poland. There is a rather high incidence in the non-Jewish population of Israel. Burkitt's lymphoma is frequent in Central and West Africa, in Uganda, New Guinea, Brazil, Venezuela and Colombia. Its geographical distribution lies in a band that embraces large areas of both tropics. This suggests that some small animal (an insect or arachnid) living in those latitudes may transmit the disease.
- Hodgkin's disease is most frequently found in Colombia (particularly in the city of Cali) and in Hawaii.

Geographical distribution countrywide A parallel aspect of the studies on the geographical distribution of cancer worldwide is its distribution within the same country. Especially significant are differences between populations which, although geographical neighbours, live in different environments. The most obvious example is the difference between urban and rural populations, which may be separated by only a few kilometres. One of the most evident environmental differences is the atmospheric pollution in cities, which includes at least ten aromatic hydrocarbons; benzo-alpha-pyrene is the most prevalent of these and is also found in cigarette smoke. In Norway, in the period 1964–66, the incidence of lung cancer in the cities was found to be more than double that in rural areas (Day and Muir 1973).

- In the state of Iowa, USA, the incidence of cancer in towns is nearly three times greater than that in rural areas. However, this does not mean that atmospheric pollution is the only factor responsible. Other factors, such as differences in smoking habits and exposure to asbestos, may play a part. Just how rash it would be to attribute the cause to the most obvious factor is shown by the following example: in Copenhagen, the incidence of testicular cancer is double that in Denmark's rural areas (Clemmesen 1965). It does not seem reasonable to ascribe this fact to atmospheric pollution, but the possibility cannot be excluded.

- Considerable and as yet unexplained differences exist in the incidence of oesophageal cancer in a number of neighbouring areas of Brittany (Tuyns 1971). There are also differences between riparian areas of Kenya (Lake Victoria) and adjacent areas in Tanzania (Cook and Burkitt 1971).
- In Iran, along the shore of the Caspian Sea, in two areas only 500 kilometres apart, the incidence of oesophageal cancer varies by six times in males and by at least thirty times in females. There are the following environmental differences between the two areas: considerable rainfall and low salinity of the soil in the area of low incidence, and a low rainfall and high soil salinity in the area of high incidence.

Custom The importance of custom is shown by the incidence of cancer in communities from which one can exclude any racial factor. For example:

- Among the members of the religious sect the Seventh Day Adventists, who abstain from smoking and alcohol, the incidence of cancer of the lung, mouth, larynx, oesophagus, bladder and cervix is much lower than the average for the rest of the US population.
- In nuns, cancer of the cervix is extremely rare, while in prostitutes it occurs frequently (Rotkin and Cameron 1968).
- Cancer of the penis is rare in populations that practise circumcision soon after birth (Jews), less rare in those who practise it at the age of ten years (Arabs) and still less rare in men with phimosis (tightness of the foreskin). A carcinogenic effect of smegma (sebaceous skin secretion) is thought to be responsible.

Occupation Carcinogenic substances can be identified by means of epidemiological investigations of different occupations. For example, the carcinogenic effect on the bladder of benzidene, alpha-naphthyl-amine and beta-naphthyl-amine was observed for the first time in industries that use these products.

Statistics compiled on workers in specific industries are significant only when considered in relation to the general population. However, the population at large is also at risk from contact with carcinogenic substances produced by industry, while workers in industry have habits common to those of the rest of the population – for example, smoking.

Relationship between cancer and age   Each type of cancer has a prevalence at certain ages.[4] A system of coordinates can be constructed, having the age of the patients (t) on the horizontal axis and the incidence (I) on the vertical axis. A curve is thus obtained that is characteristic for each type of cancer.

In the equation $I = bt^k$ where:

I = incidence
b = numerical constant
t = age
k = numerical constant

k represents the gradient of the curve, that is, the increase in the frequency of a cancer with advancing age.

Grouping together all the types of cancer that have the same incidence–age gradient, we can pick out cancers for which we may legitimately seek a common cause – for example, continuous exposure to the same environmental agent. If we find geographical differences in the incidence–age curve, we may infer that the unknown environmental factor might be present in certain countries and scarce or absent in others. We can thus restrict the field of research in which the environmental factor is sought.

An example of geographical differences (Japan–Denmark) on the incidence–age curve is provided by breast cancer, represented in Figure 14.1. The curve shows a decline in the risk with increasing age in those countries where incidence is low (Japan), while in the countries with high incidence (Denmark) the risk increases with age. This suggests a causal agent that takes a long time to produce its effect, present in those countries with a high incidence and absent or scarce in countries with a low incidence.

In terms of incidence–age correlation, the group of cancers comprising cancer of the stomach, prostate, bladder, colon, rectum, oesophagus, pancreas, pharynx, mouth, tongue, lip, penis, skin (excluding melanomas) and kidney (excluding very young patients) is fairly homogeneous. This

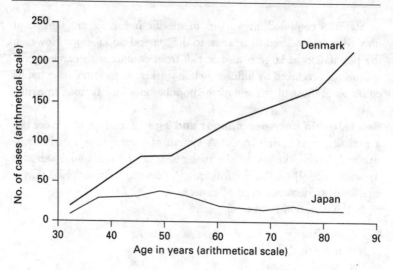

FIGURE 14.1 Graph showing the frequency in relation to age
of breast cancer in Denmark and Japan

long list might support the view that *all* cancers behave similarly on the
incidence–age curve. But statistics show that this is not true and that for
some cancers there are deviations from the mean curve. So one looks for
the factor that may be responsible for such deviations.

For example: bronchial carcinoma and laryngeal carcinoma have a
steeper incidence–age curve than the majority of other cancers. The
factor responsible for this deviation is known to be cigarette smoke.
The proof is that if the *age* of the patient is replaced with the *age of his
smoking habit*, the curve tends to coincide with the curves for the other
cancers in Figure 14.2. (Simultaneous alcohol abuse increases the risk
of cancer from smoking.)

Another example: the incidence of prostate cancer increases with
age more than any other carcinoma. It is extremely rare before the age
of 50, while it is the commonest type of tumour in men aged about 70.
The very steep incidence–age curve is in marked contrast to all the rest
(Figure 14.2). If, however, we replace the patient's age with the age minus
32 years, all the curves coincide. This leads one to suppose that the
unknown factor becomes operative after the fifth decade of life. As this
trend is similar throughout the world, we may postulate an exogenous
(external) factor.

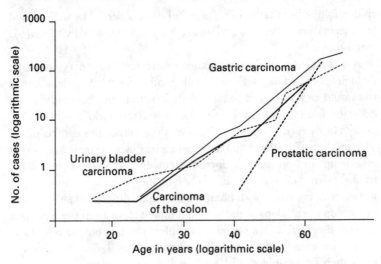

FIGURE 14.2 Graph showing the frequency, according to age, of four
types of cancer in Denmark (*source*: Day and Muir 1973)

The foregoing observations give an idea of how incongruous and
strange the epidemiological data on cancer are. But things unknown
are, by definition, strange. For example, in the pre-bacteriological era it
must have seemed strange that the plague should manifest itself by the
appearance of buboes (swollen lymph nodes), while cholera, another
febrile and deadly disease, should manifest itself by diarrhoea. And it
must have seemed odd that one fellow who had had an extramarital
escapade should be punished with gonorrhoea and another with syphilis.
These mysteries were cleared up with the discovery of bacteria, with
their predilections for this or that organ. The contradictions were resolved, and there was an explanation for what was common to all
infectious diseases (bacteria in general) and what distinguished them
(each single bacterium).

The same thing might happen with cancer. It seems to be caused by
an infinite number of different substances. The same environmental
factors, recognized or unknown, determine differences between populations of the same race or have the same effect on populations of
different races. All this seems baffling and confusing, but the confusion
is in us, not in the facts. The most tangled skein can be unravelled
eventually. One valid way of doing so would be to make better use of

epidemiology, but that requires plentiful data, collected by well-trained technicians along precise, standardized lines and evaluated by cybernetic methods.

A single electronic data-processing centre (see Chapter 15) would be enough for the whole of Europe, with another for the Americas. Better still would be a single centre for the whole world.[5] But how can data be collected from remote and technologically backward countries? Certainly not by relying on reports sent by their authorities and hospitals. The sending of leaflets and circulars (unclear even to their authors) in an attempt to instruct their doctors is equally useless, ridiculous even; we are talking of doctors who daily face the problem of how to give intravenous injections with blunt needles, and who regard a single-lens microscope, sent along with shoes and tinned foods from some mission collection centre, as 'an object that confers prestige on our hospital'.

The information must be collected *in loco* by skilled technicians and must then be examined and evaluated by other scientifically trained personnel. Finally, the data must only be fed into the computer when their accuracy is certain. If computers are given wrong information, they will give wrong answers.

An arithmetical evaluation of epidemics

If we follow the pattern of any epidemiological disease, whether acute or chronic, we find that it follows a curve that, after a rise and a period of stasis, declines with roughly the same slope as the initial rise. To reduce the phenomenon to its simplest expression, let us consider the epidemic as having its origin in a single individual who infects two other individuals. Sooner or later, each of the two first infected will infect two more in turn, and so on. We can represent the course of the epidemic by the following numerical progression:

$$1 \quad 2 \quad 2^2 \quad 2^3 \quad 2^4 \quad 2^5 \quad 2^6 \quad 2^7 \quad \text{etc.}$$

After a period of stasis (short in acute epidemics, long in chronic epidemics), the chances of contagion decrease, and in consequence the number of newly infected individuals decreases as well, which further reduces the risk of contagion – until the epidemic is extinguished. The regression of the epidemic can be represented numerically as follows:

$$2^7 \quad 2^6 \quad 2^5 \quad 2^4 \quad 2^3 \quad 2^2 \quad 2 \quad 1$$

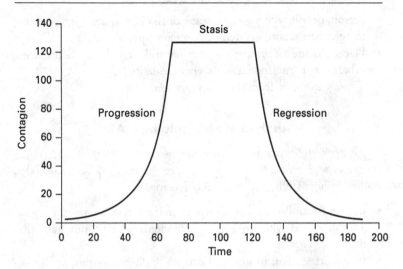

FIGURE 14.3 Computer visualization curve

The progression–stasis–regression curve can be represented as in Figure 14.3.

In ancient times – indeed, up to a few centuries ago – the progress of some well-known acute plagues followed the 'visualized' path described above. As a matter of fact, chronic, still prevalent diseases (tuberculosis, for example) follow the same path. It would be naive to think that tuberculosis had been defeated thanks solely to streptomycin and hydrazide or the BCG vaccination. But it is even more naive to believe that vaccination has been responsible for eradicating the majority of bacterial and viral diseases. While recognizing that contingent factors like better hygiene and improved nutrition have played a part in triggering the downward path of the curve, we must also recognize (as must vivisectionists) that the real cause of the decline in epidemics is the reduced infection risk.

From a practical standpoint, epidemiology can be divided into descriptive and analytical epidemiology (see Kelsey and Parker 1993).

Descriptive epidemiology (DE)

DE describes *how* a disease (or other characteristic) is distributed in a population, by taking into account three elements: person, place and time:

- Person: people with a given disease, or risk of acquiring it, according to age distribution, gender, race, socio-economic status.
- Place: disease occurrence within natural or political boundaries, urban versus rural areas, differences in latitude.
- Time: can range from days to years to centuries.

Analytical epidemiology (AE)

AE seeks to explain *why* a given disease (or other characteristic) occurs in a given population. It can take the form of case-controlled studies, cohort studies or cross-sectional studies:

- In case-controlled studies, groups of individuals with a given disease are compared with groups of individuals who do not have that disease (controls).
- In cohort studies, groups (cohorts) of individuals who, at the beginning of the study, are free of the disease, are classified according to whether they are exposed or not exposed to a defined risk (one example being the link between lung cancer and cigarette smoking). The cohort is then monitored for an appropriate period of time, after which the number of individuals who have contracted the disease (morbidity rate) or the number of those who have died of the disease (mortality rate) are compared with those who have not.
- In cross-sectional studies (or prevalence studies), the exposure to a hypothetical risk factor and the occurrence of the disease of interest are measured, at a given point in time, in a group of individuals. The number of diseased individuals who have been exposed to the risk is compared with those who have not been thus exposed.

Notes

1. Epi + demi + ology: from Greek = upon + people + study.

2. John Snow (1813–58), an Englishman and pioneer in anaesthetics using chloroform and ether.

3. Systematically examining histological slides of organs from cadavers or surgical specimens removed for diseases other than cancer, we are struck by the frequency with which 'carcinomas *in situ*' are found – that is, very small carcinomas (300–400 microns in diameter, not extending beyond the basal membrane) – especially in areas more prone to invasive cancer, such as the cervix or the prostate. This suggests that cancers are continually forming in the

organism but are blocked or destroyed by an unknown defence mechanism (which could simply be specific antibodies).

4. The incidence of malignant growths increases with age. After the age of 80 the incidence decreases, and it virtually stops after the age of 90.

5. Today each country collects its own cancer statistics, independently of others and often based on different criteria. The results are kept in cancer registers. The fragmentation is such that some countries have more than one register: for example, Germany has four. There are about eighty cancer registers throughout the world, which means that most countries do not possess even one. Italy has only two regional registers, one in Piedmont and the other in Lombardy. There are also two Atlases of Cancer Mortality, compiled from data supplied by ISTAT (Istituto Centrale di Statistica, in Rome), one of them by the Istituto di Biometria e Statistica Medica of Milan University (published by the Lega Italiana per la Lotta Contro I Tumori, Rome), the other (for the period 1971–74) edited by the Physics Institute of Milan University.

14. Computer simulation

One cannot expect judgements from computers, but they immeasurably surpass human capability when it comes to making rapid and precise mathematical calculations. Computers have no critical ability. However, they do have a prodigious memory, capable of storing millions of items of information and recalling them at the press of a button. When these two abilities are combined, a computer can produce results or deductions that differ in three ways from those of which the human mind is capable:

1. The computer produces *all* the results obtainable from a given set of facts, whereas human calculations, being directed by the will, often overlook apparently insignificant combinations that the results reveal to be none the less significant. This is because the mind 'saves' time and energy when working, while the computer, thanks to its tremendous operating speed, has practically unlimited time and energy.
2. The computer does not 'forget', that is, it does not lose any of the information it receives.
3. The computer does not make mistakes. Its calculations, however complex they may be, always lead to an accurate result. That, of course, depends on the information it receives.

Like all human activities, scientific research has a past, a present and a future. The past is the sum of ideas already acquired. The present is the time when ideas already acquired are critically assessed and projections are made about new lines of research. The future is what is expected as a result of current activity.

Choosing the research project

All research into new facts is built on existing knowledge, although a human mind capable of assimilating all previous knowledge, even regarding elementary scientific facts, does not exist. The computer, however, does have that capability. It is an immense reservoir of know-ledge, and the most versatile archive with the most rapid access to it ever devised.

The main outcome of the computer's mnemonic ability is that of avoiding useless repetition of research. It is no exaggeration to say that the volume of worthless research carried out and published every year – worthless because it has been done before – is at least a hundred times greater than the volume of research that constitutes an original contribution, however small. At this point one wonders whether re-searchers will look favourably on a tool that tells them, without mincing words: 'This research is valueless – it has already been done.' One of the aims of this book is, indeed, to challenge researchers to return to their proper sphere, so that research ceases to be 'just another way of making a living', a source of money on tap, or a machine that is no longer geared to social reality. About one hundred periodicals would suffice to include all the medical papers published throughout the world. Instead, there are more than six thousand. If one were to count all the pages, one would probably find they exceeded in number the people who read them. This is big business at work. But at whose expense?

Searching the literature

It is taken for granted, before embarking on any research, that numerous publications on the same or related subjects will be consulted. Ideally, in fact, *all* existing publications in all languages should be consulted. This poses problems, and not least because of the language difficulty,[1] but it would be still more difficult, using conventional methods, to organize all the collected knowledge in an easily accessible form.

It is here that the computer comes to our aid. We must first (this is the most crucial phase) list all the relevant topics, then read the publica-tions, underlining any of the listed topics that have been dealt with, and feed these into the computer memory. For example, in research on the causes of cancer, the topics – viruses, antibodies, antigens, chemical carcinogens, gender, age, geographical distribution, and so on – could all be of interest. These topics can be fed into the computer memory, which will, on demand, name all publications dealing with, or merely mentioning, viruses, antibodies, chemical carcinogens, etc. Moreover, it can provide us with all the combinations of two or more topics, being able to connect, for example, virus with antigen, age with geographical distribution, etc. This kind of work done by hand, using pen and paper, would occupy the researcher for the rest of his or her life and would, moreover, increase the risk of error inherent in copying by hand.

Designing the project

The computer can guide us during the designing of the project. It is the job of the programmer to utilize fully the cybernetic potential of the computer. If the programming has been done in such a way as to give the computer the option to intervene at any point, it will be able to guide us step by step, pointing out inconsistencies and preventing us from getting side-tracked. This is an indispensable function of the computer, in epidemiological research in particular, but also for large-scale statistics in general.

As I have said, the human mind can do the same thing. However, the computer does it with astronomical speed and unerring precision. For example, if an idea contained in a publication has a link with a similar idea in another published work very different in character from the first, this might escape the notice of even the most attentive reader, but it will not do so with the computer, provided that the latter has been properly instructed or programmed.

Suggestions for a creative approach

The computer does not create new ideas; the human mind does, or at least, so it seems. In reality, the mind does not create in the biblical sense of the word, but it can recall information from the memory and make connections. The construction or idea that comes from this process is new, thanks to the rearrangement of the parts that constitute it, but it still involves pre-existing parts.

A pertinent comparison is that of chemical synthesis. If we combine hydrogen and chlorine, we obtain hydrochloric acid (HCl), which is new inasmuch as it possesses qualities that are different from its two constituent elements. It is not, however, a 'creation'. The computer works in a similar way to the human mind, that is, by combining elements already there. The computer can make more varied and numerous combinations of the data stored in its memory than the human mind could ever do. The combinations offered by the computer are not in themselves 'ideas', but they can be a source of ideas for those who are open to suggestions. This requires a thorough theoretical and practical knowledge of the instrument and long practice in using it.

The computer as experimental model

Selection of the research project; searching the literature; project design; creative suggestion: all that we have said about computers so far illustrates their role as scientific research 'assistant'. Computers offer us their memory, capable of storing an indefinite amount of information, retrievable at any time without any lapses; in the twinkling of an eye they can check a vast bibliography and can guide us in designing a project. However, computers can also be used in a way that can be defined as 'more autonomous': they can be used as *experimental models*.

To make a computer into an experimental model (or simulator or mathematical model) means programming it with the maximum amount of *confirmed* information that we already have about a particular structure or function, be it mechanical, physical, chemical or biological. For instance, one can instruct the computer to simulate the respiratory system of a human being, or any other animal.

What information must we feed into the computer to perform this simulation? It will require all the data relevant to the respiratory mechanism: respiration rate; heart minute volume; dead volume; residual volume; vital capacity; pulmonary compliance, etc., and, further, the partial pressure of atmospheric oxygen; the concentration of oxygen and carbon dioxide in the blood; the haemoglobin dissociation curve; data relating to the acid-base system of the blood – in short, everything we know for certain about human respiration.

Turned thus into a kind of theoretical breathing apparatus, the computer will be able to calculate the results of the variations to which one or more of the systems comprising respiration may be subjected. What happens, for example, in the blood of a person who breathes air with a partial oxygen pressure of 120 or 110 mm Hg instead of the 'normal' (at sea level and at 21°C) 158 mm Hg? How will the composition of the exhaled air be altered? Likewise the respiration rate and heart minute volume? The computer will answer these questions correctly and rapidly, but only if it has been fed accurate information. How can we expect correct answers about human beings if we feed it information on, say, the respiration rate of the rabbit?[2]

The computer is an honest instrument – of all researchers it is undoubtedly the *most* honest. Let us not mislead it, then, with incorrect or uncertain data, or by giving it data derived from animals. If we do so, we shall be perpetuating the errors that have contaminated human physiology and medicine hitherto. We should react against such contamination and abandon all the data obtained from animals so far. It is better for a computer to receive fewer data than a massive amount, among which inaccurate data are concealed.

The computer can also be used to model the action of a drug within the body: the time it takes to be absorbed by the intestine (if taken by mouth); its concentration in the blood; the changes it undergoes in the liver and other organs and its excretion by the kidneys, or by salivation or perspiration, or via the alimentary canal.[3] Here again, we must give the computer accurate data relating exclusively to humans and avoid any false or unconfirmed information. What, for example, could the computer tell us about the metabolization of morphine in the human body if the input data included a single item (one is enough) obtained from experiments on cats? (As mentioned in Chapter 3, morphine has a stimulatory effect on cats.)

Finally, the cardiovascular system is particularly suitable for mathematical modelling. Such a model, the Mock Circulatory System (MCS), has already been built by the Hydrospace Research Corporation for the National Heart Institute (USA). It consists of a physical model linked to a computer for the programming of normal and abnormal situations, such as fatigue, shock and the action of drugs.

These three examples should give some idea of the computer as model, but the possibilities in this field are endless. Their only limitation is the skill and imagination of the researcher in exploiting the capabilities of the machine.

To exploit the computer fully, a mathematical education is needed; this is the only way to communicate with the computer, whose language is mathematics. Cybernetics departments need to be set up in faculties of medicine and surgery, and only those graduates who have completed a two-year course in mathematics and physics should be admitted to them. Such a course should be taken in the first two years of medical, biological or veterinary studies, so that a graduate who then pursues his or her post-graduate specialization of three or four years is a researcher worthy of the name, or at least has the background essential to becoming one.

The computer, and the will to use it, should be encouraged in all hospitals, both public and private, as is increasingly the case. 'Surely not in small provincial hospitals?' the conformist might say. The conformist, being a victim of the prevailing miseducation, still thinks in terms of hierarchies, in which a small provincial hospital is inferior to a city hospital, and a city hospital comes a poor second to a university clinic. But the point is that medical research on humans must 'follow the illness', and that is no respecter of hierarchies. Research based exclusively on humans must be prepared to seek its natural models (the sick) wherever they are to be found, even in 'small provincial hospitals'.

Biological science, especially human biology, differs from the other sciences in this regard – the physicist, the chemist, the geologist and the archaeologist can remove to their laboratories their material for study, whether it be stone from the Dolomites, shells from the ocean depths, fossil animals and plants from the Pyrenees, or even pieces of rock from the moon. One might say that, in these sciences, the movement of the object of study is centripetal, from the environment to the scientist, whereas in medical science, the movement is centrifugal: the research subjects must be studied wherever they happen to be, and it is the researcher who must go to them. The study of human disease must therefore be carried out where the human being is – if not within the family, then in hospital, and that means each and every hospital, even the provincial one. But even there, sufficient data cannot be collected with notebook and pencil. If all these hospitals, too, were equipped with computer terminals, their data could be transferred to larger computers for further evaluation. This would require the broadest possible exchange of information, reaching out to the periphery and culminating in centralized analysis, and presupposes cooperation on all sides.

It is easy to see what this type of organization of medical research might achieve. It is equally easy to predict the opposition that the centres of power – politicians, the pharmaceutical industry, the universities – might mount against it, for such democratization of research would rapidly undermine today's pseudo-research.

Recent advances in computing

Recent technological progress has made it possible to manufacture high-performance computers with a very large memory and extremely rapid execution. The latest supercomputers enable researchers to perform millions of operations per second. High-performance computers play two important roles in the study of living systems:

1. modelling, to obtain study data; and
2. analysis of that data through visualization.

Visualization means transforming numerical data into geometric representations. High-performance computers allow two-dimensional images to be rebuilt as three-dimensional, so, for example, enabling surgeons to simulate a surgical procedure before performing it on the patient.

Computer modelling Computer modelling offers perspectives in medical-biological disciplines such as genetics, cell biology, reproductive biology, cardiodynamics, neurology, nephrology and body dynamics.

Computer modelling in genetics Computer modelling in genetics investigates the structural evolution of the human genome and helps in the reconstruction of genetic evolutionary trees. Linkage analysis can locate and map the genes that contribute to the understanding of inherited disorders.

Computer modelling in cell biology A better understanding of the life-cycle of the cell improves our ability to control the development of various form of cancer. A more accurate simulation of cellular processes can be used to test treatment protocols before using them on patients.

Computer modelling in reproductive biology In some countries fertility is decreasing in both sexes. This suggests the need for a detailed model of the reproductive cycle, to give insight into how the environment and/ or other factors influence fertility in a given country or population. The same model can be used to study the dynamics of ageing in the mammalian reproductive system.

Computer modelling in cardiodynamics A computational model can yield information on the interactions between myocardial function and heart drugs, on the dynamics of calcium-mediated contractility in relation to cardiac preparations and on heart disease and its effect on cardiodynamics.

Computer modelling of the nervous system Supercomputers can model single neuron functions in diseases like Alzheimer's, showing how it progresses and how it might be treated. At the neurophysiological level, computer modelling can throw light on the source of rhythm fluctuations in the electric potential of the EEG.

Computer modelling of the kidney Computer modelling can represent two important mechanisms of kidney function: (1) the concentration capability of the inner renal medulla; and (2) fluctuations in tubule pressure in the physiological control mechanism.

Computer modelling of body dynamics Modelling the biomechanics of the skeleton can teach us how impact forces are transmitted through skeletal structures and can aid the design of prostheses and bio-implants. At the cellular level, collagen fibrils are arranged in a quasi-parallel pattern in the healthy ligament, while in injured tissue the arrangement is random. However, as the tissue heals, the fibrils realign in a process called collagen remodelling.

Notes

1. The scientific community worldwide should agree to publish in one language only, and that language can be none other than English. For this reason, the study of English should be compulsory for all science students.

2. The rabbit has a respiration rate of about 40 per minute, the human being 17 per minute (at rest).

3. Such a program has been used by the University of Pittsburgh, USA, in the study of drugs.

15. *In vitro* techniques

There are two ways of studying parts of living organisms *in vitro*: maintenance *in vitro* and culture *in vitro*.[1]

Maintenance *in vitro* consists of extracting from the animal the part to be investigated (fragments of tissue, organs, body systems) and maintaining it in conditions where it can survive for a limited period of time – surviving, but not reproducing itself. This is done in the following ways.

Tissue fragments are kept in physiological saline, an aqueous solution of the salts essential for cell life, which are sodium chloride, small amounts of potassium chloride, calcium, phosphates and bicarbonate. The general-purpose solutions, Ringer's and Kreb's solutions, are named after their originators. Other special solutions are formulated according to specific requirements.

Where a whole organ or body system (for example, the heart–lung system, the urinary tract) is involved, it is not only immersed in one of the above solutions but also perfused with it. For this purpose a cannula of plastic or glass is inserted into the main artery and the physiological saline introduced through it under pressure. Travelling through arteries of ever-decreasing size and eventually reaching the capillaries, the fluid perfuses the tiniest structures, supplying them with the substances necessary for a short period of survival and carrying away catabolites (waste products). It then exits via the veins.

All this must be done at the right temperature (about 37°C for mammalian organs and tissues).[2] Under these conditions, the preparation (tissue, organ, body system) is kept alive for several hours, but characteristic functions sufficiently similar to those prevailing in the living animal can be maintained for a few minutes only. After this, degeneration sets in, leading rapidly to the death of the cells.

Culture *in vitro* consists of removing small pieces of tissue and placing them immediately in an environment where the cells can not only survive but also multiply. It can be either (a) cell culture, which gives rise to the development of colonies of a single type of cell, or (b) tissue culture, which gives rise to the development of two or three types of cell, bound together in a structure resembling, but not identical with, the original tissue (Blüchel 1976).

Cell culture

Most animal and vegetable cells are capable of autonomous reproduction, but this is subject to two factors:

1. the environment (the culture medium), which must provide nutrients and remove waste products; and
2. time, which imposes limits whose effects are known, while their mechanisms remain unknown. As with complex organisms, cells, too, when artificially isolated and cultured, follow a characteristic life-cycle from birth to death, provided they retain their diploid character.[3]

Cells separated from the organism have a shorter lifespan than those living with other cells organized into tissue. Thus cells may tolerate but do not 'like' independent life. To live longer, they need to be associated with other cells, and not just sister cells but cells of a different type.

In fact, tissues are for the most part coordinated aggregates of various types of cell, one type at the service of another, obedient to laws of which we know little. Indeed, we know far too little about these interactions between cells, considering their role as the basis of multi-cellular animals and plants since their first development from single-cell life forms in the primordial swamps via cell colonies.[4] The short lifespan of most diploid cells in culture – although fibroblasts can survive for several years – contrasts with the virtual immortality of bacteria.

Bacteria – the species, that is, not the individual bacterium – live for ever, provided that they are periodically transferred to a fresh medium: that is, their source of energy and nutrients is regularly replenished.[5] In contrast, the cells of multi-cellular animals have, in culture, a life-cycle that invariably ends in the death not just of the individual cell but also of the whole colony, even if their supply of energy and nutrients is maintained.[6]

At this point we need to ask: what *is* death for a single-celled organism? There are two ways in which it can come about. The first relates to reproduction. The second occurs when reproduction stops – this is death in the human sense of the word. In the former case, the individual ceases to exist at the moment it divides into two new individuals, with no physical trace of the mother cell remaining. In the latter case, the decomposing remains of the maternal cell are left.

Culture media Cells and tissues[7] are cultured in culture media. All media are liquid or semi-solid (for example, soft agar). There are many different kinds, some for general, some for specific purposes. Some cells multiply readily in simple media, others only in specifically designed media.

1. All media must contain certain basic ingredients: ions (chlorine, sodium, potassium, magnesium, calcium, traces of iron, zinc, selenium, copper, manganese, molybdenum, vanadium); phosphates, bicarbonates, glucose[8] (or another sugar with six atoms of carbon usable by the cells, such as galactose); amino acids[9] and vitamins. The majority of cells need choline and mesoinositol. Certain cells require the presence in the medium of polyunsaturated fatty acids (like oleic acid and linoleic acid). Others do better on cholesterol. All these ingredients are normal constituents of protoplasm.

2. All cell and tissue cultures need oxygen. This penetrates the cell through the surface of the culture. Thus, in tissue cultures, if the volume of tissue to be cultured is too great, the inner part dies from lack of oxygen. The optimal concentration of oxygen varies for different tissues. Some grow well in air (21% oxygen, 78% nitrogen, 1% rare gases); others do better with an oxygen pressure less than that of air and yet others with a greater pressure. However, these pressures, while they favour the growth of certain cells, can damage or kill other kinds.

3. Cell and tissue culture vessels must contain in their atmosphere carbon dioxide (CO_2) in equilibrium with the concentration of bicarbonate in the medium (for constant and rapid control of pH). For most cell cultures, the optimal concentration of CO_2 is 2–5% (that is, similar to that of living tissues).

4. Media used for the culturing of diploid cells must contain 5–10% fresh animal serum (calf is usually used) or human serum. Therefore, a medium for diploid cell cuture cannot (with some exceptions) be completely synthetic and is not exactly reproducible at different times and locations. Moreover, it cannot be sterilized by heat.

5. The medium must be sterile, that is, free from bacteria, fungal micro-organisms and viruses. Sterilization may be done using an autoclave (a sealed vessel under pressure) for those components able to withstand heat, while heat-sensitive components, such as serum, are sterilized by filtration. The two parts are then mixed together. However, initial sterilization of the medium may not prevent subsequent contamination, and antibiotics may therefore be added to the medium: penicillin (100 units per ml), streptomycin (0.5 mg per ml) and neomycin (0.1 mg per ml). Neither sterilization by filtration nor the use of antibiotics, however, can protect cell cultures from viruses and mycoplasmas,[10] which may be transmitted in the serum or which may already be present in the tissue matrix.

6. The cultures should not be exposed, except briefly, to fluorescent light, as the shorter wavelengths (indigo, violet) transform certain substances (riboflavin, tyrosine, tryptophane) into cell toxins.

Let us return now to point 4 – the need of diploid cells (and hence primary and secondary cultures) for fresh animal serum. What substances does the serum contain? Serum contains two types of molecule:

i) molecules of low molecular weight, or *micromolecules*, such as vitamins, amino acids, lipids, choline; and

ii) molecules of higher molecular weight or *macromolecules*. These are essential to the growth *in vitro* of most diploid cells. There are exceptions, in that some diploid cells can develop in the absence of serum (Evans et al. 1964). However, such cells, placed in the medium, themselves supply the macromolecules, partly by secreting them, but mostly via the decay of those that die. Thus, even a medium not enriched with animal serum always contains a certain number of macromolecules.

The effects of serum on cell and tissue cultures are due chiefly to fetuin,[11] an alpha-globulin acid, but also to other alpha-globulins (Clarke et al. 1970), as well as gamma-globulins, insulin and CSF (Colony Stimulating Factor) (Stanley et al. 1968), a glycoprotein also found in human urine (Metcalf and Stanley 1969).

In cell cultures, serum has the following effects:

1. It helps the cells adhere to the wall of the culture vessel (plastic or glass)[12] (Todaro et al. 1965; Yoshikura and Hirokawa 1968).

2. It promotes flattening of the cells when they have adhered to the vessel wall.[13]

3. It stimulates cell multiplication; in particular, it reactivates 'stationary' cultures[14] (Todaro et al. 1965; Yoshikura and Hirokawa 1968).

4. It stimulates stationary cells to resume synthesis of DNA. This resumption occurs after a latency period of 4–15 hours, depending on the type of cell. The number of cells in a colony that resumes DNA synthesis is proportional to the quality of serum added (excessive amounts will, however, 'kill' the colony). The variations in intensity of response of different types of cell is reflected in the cell division rate of the cultured cells (Temin 1969).

5. It stimulates RNA and protein synthesis (Wiebel and Baserga 1969) and accelerates glycosis. RNA synthesis and protein synthesis are prerequisites for DNA synthesis (Müller 1969).

6. It accelerates the incorporation into the cells of uridine, guanosine and cytosine (Cunningham and Pardee 1969; Yeh and Fisher 1969).

7. It stimulates phospholipid metabolism (Peterson and Rubin 1969). This effect is proportional to the amount of serum added.

8. It protects newly seeded cells from dying. Many kinds of fibroblasts die if cultured for one or two days in a serum-free medium. The dead cells remain attached to the wall of the culture vessel, although if they die for other reasons they become detatched and float on the surface.

9. Serum, especially horse serum, is favourable to the conversion of normal embryo cells, particularly those of mice and rats, into tumour cells (Jackson et al. 1970). This transformation may, however, be due to the presence of a virus in the serum.

10. Serum of the right quality and in appropriate amounts favours spontaneous cloning.[15]

11. Serum has an as yet unexplained effect on the control of cell density, that is, the phenomenon that causes cell multiplication to cease when cells reach a certain density in the medium.

Continuous perfusion From the moment the cells, or slice of tissue, enter the medium, the composition of the latter starts to change, partly because the cells immediately start to extract nutrients from it and, to a greater extent, because the products of cell catabolism and of cell decay are added to it. Generally, these changes in composition tend to exhaust the capacity of the medium to keep cells alive, and they therefore represent a negative factor, whose impact increases over time until it brings the growth of the culture to a halt.[16] There are two ways of preventing this.

The most usual method is to replenish the medium, that is, replace part of the medium with an equal part of fresh medium. This, like all interventions, entails a risk of bacterial contamination, which would lead to the loss of the culture. Moreover, it means that the cells are subjected to a fluctuating environment. For example, if replenishment of the medium takes place every 24 hours, there will be a point of maximum 'well-being' in the first hour and a point of maximum 'distress' in the twenty-fourth hour, when the toxic waste products will have reached their highest concentration. In these conditions, metabolism, biochemical synthesis, frequency of cell division and cell movement will vary greatly over the 24-hour period.

The second method is perfusion, which means effecting a continuous influx and discharge of fresh medium into and out of the culture vessel. Various procedures that are easy to reproduce or modify have been devised for the purpose.

Rather more complicated are the devices that not only continuously change the medium but also cause the vessel to rotate so as to avoid stagnation of the layers of the medium that are in closest contact with the culture (which generally grows on the vessel walls).

Explanting and seeding The tissue to be cultured is taken from the live human being or animal. According to the specialist literature, the number of experiments on animal cells and tissues exceeds those carried out on human cells and tissues. Also, most permanent cell lines come from animals. This by no means demonstrates a necessity for using animals in this area of research. On the contrary, it merely shows that the dulling effect of routine can turn ingrained habits into rituals. In *in vitro* studies, as in experiments on animals *in vivo*, the results are unreliable or completely misleading when extrapolated to the human body and its tissues.

The primary cell line The primary cell line is obtained from tissue explants, or from cells taken by transparietal puncture from the amniotic fluid, or from blood leukocytes. To start a primary cell culture, a very small explant is sufficient – for example, a piece of human skin 1–3 mm in diameter. How is such an explant used to obtain a cell culture? The most common method is disaggregation.

Disaggregation The disaggregation of a tissue consists in the separation of its constituent cells and fibres.[17] To separate the cells, the extracellular substance, the stroma, which, like glue, joins them together, must be dissolved, and for this enzymes are used. Particular enzymes are selected according to the composition of the stroma to be dissolved and the desired quantity and quality of the cells. The enzymes must act at precise concentrations for limited periods of time, as their excessive use damages the cells, altering in particular the cell membrane. The most commonly used enzymes for this purpose are listed below.

- Pronase is obtained from the fungus *Streptomycetes griseus*. It aids cell dispersion, thus preventing the formation of cell clusters. By actively digesting dead cells and cell fragments, it effectively 'cleans' the cell suspension.
- Trypsin is slower-acting than pronase and does not always prevent the formation of cell clusters.
- Trypsin combined with EDTA[18] achieves effects similar to those of pronase.
- Collagenase: this enzyme, less commonly used than the preceding ones, is for specialized applications.

When using enzymes either for disaggregation of tissues or for detaching monolayer cultures from the vessel walls, it must be borne in mind that all enzymes damage cells. Contact time and concentration must therefore be kept to a minimum, determined experientially for each type of cell. Once the tissue has been disaggregated, the resultant uncoordinated mixture of different types of cell[19] is placed in the culture medium, where some cells die, while others (but only those capable of multiplying[20]) start, after a short latency period, to divide.

However, not all cells divide at the same rate. Therefore – depending partly on the composition of the medium – the most active ones prevail in number over the others and, after a certain time (with the cessation of multiplication and the death of some cells) they are the only active cells remaining in the culture. These cells constitute a *primary cell line*.

The cells of the primary cell line ('diploid' cells) have the following characteristics:

1. a similar form to the cell from which they originate;
2. a limited lifespan;
3. a diploid (or 'euploid') chromosome count – that is, the same as that of the parent cell;

4. the same functions as the parent cell, though not always with the full complement of functions;

5. most cells of the primary cell line need to adhere to a solid substrate (vessel wall, microsubstrate or similar) in order to reproduce, exceptions to this rule being chondrocytes, various blood cells and cells of the haematopoietic marrow; and

6. primary culture cells require a culture medium containing serum or its equivalents.

The secondary cell line By transferring or transplanting a few cells of a primary cell line to another culture vessel, we obtain a secondary cell line (or secondary cell 'strain').[21] Further subcultures (from second to third, third to fourth, and so on) are always called 'secondary' cell lines.

Despite successive subcultures and the time involved in their development, provided that the cells retain the same chromosome count (that is, the diploid state if they come from diploid cells) and the characteristics of the primary culture,[22] they constitute a *primary cell line* (PCL). However,

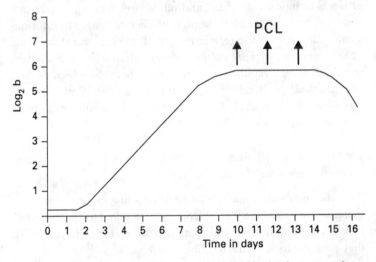

Note: 1.5–2 days: latency phase; 2–9 days: logarithmic phase; 9–14 days: stationary phase; 14–16 days: decline. Occasional permanent cell lines (see arrows) can develop from the culture line in the stationary phase.

PCL = permanent cell line.

FIGURE 16.1 Growth curve for an ideal cell colony

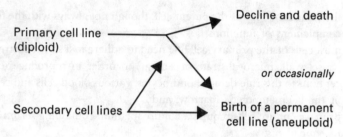

FIGURE 16.2 Diagram of cell lines

in time they tend to lose their original characteristics and become 'degraded', especially with regard to more specific functions (such as hormone production, if the cell comes from an endocrine gland). At the same time, their reproductive activity, that is, their rate of division, slows down. A logarithmic phase of growth is succeeded by a 'stationary' phase, followed by a decline that may end in the death of the entire colony (see Figure 16.1).

This is the most usual destiny of cell colonies. At times, however (after weeks or months of culture and subculture), a group of cells in a stationary culture may suddenly begin to proliferate. Such a transformation constitutes a dramatic turn in the life of a colony: a new cell line has been born, a *permanent cell line*, which behaves like a malignant tumour in that: (a) it rapidly overwhelms the other cells, which die and disintegrate; and (b) its cells, transplanted into an animal of the same species as the donor animal, develop characteristics analogous to those of a spontaneous cancer.

The permanent cell line The cells constituting a permanent cell line have the following characteristics:

1. their chromosome complement differs from that of the parent cell, therefore they are no longer diploid but aneuploid (or heteroploid);
2. they can be cultured for indefinite periods of time, during which they preserve fixed characteristics;
3. they grow rapidly, proliferating at a constant rate, each cell cycle usually taking less than 20 hours;
4. they do not require their nutrient medium to contain serum (or similar compounds);
5. they do not need to attach themselves to a substrate to reproduce but

can multiply in suspension (that is, they are anchorage-independent);

6. their proliferation is not inhibited by the density of the cell mass (that is, they are not density-dependent);

7. whatever the primary cell line from which they derive, permanent cell lines tend to conform to one of three standard types: the fibroblastic, the epithelial or the fibrocytic type (the last tending to adhere least to a substrate); and

8. the cells of permanent lines are usually malignant.

Permanent cell lines are utilized in various studies, their main advantages being:

1. Uniformity of cell type. Cultures of permanent cells can be sent to any laboratory and exchanged between laboratories, as is done, for example, with bacteria. In this way, almost perfect uniformity and reproducibility for experimental purposes are assured, even in widely dispersed laboratories. Certain permanent cell lines that have been in use for years have been given names and symbols, so that specialists can recognize and choose those with the most suitable characteristics for their research.[23]

2. They can be preserved by freezing. This allows checks to be made at any time, to see whether there are any variations in the cell line over time, after innumerable transfers.

3. When testing the effect on permanent cell lines of a chemical substance or a virus suspected of having a mutagenic effect, one can be fairly certain that the effect was caused by the substance or virus under investigation. However, when working with primary cell lines, which are composed of diploid cells, one can never be sure that the observed change is not due to the inherent instability of the diploid cells themselves.

4. Cells from permanent cell lines are easily cloned. The main limitation of permanent cell lines is their very 'standardness', which makes them less than representative of real tissues. In a sense, they resemble cultured protozoa rather than cells of human or animal origin.

Cloning There are two methods of isolating one cell from others and rendering it capable of producing a clone. The first consists of sucking up a single cell with a pipette under a microscope and transferring it at once to a microdrop of culture medium. This procedure presents technical difficulties.

The other is known as Puck and Marcus's cloning (Puck and Marcus 1955) or the plating method, and is performed as follows: a very dilute suspension of the culture is prepared, so that when a small amount is placed in the medium the individual cells are widely separated from one another. When a colony is observed to be growing under the microscope,[24] it is at once removed to another culture vessel. This method is easy but less accurate than the first method, since one can never be absolutely sure that the colony did not arise from two or more cells, rather than the single cell desired.

The first attempts (in about 1948; see Schimmer 1979) at producing a cell culture by cloning ended in failure and revealed the disconcerting fact that a single cell in isolation, even when transferred to a suitable medium, does not reproduce but dies. What the culture medium lacks are certain substances produced by the cells themselves.[25] But for these substances to pass into the medium in sufficient amounts, a sufficient number of cells must be present.

The existence of these substances has been demonstrated experimentally, and it has been found that, if a *single* cell is placed in a medium that previously contained other cells (whether of the same or a different type), it will survive and multiply by producing clones. Learning from this, cloning is now effected using 'conditioned media', that is, media which have previously been used to culture other cells.

A population of cell clones offers the advantage of almost perfect genetic uniformity of the individual cells. This is particularly useful for the study of mutagenic agents.

Cultures of microsubstrates Anchorage-dependent cells find a somewhat limited surface area at their disposal in the culture vessel, even if this is rotated. Consequently, the yield from the culture (whose development usually stops once the walls are coated with a monolayer of cells) is rather meagre.[26] To increase the yield, microsubstrate cultures have been developed (Thilly and Levine 1979). Microsubstrates are tiny beads, 50 to 100 microns in diameter, which are added to the culture medium in suitable amounts. The cells adhere to the surfaces of the beads and multiply. Cultures on microsubstrates can increase the yield of a culture 10- to 20-fold. The cells are removed from the beads in the same way as they are removed from culture vessel walls, that is, by using the proteolytic enzymes pronase, trypsin and collagenase. Culturing on microsubstrates is particularly suitable for the study of viruses.

Mathematical representation of the development of a culture A culture medium can be seeded with a single cell (cloning) or a number of cells (plating). In both cases, its development follows the pattern illustrated in Figure 16.1, with the following phases:

1st phase: latency[27]
2nd phase: logarithmic multiplication
3rd phase: stationary phase
4th phase: decline and eventual death of the culture

The phases vary with cell type, composition of the medium and other factors. What follows is the description of an ideal culture. The highest multiplication rate of cells takes place during the logarithmic phase.

Logarithmic phase After seeding with a single cell, the first generation consists of two cells, the second of four cells, the third of eight cells. The number (b) of cells in each generation is therefore expressed by the following equations:

1st generation: $b = 1 \times 2 = 2$
2nd generation: $b = 1 \times 2 \times 2$ (i.e. 1×2^2) $= 4$
3rd generation: $b = 1 \times 2 \times 2 \times 2$ (i.e. 1×2^3) $= 8$

Or, from seeding with a single cell and calling the number of generations 'n', we find:

$$(1) \quad b = 1 \times 2^n$$

If, on the other hand, seeding is done with a number of cells 'a' (a>1), equation (1) is substituted by:

$$(2) \quad b = a \times 2^n$$

This equation states that, during the development of the culture, the number of cells is an exponential function of 2, which considerably simplifies the calculations by referring to the logarithm of the number of cells rather than to the number itself.

For instance, if we use a Cartesian system of coordinates, with the abscissa representing growth time and the ordinate representing the logarithm to base 2, we get a straight line for periods of constant increase (Figure 16.1, days 2 to 8). Usually, however, the seedings contain a large number of cells. As a result, it is more convenient to use base

10 rather than base 2 logarithms, bearing in mind that the base 2 logarithmic scale stands in the following relationship to the base 10 scale:

$$\log_{10} y = \log_2 y \times 0.3010$$

where y is any number.

Returning to equation (2), this can be expressed with the base 2 logarithm by:

$$\log_2 b = \log_2 a + n$$

Using base 10 logarithms instead, the equation becomes:

$$\log_{10} b = \log_{10} a + n \log_{10} 2$$

but, since $\log_{10} b = 0.3010$, we can also write:

$$\log_{10} b = \log_{10} a \, (n \times 0.3010)$$

This equation allows us to find the values of 'n', or the number of generations produced from the moment of seeding to the moment of examination. The solution of 'n' is thus:

$$(3) \quad n = \frac{\log_{10} b - \log_{10} a}{0.3010}$$

Then, if we wish to determine the mean generation time (G) during the same interval, since:

$$G = \frac{\text{time passed}}{\text{number of generations}} = \frac{t}{n}$$

then

$$(4) \quad G = \frac{t}{\dfrac{\log_{10} b - \log_{10} a}{0.3010}} = \frac{0.3010 \times t}{\log_{10} b - \log_{10} a}$$

The above equations allow the fundamental parameters of a cell population to be calculated, that is: the number of cells present at seeding (a); the number of cells after a given time (b); the number of generations (n); the mean generation time (G).

This, however, concerns calculations valid only for constant values.

In particular, the mean generation time (G) is not constant during the whole cycle of development, and seeding is in fact followed by a latency phase characterized by a very long mean generation time. This is succeeded by the logarithmic phase, which follows the exponential laws just mentioned, that is, the stationary phase and then decline.

The logarithmic phase is characterized by constancy of generation time. This constancy allows us to represent the exponential function of cell multiplication over time by a straight line. Of course, not all cells in a culture divide, and not all those dividing do so at the same rate. It is by virtue of the large number of cells in a colony, and the high percentage of those actively multiplying, that the phenomenon takes on statistical consistency.

Actually, even during the logarithmic phase, there are some arrested cells which are incapable of multiplying. However, their presence does not alter the general trend of the phenomenon overall, which can be represented as though all the cells behaved in the same way at the same time.

Stationary phase – decline and death The shift from the logarithmic to the stationary phase is followed by a lengthening of the mean generation time and a reduction in the percentage of cells actively multiplying. The generation time tends towards infinity, which means that at a certain moment multiplication ceases. However, this does not mean that the majority of cells do not remain alive for some time.[28]

During the stationary phase, represented in Figure 16.1 by a line parallel to the abscissa, the number of cells that die is approximately the same as the number of cells that grow and multiply. However, this condition does not last long; the cell population eventually starts to decline as the death of an increasing number of cells occurs, until the death of the entire culture takes place. During the phase of decline, the glycolytic metabolism of the cells slows down, glycogen and lipids accumulate in the cytoplasm and – in fibroblasts – the ability to form collagen fibres disappears.

Generation time The generation time (G) varies, not only with cell type but also with the age of the cell donor. This is very evident in fibroblasts: those taken from a foetus grow more rapidly than those taken from an adult, and the older the donor, the slower the growth of the fibroblasts in culture (Martin et al. 1970). Also, fibroblasts taken from children affected by the genetic diseases progeria and Werner's Syndrome[29] grow slowly, as they would in the elderly (Goldstein et al. 1969; Martin et al. 1970).

Inhibition and cessation of growth Why does a cell culture, at a certain stage in its development, stop growing? This is a problem of universal significance, reflected in the older questions: Why do animals stop growing when they reach a certain size? Why does an organ only grow to a certain size? and the allied question: Why do all living organisms have characteristic shapes and dimensions that determine their appearance and distinguish them from one another? The universal nature of the problem suggests the importance of investigating these questions *ab ovo*, that is, in the smallest units of the organism, the cells.

When a primary cell culture (diploid culture) reaches a certain size, its cells cease to multiply.[30] Something must 'inform' the individual cell that the state of cell community or colony has been attained. We are far from understanding how this happens, but certain significant facts have been established.

One factor that seems to inhibit cell multiplication is *contact between one cell and another.* The term used to describe this phenomenon is contact inhibition, or topo-inhibition.[31] Contact between cells is, in turn, a result of crowding within the culture. Clearly, the more crowded a culture, the more its cells are forced into mutual contact. But by what mechanism is cell multiplication inhibited? One important mechanism is the inhibition of the movement of cell membranes, especially the cytoplasmic membrane.[32] Wave-like movements continuously pulsate through this membrane and are particularly pronounced on the pseudopodia.[33] These peristaltic waves can reach a height of 5 microns, which is considerable compared to the size of the cell as a whole. The movements of the part of the membrane adhering to the wall of the culture vessel allow the cell, newly formed by cell division, to move into its place, occupying an adjacent space.[34] When the cell makes contact with another cell with its leading edge, movement stops, and the edges of the two cells adhere firmly to each other. Later, however, the same cell can resume motion in a different direction, giving up its place to another emerging cell. To do this, it has to disengage itself from one or more of the cells to which it has already adhered. Pulling away takes considerable 'effort'.

Thanks to these shifts in position by the cells, the culture spreads like a drop of oil, forming a kind of mosaic pattern on the vessel walls. These movements and the peristaltic motion of the cytoplasmic membrane are clearly seen when a 'wound' (that is, the laceration caused by removing some of the cells) is caused to the culture. The cells at the edge of the wound start to move and, by multiplying and positioning themselves appropriately, soon reconstruct the missing part. This closely resembles what happens in tissues *in vivo*.

Other factors, apart from contact inhibition, contribute to cessation of growth of a culture, namely, exhaustion of certain substances in the nutrient medium or serum and accumulation of catabolites excreted by the cells. Where continuous perfusion is used, these factors are irrelevant, however, and the production by the cells of inhibiting substances, known as chalones and comparable to hormones, has been postulated.

The nature of adhesion between cells The cells of a monolayer culture adhere tenaciously to one another by means of two types of bond.[35] The first type acts in the initial phase and is a physical bond due to electrostatic attraction, van der Waals forces,[36] or bonding between hydrogen ions. Electrostatic attraction occurs mainly between the peptides and proteins of the cytoplasmic membrane, so that when cell cultures are treated with proteolytic enzymes, which digest proteins and peptides, the culture disintegrates.

The second bond is formed at a later stage: in the space of about 100Å that exists between the edges of the two cells a substance called desmin is deposited which consolidates the adhesion. This substance can also be digested by proteolytic enzymes.

Intercellular adhesion has significant implications for the study of malignant tumours. The cells of these tumours, when cultivated *in vitro*, adhere only weakly to each other or not at all. In the culture medium, therefore, they tend to grow in suspension. This seems to be due mainly to a fairly high negative charge on their cytoplasmic membrane. The electrical charges of two adjacent cells repel each other, pushing the cells apart. This throws a great deal of light on the tendency of malignant tumours in the living organism to disintegrate and thus liberate cells, which are carried in the blood and the lymph to distant tissues and organs, to form metastases. No *in vivo* research would ever have been able to reveal a fact so significant for our understanding of malignant tumours.

Tissue culture

Cultivating a tissue means allowing all its constituent cells and fibres to develop *in vitro*, so that they can harmoniously reconstruct the structure from which they derive – to produce, for example, a large piece of skin from a small fragment, or a number of liver lobules from a fragment of liver tissue. This ideal result has not yet been widely achieved, but partial successes have been sufficient to encourage further development of existing methods and promote a search for new ones.

Tissue placed in a culture medium does not develop harmoniously in every part, mainly because one type of cell multiplies at such a rate as to overwhelm the others, so that only a single cell line is obtained from the culture. For example, a skin sample produces a *fibroblast line*. These cells, deprived of their natural contact with the other components of the tissue (other cells, fibres, membranes), tend to lose their original characteristics. They survive for a limited time (which demonstrates a generic 'tolerance'), or they transform themselves into permanent cell lines with neoplastic properties. This is incontrovertible proof that neoplastic cells, *in vitro* or *in vivo*, have no need of other cells; they are independent, anarchic, and, by virtue of their capacity to appropriate nutrients at the expense of other cells, predatory.

In *cell culture*, an abundant yield is usually desired. Vigorous growth and a prolonged logarithmic phase indicate that the cells 'appreciate' the environment provided for them.

In *tissue culture*, on the other hand, slow, circumscribed growth is desirable. The ideal environment would be that in which the tissue stopped growing on reaching a certain critical size, as it does in living creatures, where only tumours continue to grow indefinitely, while normal tissues, whether in the course of physiological growth or wound healing, stop growing 'at the right moment'.

In vitro tissue, deprived of blood, absorbs nutrients and oxygen (and eliminates catabolites and CO_2) through its external surfaces. If, however, the tissue grows too much, the surface area is too small in proportion to volume, and parts of the tissue, particularly the inner parts, die.

The ability to test the effects of various agents (toxins, antigens, antibodies, hormones, viruses, ionizing radiation) on complete tissues *in vitro* would overcome the following objection as to the comparability of *in vitro* and *in vivo* testing – namely that, because an animal is a coordinated complex of organs and functions, substances tested on it undergo a coordinated series of transformations in more than one organ or tissue, while in cell cultures, or cultures of tissue fragments, the same substances attack the cell directly 'in its raw state'. Moreover, the cells attacked are not like normal ones, since they have lost some of their functions and are living in an unnatural state, deprived of contact with other cells. For example, epidermal cells cultured *in vitro* are no longer in contact with the basal membrane or the dermal mesenchyma, and liver cells cultured *in vitro* have no further contact with the reticular endothelium. With improved methods of tissue culture, many new avenues would be opened up: for instance, the effect of a substance on kidney tissue *in vitro* could be studied after subjecting it to metabolic processing by a passage through liver tissue *in vitro*.

Obviously, this would mean dealing with *human* tissue (from kidney, liver, heart, nervous system, endocrine glands, etc.). No one would prevent a veterinarian doing the same thing in the case of dogs, cats or calves, provided that these experiments would clearly benefit the said animals. In the same way, research for the benefit of humans could progress with the small but sure steps we demand of an exact and responsible science. The remainder of this chapter will show that this is not merely a Utopian vision.

Working with human cells: a responsible research method
The complex structure of tissues, the ordered arrangement of their many constituents, might suggest a centralized organization, as if an architect had arranged the cells, each in its proper place, like building-blocks with no will of their own. But this is not so. *In vitro* cultures have demonstrated a surprising fact: the 'will'[37] to unite and form organized structures is inherent in each individual cell.[38] Here are some examples:

- When embryo tissue is disaggregated, an uncoordinated mixture of various cell types suspended in the culture medium is obtained. But if the suspension is left undisturbed for some hours, the cells re-organize to form a structure similar to the original tissue (Weiss and Taylor 1960).
- If the kidneys from chick embryos are disaggregated and the result-ant cell mixture is spread on the egg membrane, the cells soon reorganize, blood vessels appear and typical kidney tissue develops (ibid.).
- Disaggregated skin of chick embryos reorganizes to form new skin with typical feather-bearing matrices.

These and other similar experiments demonstrate that the cells have a definite 'will' to relate to each other and to form the structure for which they were originally designed. The ways in which these aggregations and related movements arise have been observed and filmed. If cells of different types are mixed together and suspended in a liquid medium, a surprising fact is observed: the cells move in an apparently uncoordinated way, but as soon as two 'sister' cells touch, they unite and do not separate again. Others join the first two, and in this way a cluster of cells of the same type is formed. This is not a static association: on the contrary, the cells within it are constantly moving about, gliding over each other, not separating, but changing position, as if each cell were seeking the most suitable place for itself.

The following phenomenon is equally surprising: if various types of cell from one animal species (for example, cells from a mouse embryo) are mixed with those of another species (from a chick embryo, for example), the cells from the mouse embryo join with those of the chick, provided that they are of the same type, that is, mouse epithelial cells unite with chick epithelial cells, mouse fibroblasts with chick fibroblasts, and so on (Moscona and Moscona 1952). In other words, attraction occurs between cells of the same kind from different animals, rather than between different cell types from the same animal.

Tissue culture methods are rather more varied and less standardized than cell culture methods. This follows, in part, from the natural differences between tissues and in part reflects the fact that such methods are still at the pioneering stage. Understandably, the difficulties increase in proportion to the complexity of the tissue to be cultured. We shall mention just a few simple procedures used in tissue culture, to give an indication of the ingenuity the experimenter must possess and to show how stimulating this kind of research can be – research on which much of the future development of medical science will depend.

The vaginal wall and the skin are both relatively simple tissues.[39] If small pieces of these tissues are placed in *in vitro* culture conditions, the dermis shrivels and the epidermis totally envelops it, forming a kind of cyst, within which, due to the poor permeability of the epidermis, the dermis 'suffocates' and degenerates. To avoid this, the following measure is taken: the skin or vaginal mucosa, instead of being placed directly on the culture medium, is placed on a piece of rayon, the dermis in contact with the fabric (Fell 1972). The mesenchymal tissue that constitutes the dermis then develops by penetrating the mesh of the rayon, and the epidermis can no longer envelop it. If histological slides are subsequently required, the rayon can be dissolved away using acetone.

Cultures of normal epithelial cells are useful for the study of how such cells are transformed into cancerous ones by the action of chemical compounds, viruses and radiation. However, unlike epithelial cancer cells, normal epithelial cells are somewhat difficult to culture *in vitro*. Why is this?

In living tissue, epithelial cells, such as those of the epidermis of the vaginal wall, depend intimately on the mesenchyma that forms the dermis beneath, and still more on the basal membrane.[40] When the epidermis is separated from the dermis and placed in a culture medium, it does not keratinize (that is, it is incapable of maturing), and after a few days it degenerates and dies. If, on the other hand, it is placed in contact with the dermis again, its cells multiply, develop in the normal way and produce basal membrane. This happens even if the epidermis is applied to a dermis that has been 'killed' by repeated freezing and thawing. If instead it is killed by heat, it loses its ability to keep the epidermis alive. We may therefore reason that if the dermis when 'killed' (but not denatured by heat) keeps the epidermis alive, allowing it to mature, an artificial membrane of similar chemical composition to that of dermal collagen might have the same property. Experiments have confirmed this hypothesis. If the epidermis is placed on a layer of collagen gel, the cells multiply, keratinize normally and sometimes even produce a basal membrane.[41] It is an interesting fact that keratinization does not occur if the epidermis is placed on collagen different from that of the dermis. The dermis contains a specific factor for epidermal development that other connective tissues lack.

These findings have been strikingly confirmed. If a piece of epithelium of the submaxillary gland of an embryo is cultured while in contact with mesenchyma taken from any other part of the body, it forms only a small mass of undifferentiated epithelial cells. If, on the other hand, it is cultured in contact with the mesenchyma destined to form the capsule of the gland, it develops, forming true glandular acini. Likewise, the mammary gland develops normally – that is, it forms acini and glandular ducts – only when it is cultured in contact with mammary mesenchyma and not with any other kind of mesenchyma (Sakakura et al. 1976). This specific capacity of the mesenchyma to instruct epithelial structures is one of the most important discoveries in embryology of recent decades.

But there is an even more important fact that bears on possible practical developments. Only normal epithelial cells depend for their growth and differentiation on the mesenchyma and basal membrane, while cancerous ones grow independently of these structures.[42] These findings would have been impossible without the contribution of *in vitro* tissue culture.

Once it was established that the 'health' of the epithelial cell depends mainly on contact with the basal membrane, attempts were made to construct artificial basal membranes. Technical data can be obtained from the original published paper (Reid and Rajikind 1979), but the main points are outlined below. The basal membrane is composed of:

1. collagen proteins;
2. adhesive protein, LETS (Large External Transformation Substance); and
3. mucopolysaccharides (or glucosaminoglycanes).

For the artificial basal membrane, collagen is extracted from the skin or tendons; these are tissues that contain mainly Type I collagen, but there is also a small amount of Type IV in the skin, deriving from the basal membrane that separates dermis and epidermis. The LETS is harvested from cultures of fibroblasts, on whose surfaces it is found in abundance, while mucopolysaccharides are prepared by the method described by Hall (Hall 1976).

In order to manufacture the Reconstituted Basal Membrane (RBM), 50 g of LETS and 50 g of mucopolysaccharides are added to 1.0 ml of solution no. 1 (collagen extract). The mixture is allowed to gel into a very fine film in a culture vessel (about 1 mg of the mixture for a container 35 mm in diameter). Epithelial cells are transferred from a primary culture onto the film, and the whole is then placed on a culture of fibroblasts.[43] This produces a typical skin, with its three components: epithelium, basal membrane and mesenchyma.

The results show that this is far from a mere technical exercise. The epithelial cells, which grow only slowly when cultured on their own *in vitro*, survive for a long time in this complex type of culture (known also as sociocellular) and retain their principal physiological properties.

Another structure that can be reconstituted *in vitro* is the vascular wall: bovine endothelial cells cultured on smooth muscle cells from rats have produced a structure similar to the wall of a blood vessel, which remained intact for several months.[44] A vascular wall formed in this way could be useful for research into thrombosis, atherosclerosis, transparietal migration of leukocytes and the ability of cancer cells to penetrate vascular walls.

In vitro methods: assessment and prospects

Even if cell and tissue cultures had nothing more to offer – an absurd assumption, in my view – their achievements to date amply justify the effort invested in them. This is clear merely from examining those areas where investigation could not have been done by any other means – for example:

- Embryology: demonstration of the inductive function of mesenchyma for their respective epithelia.
- Cell physiology: demonstration of (a) the indispensability of the basal membrane for the survival of the epithelium; and (b) the fact that the basal membrane is largely secreted by the epithelial cells.
- Somatogenesis: self-limitation of the growth of tissues – an insight into the 'mystery' of the form and size of living organisms.
- Pathology: demonstration of (a) the independence of cancer cells from the basal membrane and the mesenchyma; (b) the fragility of the bonds that hold cancer cells together; and (c) the 'spontaneous' transformation of normal cells into cancer cells.

This last is the most startling phenomenon – and the most promising for research into the causes of cancer. When an animal or human 'spontaneously' contracts cancer, all we can do is accept the fact. All we know about their condition is that one of their cells has started to proliferate 'like mad'. And by the time we realize that this runaway proliferation is taking place, the cells already number several million and are likely to continue on the same course.

We can observe this same transformation in *in vitro* cultures, from the initial stage, when a primary (euploid) cell line suddenly becomes a permanent (aneuploid) cell line, likely to be composed of cancer cells. We see the chromosomes increasing until they double in number (tetraploidism), as if a new kind of animal has emerged from the preceding one. The new cells no longer recognize the euploid cells as their sisters – they attack and destroy them.

Observing these phenomena through the microscope, we feel that we are close to discovering the cause – but what is it? Is it a virus already present in the culture? How did it get there? Is it from the organic substances (calf serum) that constitute the culture medium? Or was it already present in the explant? Perhaps it is not a virus at all, but an airborne chemical contaminant, or a chemical in the glass or plastic containers used. Or is it due to irradiation from an external energy source, such as cosmic or ultraviolet radiation or X rays? Whatever it may be, we seem to be closer to it in these experimental conditions than by using any other methods.

The potential for cell and tissue cultures is unlimited, as continuing improvements push back the frontiers of investigation. There are many possible areas of research:

- experiments on viruses;
- experiments on hormones and endocrine glands;
- toxicological experiments;
- experiments with mutagenic, teratogenic and carcinogenic substances;
- immunological studies; and
- the study of enzymopathies.

Experiments on viruses Cell cultures are suitable for investigation of the following:

- virus culture;
- viral metabolism;
- pathogenic action of viruses on cells;
- mutagenic and carcinogenic action;
- research into anti-viral drugs;
- production of anti-viral vaccines; and
- production of interferon.

Virus culture A virus is the smallest piece of living organic matter. Although, like all living things, it is able to reproduce, it cannot lead an autonomous existence – it can live only in another cell, utilizing the latter's enzymes and metabolic apparatus.[45]

For many years virus cultures used the largest known cell, the egg of a chicken or other bird. With the advent of cell cultures, viruses could be cultured on somatic cells, which could be selected for their suitability for each of the many types of virus in existence.[46]

One of the advantages of using cell and tissue cultures, rather than studying viruses *in vivo*, is that cell and tissue cultures do not contain antibodies (which form rapidly in the living organism to protect it from viral attack). This permits us, on the one hand, to study the cell's ability to defend itself when it has to fight the virus 'single-handed', and, on the other, to identify the mechanisms whereby the virus attacks the cell and utilizes its contents and energies without, as it were, being stabbed in the back by the antibodies that would, *in vivo*, be produced in self-defence by the organism.

If the specific antibody for a particular virus is added to the culture medium, the infectivity of the virus for the cell is wholly or partially blocked. This is an invaluable way of assessing the effect of anti-viral antibodies (Moffat 1973).

Some viruses are more suitable than others for general virological investigation. One of these is the SV-40 virus (or monkey virus 40), which is particularly suitable for the study of viral DNA, the transcription and translation mechanisms involved, and the interactions between DNA and proteins.

Some years ago, the SV-40 virus contaminated batches of anti-poliomyelitis vaccine. This was discovered only after the vaccine had been distributed and used. We do not know what, if any, will be the consequences of this. We do know, however, that the SV-40 virus changes normal human cells (diploid and euploid) into cancer cells *in vitro*. Perhaps it is no coincidence that we are now beginning to hear reports of the potential carcinogenic effects of polio vaccine.

Adenoviruses are useful for the study of replication of cancer-producing DNA viruses.[47] Thirty-one different types of adenovirus, pathogenic in humans, are known, and some of them replicate[48] actively in HeLa cells. This allows many features of the genome[49] of these viruses to be identified. In the more 'permissive'[50] human cells, they replicate to produce about 200,000 viral particles (called virions) per cell.

Viral metabolism The culture of viruses in cells *in vitro* permits identification of the substances essential to their replication, and this could be a first step towards the discovery of virostatic substances: when it is known that a certain metabolite is essential for a living organism, it is possible to find the corresponding antimetabolite to inactivate it. For example:

- The polio virus replicates actively in HeLa cells, provided that the culture medium contains glutamine. Presumably an antimetabolite of glutamine could stop replication of the polio virus *in vivo*.
- Thiol compounds[51] are necessary for the growth of the vaccinia virus and of the GD-VII virus (which causes encephalomyelitis in the mouse). This is shown by the fact that the growth of these viruses is inhibited by the presence in the medium of mercuric benzoate-p-chloride, which binds and inactivates thiol compounds. The growth of the virus is, however, reactivated by adding glutathione, a sulphur compound that binds benzoate-p-chloride and hence prevents its action on the thiol compounds.

These examples are based on the *addition–subtraction method* used in virology, which consists in subtracting a substance from the environment of an organism to establish whether it has an essential role, or adding a substance to see whether this inhibits the organism's development or even kills it, or whether, on the contrary, it neutralizes a harmful substance already present.

This is an old method that was used *in vivo*, often with misleading results. Moreover, it cannot be extrapolated to humans. The example of vitamin C is a case in point. Subtracting it from the diet of the usual laboratory animals causes no harm, whereas its absence from the human diet leads to scurvy. Nevertheless, cell culture is undeniably the only viable method for the study of viral metabolism. It would be unthinkable to study it in the live animal.

Pathogenic action of viruses on cells If a cell is 'permissive' towards a certain kind of virus, it undergoes changes that either cause its death or transform it into a cancer cell. The virions swarm from a dead cell in search of other cells to penetrate and in which they can replicate.

The cells of a monolayer culture inoculated with a virus take on a granular appearance, tend to become spheroid and finally break up and die. The phenomenon appears to the naked eye as a formation of plaques, or thickened areas, on the thin, homogeneous monolayer. The number of plaques and the speed with which they form are used as criteria for assessing the infectivity of the virus for that particular type of cell. This gives indications of viral tropism towards various organs and tissues in living organism and of the way in which they attack and damage them.

Mutagenic and carcinogenic action The transformation of a diploid cell line into a permanent cell line indicates a genetic mutation in the cell, which becomes aneuploid and takes on neoplastic features, including the capacity to multiply indefinitely. In some cases the reasons for this transformation remain unknown, but often the cause is revealed to be an accidental viral contamination. On the other hand, the transformation often, though not always, takes place when a cell culture is deliberately infected with viruses.

The most interesting feature of these observations lies in the following facts: while in many animals the cause of malignant tumours has been found to be a virus, in humans the cause is (almost) certainly viral only in Burkitt's lymphoma. Turning from the whole organism to the *in vitro* culture, however, one finds that human cells are mutated by certain viruses (for example, the SV-40 virus) as readily as are the cells of other animals. This shows the potential dangers for people working with cell cultures (Barkley 1979).

Cell cultures are dangerous when deliberately infected with a virus but are even more so when, unknown to the experimenter, they contain a carcinogenic virus in its latency phase. For example, human lymphocyte cell lines may contain the Epstein-Barr virus, which is carcinogenic for human cells. Therefore, cell cultures and permanent cell lines in particular should always be handled with the utmost care. Serious laboratory infections have already occurred, in particular monkey B virus (*Herpesvirus simiae*) and Marburg virus infections (Hull 1973).

It is estimated that about 80% of viral infections originating in laboratories have arisen from inhalation of the virus, or of cells or cell fragments contained in aerosol formed in the air around the culture.

Research into anti-viral drugs As far as we know, viruses do not possess enzymes of their own but utilize those of the host cell. All the drugs that kill a parasite (bacterium, fungus, protozoon) act by blocking one or more enzymes indispensable to the life of the parasite. In the case of viruses we lack a specific target and have to test a range of chemical or antibiotic substances.

Cell cultures are the ideal tool in the quest for anti-viral drugs. The method consists of adding the potential anti-viral agent, in a concentration harmless to the cell, to the infected culture. If the anti-viral effect exists, the culture will not undergo the characteristic changes (granular changes, rounding of the cells, plaque formation). Should the supposed anti-viral agent 'kill' the virus, the infected culture will no longer be able to infect other cultures.

Numerous experiments have been conducted, some with partial success, using analogues.[52] For example, many amino acid analogues have been tested as anti-virals, in particular alanine, tryptophan, methionine and phenylalanine. Certain purines, pyrimidines, nucleosides and vitamin B_{12} have also been tested. Results of considerable theoretical interest have been obtained and have clarified certain features of viral metabolism.

Production of anti-viral vaccines Most anti-viral vaccines are produced by means of cell cultures. Live animals are still used in the production of smallpox, rabies and poliomyelitis vaccines, but methods are being sought to produce these also *in vitro*.

A constant menace lurks in vaccine prepared from live animals: any animal may be a carrier of another virus, which could be as dangerous or more dangerous to humans than the target virus – a cancer-causing virus, for example. (A comparison may be made with the dangers lurking in xenotransplantation – animal-to-human transplants.)

A strain of diploid cells, the WI-38 strain, taken from the lung of a human embryo, has already been used to produce numerous vaccines, including polio vaccine and the rubella vaccine Almevax, made by Burroughs Wellcome.

The AM-57 cell line can also be used to isolate the polio and Coxsackie B viruses.

Production of interferon Interferon is an inhibitor of viral replication. It is a protein produced by many cells cultured *in vitro*, by malignant tumour cells and probably by all the cells of a living organism. The production of interferon is induced mainly by viruses. Interferons that differ slightly from the anti-viral ones are induced by other microorganisms (*Rickettsiae*, *Mycoplasma*, gram-negative bacteria), by bacterial toxins, by statolone and helenine (polysaccharides of certain fungi of the genus *Penicillum*) and by phytohaemagglutinin (a vegetable compound).

Interferon production is triggered either by live viruses or by viruses inactivated by heat, UV rays or formalin. Viruses of different species vary in their ability to induce interferon production: the myxoviruses, paramyxoviruses, arboviruses (all RNA viruses) are good inducers, while most of the adenoviruses lack this capability altogether.

Once produced by the cells, the interferon passes rapidly into the bloodstream. Different cells (of the same organism) produce interferon *in vitro*, in different amounts when exposed to different viruses, which means that cells that do not produce interferon, or do not produce enough of it when stimulated by one virus, may do so when exposed to another.

Properties of interferon The anti-viral activity of interferon is non-specific, which means that the interferon induced by one virus acts also on other viruses. Interferon produced in one animal species has little or no effect on other species.[53] In other words, interferon is virus non-specific, but species-specific.

Although interferon may not yet have yielded the hoped-for therapeutic results (that is, inhibition of viral replication in cells invaded by a virus or cancer cells), its production continues with the object of finding out why a substance so promising in theory should be so disappointing in practice.

Cell culture is one of the most suitable means of producing interferon. Monolayer diploid cultures are the ideal, optimal production being achieved about one week after the culture reaches confluence.[54] Cells cultured from recent explants give better yields than those which have undergone frequent subculturing.

In addition to diploid cells, some permanent (aneuploid) cell lines are good interferon producers. Unlike the diploid cells, the number of secondary cultures obtained from aneuploid cells does not affect interferon production. This reflects the generally stable character of permanent cell lines. The same stimuli that induce the production of interferon *in vivo* function similarly *in vitro*. *In vitro* as *in vivo*, the best triggers are the RNA viruses, especially the myxoviruses, arboviruses[55] and paramyxoviruses, whether active or inactivated.

The techniques for interferon production using human RSTC-2 cells infected with *Arbovirus chikungunya* are described by Friedman (Friedman 1979).

Experiments on hormones and endocrine glands There are two possible approaches to the study of hormones using cell and tissue cultures: (a) culture of cell or tissue explants from endocrine glands; and (b) *in vitro* tests for the action of various hormones on tissues and cells.

Endocrine cell culture This is an extremely wide and largely unexplored field of research. The endocrine glands are numerous, and even more numerous are the hormones, while the number of cell types on which hormones can be tested is enormous. I shall select here a few of the more significant findings.

Endocrine cells *in vitro* secrete, unchanged, the hormones that they secrete *in vivo*. For example, pituitary cells secrete prolactin, growth hormone (GH, also known as STH = somatotropic hormone) and adrenocorticotropic hormone (ACTH). These hormones are, in addition, secreted by certain pituitary tumours. One such tumour maintained its hormone-secreting property *in vitro* for 15 years (Tashjian 1979). Cortisone stimulates GH production in cultured human pituitary adenomas and in cultures of normal human pituitary gland (Kohler and Bridson 1973).

Parathyroid tissue cultured *in vitro* secretes parathormone. An excess of calcium in the culture medium inhibits secretion, while a low calcium level stimulates it, as it does *in vivo*. Human tumour cells producing calcitonin have been cultured, and the results confirm that high calcium levels in the medium stimulate this production (Gantvik and Tashjian 1973).

Another example is cell line Y_1, derived from cells isolated from a tumour of the suprarenal cortex of a mouse. This cell line had continued, since 1964, to secrete steroid hormones and is so sensitive to stimulation by ACTH that it can increase hormone production tenfold (Schimmer 1979).

Now that the basic fact that the endocrine cells secrete their hormones *in vitro* has been established, the potential applications are endless. In cell cultures we can observe cells developing functions; we can check how they react to various stimuli, what increases secretion, what inhibits it and how hormones from different glands interact with each other. We may be able to culture organs with related functions in tandem: the pituitary and suprarenal gland cultures, for example, or cultures of the thymus and the gonads, or the suprarenal glands and the gonads. Working hypotheses that today seem far-fetched will be easy to realize, once more refined techniques are evolved.

In vitro *testing of the actions of hormones on tissues and cells* Here, too, the potential is enormous, as past achievements already indicate (Fell 1965a):

- The prostate, maintained *in vitro*, responds readily to sex hormones. In the absence of male hormones, its epithelium flattens, and secretion stops almost completely; but with the addition of testosterone to the perfusion liquid, the epithelium increases in height and starts to secrete actively.

- The epithelium of the mammary gland rapidly degenerates in the absence of sex hormones, but it survives longer in the presence of hydrocortisone and aldosterone and, with the addition of prolactin[56] and somatotropin (both pituitary hormones), takes on the appearance of the lactating gland.[57]

- Bony tissue: the presence of parathormone in the perfusion liquid causes rapid calcium depletion and reabsorption of bony tissue, as *in vivo*.

- HeLa cells: the cells of the permanent HeLa cell line proliferate more actively if progesterone or oestradiol or a mixture of both is added to the culture medium. Testosterone, on the other hand, has an inhibitory effect. This is nullified, however, by the simultaneous presence of oestradiol and progesterone. Thus, although the HeLa line is one of the oldest permanent cell lines, its cells still 'remember' their origin in the epithelium of the cervix and behave accordingly in the presence of sex hormones (Hiroyoshi Endo et al. 1965).

- HTC cells: the glucocorticoids (suprarenal hormones) induce in HTC cells[58] synthesis of the following enzymes: tyrosine aminotansferase, ornithine decarboxylase and glutaminosynthetase. They reduce the activity of phosphoesterase and a plasminogen-activating enzyme (Thompson 1979).[59]

- Myocardial fibres: these can be cultured from explants from human and animal embryos. These fibres retain in culture their characteristic contractile capacity. Various substances act on the fibres *in vitro*, increasing or decreasing their ability to contract. For example, at a concentration of $10^{-6}M$ acetylcholine[60] reduces contractility, while the cardiac glycosides (particularly digitalis and strophanthin)[61] increase it.

Toxicological experiments Substances intended for human use must undergo toxicity testing on *human* cell and tissue cultures. Testing them on cultures of animal cells would be as erroneous as experimenting on live animals with the absurd objective of extrapolating the results to humans. Besides, it is just as easy to culture human cells as those of animals: surgeons can supply any type of freshly removed body tissue, while foetuses of varying ages are available from gynaecological departments.

Creating the proper conditions for human, rather than animal, cell and tissue culture is merely a matter of organization. There is no point in culturing animal cells and tissues, except to practise techniques. But one can practise to greater advantage on human explants and may even thereby discover some technical refinement specific to human tissues.

The objection may be made that chemical substances undergo a series of changes in the living animal (principally in the liver), so that on arrival at the target cells they are no longer the substance originally administered, which has obvious implications if it is being tested for potential use as a drug. This is true, but it is also true that we can never know *a priori* if a substance is metabolized in laboratory animals in the same way as it is in humans. Therefore the results of animal experiments may be not only misleading but also dangerous – anything misleading is potentially dangerous.

On the other hand, the changes that take place in human organs, particularly the liver, are known for almost all the chemical groups to which the various potentially therapeutic substances belong. It is therefore possible to test not the substance itself, but its metabolites (that is, the products of these changes), and since toxicity tests can be performed on a large number of different cells, or even on whole complex tissues in culture, reliable and readily reproducible results can be obtained.

Comparison of these results with those obtained on animals is irrelevant, since, for the following reasons, we should not be comparing like with like:

1. Results of toxicity tests in on human cell cultures may be incomplete, but they are certainly relevant to man.
2. Results of toxicity tests on animals, on the other hand, are comprehensive, but they are *valid solely for that particular animal species*. Sometimes, by the chance of statistical probability, they coincide with results in humans, but we can only know this *a posteriori*, that is, after testing on humans.

Experiments with mutagenic, teratogenic and oncogenic substances The problem of mutagenic and teratogenic[62] substances had long been recognized but was of little concern until 1961 when, tragically, the public was made vividly aware of it, following the thalidomide disaster. Thalidomide did, however, teach us one lesson – the absolute futility of testing teratogenicity on animals.

We tend, when considering teratogenicity, to think only of its physically deforming effects, overlooking another rather disturbing question: how many children, who appear normal at birth but seem at school age to be 'not very intelligent', or withdrawn, or restless, owe these deficiencies to brain damage caused before birth?

We should remember a very important but neglected fact. Most substances (and viruses) are said to exert their teratogenic effect in the first trimester of pregnancy, that is, in the period when the internal organs are being formed. But the brain continues to 'form', not only throughout the foetal period but also long after birth, for twelve or more years. The possibility cannot be excluded, therefore, that substances ingested by the mother after the first trimester may influence brain development.

Teratogenicity and carcinogenicity are closely related: numerous teratogenic substances have been shown to be carcinogenic; conversely, all carcinogenic substances are also teratogenic. Cell and tissue cultures can reveal relatively easily the cancer-causing capacity of a substance. But if it is carcinogenic, it is almost certainly also teratogenic; care must therefore be taken to prevent its absorption, even in minimal amounts, by pregnant women.

The number of substances teratogenic for humans is enormous (see also Chapter 5). They are listed below by category (but each category contains dozens of teratogens):

- General and local anaesthetics act on the foetus, not only through the mother but also through the male sperm (Sullivan 1979).
- Analgesics: codeine (Saxen and Saxen 1975), aspirin and other salicylates (McNeal 1973; Richards 1972), phenacetin and paracetamol (Schenkel and Vorherr 1974).
- Anticonvulsants: phenobarbitone, phenytoin, primidone, troxidone, pheneturide, methylphenylbarbitone, and diazepam (Hill 1973; Lowe 1973; Speidel and Meadows 1972).
- Cancer drugs: the most powerful teratogens for humans are found among the following: alkylating agents, cytotoxic antibiotics and steroids. The risk of congenital deformity in the babies of women who take alkylating agents is as follows: busulphan: one in 14; chlor-

ambucil: one in three; cyclophosphamide: one in three; nitrogen mustards: one in four (Schardein 1976). Some of the anti-metabolites are certainly teratogenic for humans – for example, the folic acid antagonists (like aminopterine), the nicotinamide antagonists, the purines and pyrimidines, methotrexate, 6-azauridine, azathioprine and cyclophosphamide (Scott 1977).

- Anticoagulants: the coumarins (such as warfarin) are teratogenic (Pettifor and Benson 1975).
- Lithium carbonate: this salt, used in the treatment of manic depression, is teratogenic (Schou et al. 1973).
- Antibiotics: aminoglycosides, such as streptomycin, dihydrostreptomycin, kanamycin and gentamycin damage the acoustic nerve and cause deafness in varying degrees (Ganguin and Rempt 1970). Tetracycline causes changes in the teeth and bones (Greene 1976).
- Antimalarials: quinidine is teratogenic in doses used to procure abortion (2–4 g) (Sullivan 1979).
- Hormones: prednisolone, taken during pregnancy, causes death or malformation of the foetus in a significant percentage of cases (Warrel and Taylor 1968). Synthetic hormones like ethisterone and norethisterone masculinize female foetuses, as does testosterone (Cahen 1966). Oral contraceptives combining oestrogen and progestogen taken during the first weeks of pregnancy, before the mother has become aware of it, damage the foetus, particularly the heart (Heinonen et al. 1977; Levy et al. 1973; Nora and Nora 1973).

The teratogenic effects of all the above drugs were discovered clinically, *when the damage was already manifest*. However, thousands of tragedies could have been avoided if, instead of doing teratogenicity tests on animals, the link between the following facts had been recognized and exploited:

1. the ease with which the carcinogenicity of a substance can be tested on human cell cultures (using, where necessary, a large number of mesenchymal and epithelial cell lines); and
2. the fact that probably all carcinogenic substances are also teratogenic. Thus, proven carcinogenicity equals proven, or extremely probable, teratogenicity.

It is to be hoped that more account will be taken of these facts in future.

Teratogenicity tests can also be done on bacterial cultures (the Ames test – see Chapter 16).

Immunological studies In the living subject, immunoglobulins (antibodies) are produced by the lymphocytes. *In vitro* the lymphocytes continue their function of producing various types of immunoglobulins. There are about five hundred lymphocytic cell lines, which, many years after explantation, continue to produce immunoglobulins (Matsuoka 1973). Immunoglobulins produced *in vitro* are assigned a type, after causing them to react with the corresponding antigen by means of immunofluorescence or immunoelectrophoresis.

Study of enzymopathies Enzymopathies are illnesses caused by a change in, or lack of, one or more enzymes and may be congenital or acquired.[63] They can affect nitrogenous substances, carbohydrates, lipids or pigments. Cell culture, linked with clinical observation, is the most valid experimental method for the study of enzymopathies. Congenital enzyme disorders can be studied in cultured cells from amniotic fluid or aborted foetuses.

Cultures containing practically all the different types of cell of an organism can be prepared from aborted foetuses. Each foetus, therefore, if well utilized, represents an enormous experimental resource. Enzymopathies and the metabolic disorders deriving from them are extremely numerous. Some general observations on them are made below:

1. In most enzyme disorders, the defect is present in all or most of the cells of the organism. Cell cultures allow differences in the effects of enzyme defects on different cells to be observed.
2. Congenital enzyme disorders offer natural experimental models, in that a substance is lacking in the organism, allowing us to observe the results of this lack. Other cases offer models by addition, since the absence of certain enzymes causes substances to accumulate in the cells and interstitial fluids. The nature of these substances and their secondary effects on cell metabolism can be studied *in vitro* with a precision that would not be possible by any other method.
3. Certain enzyme disorders affect not all the organs, but only one or two, most commonly the liver and kidneys. Dysfunction of these organs, whose task it is to cleanse the organism of various substances, has consequences for all the other cells, for example, the accumulation of non-eliminated substances (storage disease). Hence, even in organ-specific enzymopathies, important information can be obtained from the study *in vitro* of all the cells and tissues, not only those in which the enzymatic defect resides.

A review of the literature indicates that cell culture is still used to an insignificant degree, even though it represents the most promising route to understanding not only the mechanisms of enzyme-linked metabolic disorders, but also many features of normal metabolism.

Notes

1. The Latin term *in vitro* arose from the fact that a few decades ago the containers for cell and tissue culture (and earlier still for bacteria, fungi and protozoa) were made of glass (Petri dishes, Roux flasks, etc.). The founder of modern cell and tissue culture is considered to be the American Ross Grenville Harrison, who, using nervous tissue taken from a frog and placed in a drop of lymph from the same animal, saw the nerve fibre (neurite) emerge and develop from the body of the nerve cell. Even earlier, however, between 1880 and 1885, V. Roux had kept chick embryos alive in physiological saline for a few days (Roux 1885), and F. Arnold, in 1887, had cultured amphibian lymphocytes (Arnold 1887). The foregoing experiments are examples of *maintenance in vitro* rather than *culture in vitro*. The first person to succeed in culturing a large number of cells *in vitro* was Alexis Carrel, who kept a cell line alive and active for 34 years (Carrel 1923).

2. Above 42°C the cells die. At about 4–5°C the cells survive but do not multiply.

3. Somatic cells are *diploid*, which means that their chromosomes are arranged in pairs. The somatic cells of the human species have 46 chromosomes, forming 23 pairs. In addition to the somatic cells, the organism contains the sex cells, the ovum and spermatozoon, which are *haploid* (from the Greek for 'simple'), that is, they possess 23 single (unpaired) chromosomes. The two haploid sex cells, when united, reconstitute a new diploid cell, in which each pair of chromosomes develops out of a male chromosome from the spermatozoon and a female chromosome from the ovum. *Euploid* (from the Greek 'well-made') means endowed with a normal complement of chromosomes. *Aneuploid* is the opposite (from the Greek 'without' + *euploid*) of euploid: an aneuploid cell has an abnormal number (too many or too few) of chromosomes. *Heteroploid* is synonymous with aneuploid.

4. A colony is the union of a number of cells of the same type. It occurs when the two cells that result from division remain united but continue to multiply, remaining joined until they form a colony. It is thought that it is in this way that the first metazoa (multicellular animals) came into being. Subsequently, some cells of the colony became differentiated, assuming particular forms and functions useful to the community of cells.

5. Thus bacterial survival appears to be closely linked to the sources of energy and matter. If these sources do not come to an end, their life appears likewise to continue indefinitely. However, we find that a community of bacteria, or colony, is governed by laws similar to those that apply to metazoan cells *in*

vitro: at a certain point their development stops, even when the individuals which form the colony are alive and capable of continued existence. This arrested growth is not caused by exhaustion of the nutritional elements in the medium, nor by the accumulation of toxic waste products. What, then, could be the cause? It is thought that secretions may occur in the colonies that exert a bioregulatory effect on the growth and proliferation of bacteria.

6. The maximum survival of human diploid cells extends to the fiftieth generation (Hayflick 1965; Hayflick and Moorhead 1961). By this time each cell of the colony has generated 2^{50} cells. The colony then dies or is transformed into a permanent, aneuploid, line.

7. Tissue culture is also called organ culture, but this is a misleading term, which suggests the possibility of culturing an entire organ, such as a heart, a liver or a spleen, in a culture medium. The term tissue culture is more appropriate, since one can actually obtain *in vitro* pieces of tissue similar to those from which they derive. Foetal tissues mature similarly *in vitro* and *in vivo*.

8. Glucose is the main source of energy for cells *in vitro*, which, however, are also capable of obtaining energy from the de-aminization of amino acids.

9. The need of cells cultured *in vitro* for the amino acids considered essential for the nutrition of the whole organism (arginine, cystine, glutamine, histidine, tyrosine, isoleucine, leucine, lysine, methionine, phenylalanine, threonine, tryptophan and valine) suggests that the majority of cells may lack the enzymatic systems necessary for the synthesis of these amino acids. Certain cells require serine. Neoplastic cells, particularly those of certain leukaemic lines, need asparagine. Also essential are folic acid and vitamin B_{12}; these two compounds and the amino acids listed above are found in fresh serum.

10. Mycoplasmas are particularly liable to infect cell cultures, as they are resistant to most antibiotics. Moreover, their presence can pass unnoticed because they do not, as a rule, markedly alter the appearance of the culture. Mycoplasmas profoundly change the cells, one of the commonest contaminants being *Mycoplasma pulmonis*.

11. Fetuin is the principal globulin in the foetal blood of various animals (Pedersen 1944). Human serum contains an alpha-globulin that is different from fetuin but has similar properties (Holmes 1967).

12. The substance that causes the cells to adhere to the wall of the container (or other substrates, such as the microspheres described later) is a protein of high molecular weight known as LETS (Large External Transformation Substance), also called fibronectin or CSP (Cell Surface Protein).

13. The cells, as long as they remain suspended in the liquid medium, are round. When they adhere to the wall of the culture vessel, they remain round for a while then slowly flatten, so that the surface area available for adhesion is considerably increased.

14. A stationary cell culture is one in which cells, though alive, have stopped multiplying.

14. Cloning is the development of a colony from a single 'parent' cell. The

clone is a 'pure cell line', in which all the cells, originating from a single cell, have an identical genetic make-up. For spontaneous cloning to occur in a culture, the cells need to attach themselves to the wall of the vessel, each separated from the others, before they begin to multiply. This separation can be obtained by adding sera or mixtures of sera to the medium, from different animals and in suitable proportions (Ham and Sattler 1968; Ham et al. 1970). Cloning can also be achieved by other techniques.

16. The environmental modifications that have the most deleterious effect on the vitality of cells in culture are: lowering the oxygen pressure, a decrease in pH (acidification) and glucose depletion. These are the same factors that depress cell vitality *in vivo*.

17. Fibroblast cultures can be obtained from human skin without disaggregating the tissue: the fibroblasts at the edges of a piece of skin placed in culture medium develop rapidly, expanding like a drop of oil. The first experiments in cell culture were done using very small whole explants, that is, without disaggregation.

18. EDTA is the bisodium salt of ethylene-diaminotetracetic acid.

19. In the case of a skin explant, for example, we will have all types of epidermal cells (those of the basal, granulose and horny layers), all types of dermal cells and those of the blood and lymph vessels (fibroblasts, fibrocytes, histiocytes, endothelial cells, pericytes, smooth muscle cells, mast cells and cells of the peripheral autonomic nervous system). Besides these, we will have the blood cells: red blood cells, neutrophils, eosinophils, basophils, lymphocytes and monocytes.

20. Not all cells are capable of division. Of the epidermal cells, for instance, only those of the basal layer reproduce.

21. As diploid cell cultures generally grow adhering to the wall of the culture vessel, they have to be detached before they can be transferred to another vessel. For this, enzymes are used (pronase, trypsin, collagenase). Once detached, the cells resume their spherical shape. However, having attached themselves to the wall of their new container, they again become flattened and after a short time lag start to multiply once more. Transfer to a new vessel is usually done when the cell colony has become overcrowded to the point of inhibiting further growth.

22. Fibroblasts are among the human cells that maintain the integrity of their chromosomes and principal biochemical functions for some months and are readily obtained from skin explants. Human cell physiology studies can be conducted using these cells.

23. One of the first permanent cell lines obtained in the laboratory was the HeLa line. These cells were isolated from an epidermoid cancer of the cervix of one Henrietta Lache (hence the letters HeLa). The cells of the HeLa line contain between 50 and 350 chromosomes, instead of the 46 that are normal for humans. These cells favour the growth of a great many types of virus. Another very old permanent cell line is the Hep-2 line, derived from human epithelial cells.

24. In order to study cell cultures adhering to the walls of the culture vessel, inverted microscopes – in which the lenses lie beneath the object and the light above it – have been developed.

25. Some of these substances are known: for example, CO_2, pyruvate and some inessential amino acids, particularly serine.

26. When a single layer of cells has covered the whole wall of the container, the culture is said to have reached 'confluence' ('flowing together'). After this, the growth of the culture declines rapidly and comes to a standstill.

27. The duration of the latency period depends on the type of cell, the density of seeding, the composition of the culture medium and any manipulations previously performed on the cells (mechanical or enzymatic actions).

28. The proportion of dead to live cells in a culture can be counted by treating the culture with a solution of Trypan Blue, which stains the live cells but not the dead ones.

29. Progeria (or Hutchinson–Gilford's Syndrome) is an autosomal illness, caused by recessive genes and characterized by premature ageing (Gilford 1904; Hutchinson 1886). Even in the first year of life, hair and teeth show poor growth. At maximum growth, the height does not exceed 130 centimetres, and the subject has the appearance of an old person. Death usually occurs by the age of 25. Werner's syndrome, another autosomal recessive hereditary disease, is characterized by physical underdevelopment (average height about 140 cm), lack of sexual development, greying hair and baldness towards the age of 20. Between the ages of 35 and 40 the subject resembles someone 80 years old or more. Death occurs around the age of 47 (Werner 1904).

30. This generally occurs when the cell population has reached confluence. Certain cultures, however, especially permanent cell lines, continue their logarithmic growth even after confluence (provided that the medium continues to supply the necessary nourishment).

31. 'Contact inhibition of cell movement', or 'contact inhibition of cell replication' (Abercrombie and Heaysman 1954), or 'density-dependent inhibition of growth'.

32. The cytoplasmic membrane envelops the entire cell. Inside the cell, however, other membranes are found: the nuclear membrane around the cell nucleus, the mitochondrial membranes, and the membranes that form the reticular apparatus, a complicated network of canals.

33. The pseudopodium is a projection that forms at the edge of certain cells when they move in a particular direction. It starts off as a small projection but gradually becomes larger, until first the cytoplasm and then the nucleus pass into it entirely. When the process is complete, the cell is found to have moved itself from its previous position into the pseudopodium. Movement by means of pseudopodia is very evident in amoebas and in the polymorphonuclear leukocytes in the blood.

34. This is true of cells that develop in a monolayer, that is, those that adhere to the wall of the culture vessel.

35. Adhesion does not mean that the two edges of the cells are in contact – the electron microscope has revealed a space between them of about 100Å (Å = one-thousandth of a micron, that is, 10^{-8} cm).

36. Van der Waals forces establish themselves between the atoms of two adjacent molecules. They are non-polar forces, that is, independent of electrical charge.

37. The hypothesis that 'intelligence' (and hence 'will') is not concentrated in the brain but distributed throughout the cells of multi-cellular organisms and also present in mono-cellular organisms was first suggested by the philosopher Albert North Whitehead (1861–1947).

38. The first demonstration of this fact was performed on the marine sponge. The sponge was broken up to obtain single cells in suspension. When allowed to settle, they reorganized themselves in the form of a sponge.

39. The skin has two layers: the epidermis and the dermis. The epidermis is an epithelial tissue, the dermis a mesenchymal tissue. The blood and lymph vessels are found in the dermis; the epidermis is nourished by interstitial fluid, which seeps from the blood and lymph vessels and penetrates between the epithelial cells, carrying nutrients and oxygen to them. Thus the epidermis cannot live without the dermis.

40. The basal membrane is a thin (1–2 microns) homogeneous structure that separates the dermis from the epidermis. The basal epidermal cells (that is, those multiplying most actively) lie on the basal membrane. The substance that forms the basal membrane is secreted mainly by the epithelial cells but also partly by the mesenchymal cells of the underlying dermis.

41. This 'basal membrane' is probably incomplete, lacking the part normally produced by the mesenchymal cells.

42. In the living organism, the first sign of the change from a tumour *in situ* to an invasive tumour is the rupture of the basal membrane by the cancer cells and their penetration of the underlying mesenchyma.

43. The best socio-cellular cultures are obtained by exploiting the affinity between any epithelium and its corresponding mesenchyma. Thus, for pancreatic cells, fibroblasts obtained from the pancreatic stroma should be used; for mammary gland cells, fibroblasts from the mammary stroma; for the epidermis, dermal fibroblasts.

44. This case is another example of the vivisectionist tradition of carrying out experiments with animal tissues that could just as easily be done on human tissues. The advantage of the direct method would be the circumvention of fanciful hybrids (of the ox–mouse type) that are unlikely to contribute to the success of the experiment.

45. Viruses vary in size between 20 and 200 nanometres (1 nanometre = one-thousandth of a micron, that is, a millionth of a millimetre). They fall into two groups: RNA and DNA viruses.

46. Certain viruses attack only the cells of mesenchymal origin, others only

those of epithelial origin. Some attack both types of cell. The viruses pathogenic for humans are classified as follows:

a) Picornavirus $\begin{cases} \text{Rhinovirus} \\ \\ \text{Enterovirus} \end{cases}$ $\begin{cases} \text{Poliomavirus} \\ \text{Coxsackie virus} \\ \text{Echovirus} \end{cases}$

b) Reovirus   e) Paramyxovirus   h) Herpesvirus

c) Arbovirus   f) Rabies virus   i) Poxvirus

d) Myxovirus   g) Adenovirus   j) Unclassified viruses

47. Oncogenic viruses are those that give rise to malignant tumours in certain animals. In humans there is only one virus which (almost certainly) causes a malignant tumour: the Epstein-Barr virus, the (probable) cause of Burkitt's lymphoma, frequent in Central Africa and occurring sporadically elsewhere in the world. The Epstein-Barr virus is also the cause of most cases of infectious mononucleosis.

48. 'Replication' is the term used for viruses; it corresponds to 'reproduction' or 'multiplication' in bacteria, fungi, protozoa and metazoan cells.

49. The genome of a virus is that part of the DNA (in DNA viruses) or RNA (in RNA viruses) that contains the genetic information. The viral genome cannot replicate itself (whereas the chromosomes of cells and bacteria can), but it 'transcribes' the genetic information onto the genome of the host cell, which provides the material for building new viral particles (virions).

50. The cells in which viruses replicate particularly actively are called 'permissive'.

51. Thiol compounds are those containing the group $-SO_2-OH$ (sulphoxyl group).

52. Analogues are substances that structurally resemble another substance (which may be essential for the life of an organism), without, however, possessing all its properties. When the essential substance is substituted with the analogue, an entire metabolic pathway can be blocked, with grave or lethal consequences for the target organism.

53. Due to the aforementioned properties, interferon behaves conversely to the antibodies: (a) antibodies are specific to the viruses and other micro-organisms instrumental in their production; and (b) the antibody produced by one animal species is active also in other species. Hence, viral antibodies are virus-specific and species-nonspecific.

54. That is, a week after the whole surface of the culture vessel has been coated with a monolayer of cells.

55. One of the more potent arboviruses is the chikungunya virus.

56. Prolactin is also called mammotropin. It is secreted by the anterior lobe of the pituitary gland.

57. Mammary cells cultured *in vitro* produce the milk proteins alpha-lacto-globulin and alpha-lactoalbumin (Larsen and Andersen 1973).

58. HTC cells come from a rat liver tumour (hepatoma).

59. Plasminogen is the precursor of plasmin, the active portion of a proteolytic enzyme whose function is to break down fibrin (fibrinolysis).

60. 10^{-6} = one-millionth of a gramme molecule of acetylcholine, or 0.124 mg, since the molecular weight of acetylcholine is 124.

61. The cardiac glycosides are not hormones, but drugs of plant origin. They are included in this section because of their close links with the subject matter.

62. A mutagen is a substance that changes the genetic code of the cell, while a teratogen is a substance that causes deformities. But since the deformities are generally due to changes in the genetic code, the two terms are used interchangeably.

63. Various toxins can alter one or more enzymes, causing an acquired metabolic disorder. The commonest are the heavy metals (lead, mercury, gold, silver, bismuth, copper, cobalt, cadmium, tungsten, osmium), uranium salts and endogenous (developing within an organism) toxins arising from extensive burns and gangrene.

16. Other methods of biomedical research

Epidemiology, computer models, and cell and tissue culture *in vitro* are the three basic methods used in modern biomedical research. But alongside them (and partly deriving from them) are many others that awaken new hope: the hope that biomedical research may already be on the way to radical renewal. Let us look at just a few of the most important of these.

The Ames test for mutagenicity

In the Ames test (Ames 1971; Ames et al. 1973) the test substance is placed in a culture medium favourable to the growth of *Salmonella typhimurium*,[1] a bacterium whose genetic code is known. A mutant strain of the bacterium that does not require histidine for growth is obtained.[2] If the substance is mutagenic, it restores the histidine requirement of the bacterium. Although the substance itself may not be mutagenic (and not, therefore, carcinogenic), it may become so as a consequence of the changes it undergoes in the organism, particularly in the liver. An extract of fresh liver is therefore added to the medium, on the assumption that liver enzymes act *in vitro* as *in vivo*. The Ames test has many advantages:

- speed, due to the rapid growth of *Salmonella* (and of bacteria in general);
- simplicity, as with most bacteriological methods;
- low cost;
- the possibility of testing many substances at the same time; and
- reproducibility (in the same laboratory or elsewhere), the only condition being that the same strain of *S. typhimurium* be used.[3]

By the mid-1970s 300 substances had been tested satisfactorily by the Ames method (McCann et al. 1975). There is still plenty of scope for further refinement of the test, using bacteria other than *S. typhimurium*. With due care, its use could be extended to fungi and protozoa.[4] It has been rendered more sensitive by using *Salmonella* treated with pKM-101 plasmid.[5] Thus modified, the Ames test, when applied for validation purposes to substances already known to be carcinogenic (but for which animal?) can claim 80–90% accuracy, while the original method without plasmid achieves only 60–65%.

A critical evaluation of the Ames test arouses some doubt as to the legitimacy of extrapolating its results to human pathology, particularly regarding the use of liver extract to metabolize certain substances *in vitro* before submitting them to the test.

The Draize test

Irritants can enter the eye accidentally or be placed there for therapeutic purposes. The substances that most often come into accidental contact with the eye are soaps and shampoos, hair dyes, eye make-up and face creams. The principal ophthalmic drugs are decongestants and anti-bacterials. We need to be sure that none of these substances will cause irritation of the conjunctival membrane, or that any irritation will be short-lived and without harmful consequences.

In 1944, J. H. Draize (Draize et al. 1944) proposed an *in vivo* test using rabbits, whose eyes are particularly sensitive, especially to alkaline substances.[6] The test substance is dripped into the lower eyelid of one eye of the animal, the other eye serving as a control. The results are monitored at regular intervals on seven successive days. An assessment is made on the basis of whether the cornea of the eye becomes opaque and whether there is inflammation of the iris and conjunctiva, the degree of irritation being measured on a scale from 0 to 110. Decades of Draize testing have shown:

1. that it is a crude and unstable test that distinguishes merely between severe irritants and non-irritants, with no intermediate gradations (Ballantyne and Swanston 1977); and
2. that the method is not easily reproducible and gives divergent results even in the same laboratory, let alone different ones.

In a study carried out in 24 American laboratories using ethoxylauryl alcohol, one laboratory gave it a score of 7 on the irritant scale, while another awarded it 79 (Thompson 1979). This means that the first judged the substance to be virtually innocuous, while the other deemed it a severe irritant.

Since a method producing such dissimilar results is unacceptable, more reliable methods have been investigated. One of these is the Simons method.

The Simons method

The method proposed by Simons (Simons 1980) uses cells of the L-929 mouse strain. The cells are placed in MEM (Minimum Essential Medium) containing glutamine and non-essential amino acids, combined with 10% calf serum. After 24 hours the test substance is added. After another 24 hours, the cells floating on the surface of the medium (that is, the cells that have died and so become detached from the wall of the culture vessel) are transferred to another vessel containing an isotonic solution. The cells still adhering to the wall (the live cells) are detached from the wall using trypsin solution[7] and added to the dead ones. A pool of dead and live cells is thus obtained, which is stained with Trypan Blue.[8] The proportion of live (stained blue) to dead (uncoloured) cells is counted under the microscope, and the results are expressed on a scale of 0 to 110, as in the Draize test.

The *in vitro* Simons method gives results that are more reproducible than those of the Draize test. Again, it does not permit the degree of irritation caused by a substance to be precisely established, merely distinguishing irritants from non-irritants. It has nevertheless opened up a new avenue of research, allowing the Draize test to be abandoned as inaccurate and unreproducible. Moreover, the Simons method has ample potential for improvement, whereas the Draize test has not, as shown by the fact that it has remained unmodified for more than fifty years. Finally, the Simons test, like all *in vitro* methods, is less expensive than the *in vivo* test.

Bettero's method

This method is one of the most important examples of how a *non-scientific* method, like the Draize test, can be replaced by a *scientific* one, that is, one that is accurate and reproducible.

The test is performed on human tears, which have the function of diluting and removing irritating substances that come into contact with the conjunctiva. Under normal conditions, tears contain only traces of chemical mediators of inflammation, but irritating substances of any kind and specific allergens (in allergic subjects) bring about a rapid increase in the above-mentioned factors. The test consists of demonstrating such an increase after applying the test substance to the *human* conjunctiva. The chemical mediator most commonly used is histamine, but others, such as serotonin and leukotriene 4, can also be used.

Fifty microlitres of saline solution containing a known quantity of histamine and fluorescamine is applied to the lower eyelid. After ten seconds, 20 microlitres of the resultant liquid (a mixture of tears and the histamine–fluorescamine solution) are drawn off with a special pipette. The procedure is repeated with a second application of the solution under investigation to the eye. If this solution is an irritant, the histamine level will be higher after the second application than the first.

Bettero's test has the important feature of 'personalization', that is, it can be performed on people who complain of conjunctival irritation caused by substances which do not have this effect on the population in general. This is typical, for example, of allergens, which only trouble 'allergic' persons.

Inhibition of enzymes as an *in vitro* toxicity test

Toxic substances act, in general, by inhibiting one or more enzymes or co-enzymes. Permanent inhibition is the more rapidly fatal, the more important the broken metabolic pathway for the life of the cell. For example, hydrocyanic acid causes almost instantaneous death because it blocks cytochrome activity, indispensable for cell respiration, in all the cells of the organism.

On this basis, it is possible to test a putative toxic substance on those enzymes so far isolated, and there are likely to be more of these, thanks to progress in biomedical research. If the target enzyme for a particular toxic substance is not known, tests are carried out on all available enzymes. Where it is known, the substance can be tested in various concentrations to obtain a useful quantification of the process. Moreover, it is possible by enzyme testing to identify antidotes, that is, substances capable of blocking the action of the toxin on a specific enzyme. One example of the enzyme inhibition method where the target is known is that of organophosphates.

In vitro neurotoxicity tests on organophosphates Organic compounds of phosphorus (organophosphates) are used either singly or in association with other substances such as insecticides. They are also used in small quantities in the manufacture of some drugs. In industry, they are components of certain lubricants and substances used in the manufacture of synthetic resins. Humans thus have plenty of occasions for contact with these compounds. Pesticides especially can be ingested accidentally, or even deliberately in suicide attempts. As an insecticide, phosphorus mainly takes the form of ToCP (tri-ortho-cresyl phosphate).[9]

If chickens are given organophosphates, they are affected after about two weeks by a characteristic paralysis. However, testing these substances on chickens only demonstrates chronic toxicity, not the acute form of poisoning (Johnson 1980). Acute and chronic organophosphate poisoning are two distinct phenomena, with different biochemical mechanisms:

1. Acute toxicity is due to inhibition of the enzyme acetylcholinesterase; phosphorus inactivates it by binding to its active part.[10]
2. Chronic toxicity occurs in two stages: in the first stage, the organophosphate inhibits the enzyme neurotoxic esterase (NTE) (Johnson 1977); in the second stage, a phosphoryl group remains permanently attached to the NTE, which, in turn, binds firmly to the cell membranes of the nervous tissue (Aldridge and Johnson 1977).

An *in vitro* test based on this knowledge has been developed to replace the *in vivo* test on chickens. The *in vitro* test has the following advantages:

1. It enables toxicity to be quantified (rather than the mere generic distinction between toxic and non-toxic).
2. It is much faster and more economical.

The test consists of testing the substance suspected of containing toxic amounts of organophosphate on a preparation of NTE, which is allowed to act on the specific substrate. If the activity of the enzyme is blocked by the compound under examination, the substrate does not undergo any change, thus demonstrating the presence of a toxic organophosphate or other substance having the same mechanism of action.

Radioligand binding assay (RBA)

There are about seventy thousand synthetic chemicals in common use, with an increment of some five hundred each year (Shayne 1933). That implies a need for rapid and economical methods to distinguish active from inert substances, whether synthetic or natural. It is estimated that only about one in ten thousand compounds turns out to be useful. Testing all substances *in vivo* would require an enormous number of animals and unacceptable costs in terms of time and money.[11] Moreover, any attempt to obtain qualitative information from animal testing produces false results, as stressed earlier in this book. The RBA (Sweetman et al. 1933) is a reliable method of distinguishing active from inert substances, of particular relevance in the identification and subsequent monitoring of pharmaceuticals, cosmetics, household and other products to which humans and other animals are exposed. The basic RBA method measures the radioactivity of cells made radioactive by binding to a substance treated with a radioisotope.

Limits and requirements of the RBA   The RBA shows whether a substance acts on cells or not but does not inform us whether such action is harmless or toxic.

Two components are needed for the RBA: cultured cells and a radioligand. Each cell of the billions that constitute an animal has encoded in its DNA all the attributes of the entire organism. Therefore, all functions can be studied in a single cell of the organism. By cloning, the same cell can be replicated by the thousand, producing cells identical to the parent cell. If the activity of a substance in humans is to be studied, the RBA should be performed on *human* cell cultures – unless there is an interest in other species for veterinary use. To understand the role of the cell culture in an RBA, the term radioligand needs to be further defined.

A *radioligand* is a substance (natural or synthetic) presumed capable of acting on the cell. In order to become a radioligand, the substance must be labelled with a radioactive isotope. If the cell or cell culture becomes radioactive, it proves that the substance has found in it a link in the form of cell receptors.

Cell receptors (Parascandola 1981) (or chemical messengers) are specific proteins by means of which a substance can act on cells, whether beneficially or otherwise. The role of receptors in biological systems was known early in this century, but it was not until 1956 that the binding of a substance to cell receptors was linked to its efficacy. The RBA is based on the binding of the radioligand to cell receptors. In the absence of receptors, the substance – even if it comes into direct contact with the cell – will remain inactive.

The amount of binding between ligand and receptor depends on the rate of decay of the isotope in minutes (dpm). Since in most cases the radioligand reacts non-selectively with other (non-receptor) proteins of the cell membrane and with the fibreglass filters used to terminate the binding reaction, the specific dpm is calculated by subtracting the non-specific dpm from the total dpm (specific binding = total binding minus non-specific binding). The greater the ratio of total binding to non-specific binding, the more reliable an assay will be as a tool for drug discovery.

Structure-activity approaches for predicting toxicity in humans (SAR)

SAR methods predict the toxicity of chemicals according to their structure. The prediction may be either:

a) qualitative (mutagen versus non-mutagen – for predicting carcinogenesis, teratogenicity, mutagenesis), or

b) quantitative – for predicting LD-50 values.

An overview of drug structure and activity is provided in *Burger's Medicinal Chemistry* 1980.

Unlike the RBA, the SAR predicts toxicity for humans. What about other animals? The concept of the biological activity of a compound as a direct function of its structure is now a century or more old, but SAR methods have become a useful toxicological tool only in the last fifteen years or so.

Notes

1. *Salmonella typhimurium* does not require a special culture medium; it grows very well in simple agar, in TSA (tryptic soya agar) or BHIA (brain heart infusion agar) .

2. The strain of *S. typhimurium* able to grow in the absence of histidine is obtained by growing the bacterium in media containing the substance in ever-decreasing amounts until it undergoes the necessary mutation.

3. There are many serological strains of *S. typhimurium*.

4. Various species of unicellar algae have already been used, a development inspired by the Ames test.

5. The plasmids are structures found in the nucleus outside the chromosomes. Like chromosomes, they are made of DNA and are capable of replicating themselves. Some provide the genetic information needed to guarantee transferability to other species or to other strains of the same species.

6. Differences between the rabbit eye and the human eye: (1) the thickness of the cornea: 0.037 in the rabbit; 0.05 in humans; (2) in the rabbit eye there is a third eyelid; (3) lacrimal secretion in the rabbit eye is very slight; (4) pH of the lacrimal secretion is 8.8 in the rabbit, 7.1–7.3 in humans.

7. Trypsin is used in an end concentration of 0.25%, that is, 250 mg of trypsin to every 100 ml of cell suspension.

8. Trypan Blue is used in the dilution 1:10, that is, 0.2 ml of the matrix solution to 0.9 ml of cell suspension.

9. In 1930, in the southern USA, thousands of people were afflicted with Ginger Jack paralysis, after consuming a non-alcoholic drink (a 'ginger') originating in Jamaica. The drink had been smuggled in and contained organophosphate (Smith and Elvove 1930). In Morocco, in 1959, ToCP poisoned about ten thousand people. Insecticides containing organophosphates are Mipafox, Trichlorphon and Dipterex. Sporadic poisoning occurred between 1920 and 1930 among persons suffering from tuberculosis who were treated with phosphocreosote (a compound of phosphoric esters and phenols derived from tar). The symptoms of organophosphate poisoning appear 8 to 14 days after exposure. They are: asthenia, followed by ataxia and paralysis of the lower limbs. In the most serious cases, paralysis also affects the arms. Organophosphates are also thought to be a substance responsible for ME (myalgic encephalomyelitis, also known as chronic fatigue or postviral syndrome).

10. The acetylcholinesterases are a group of enzymes which act at motor-nerve endings. They inactivate acetylcholine formed during the passage of the nerve impulse from the nerve to the effector muscle, so that subsequent impulses find the muscle fibres ready for the next contraction.

11. A Centre for Alternatives to Animal Testing was founded in Baltimore, MD, at the Johns Hopkins University of Hygiene and Public Health in 1981 (CAAT).

Epilogue

To fight with the weapons of science against experimentation on animals for human medicine – a methodology with historical roots going back to Claudius Galen in the second century AD – could be considered foolish by anyone accepting that vivisection is a sound and irrefutably scientific method.

On those grounds, then, it seems that anti-vivisectionists are the foolish ones, since they oppose that 'scientific' method using a truly scientific argument: that no animal can be taken as an experimental model for any other animal, humans included.

When I started campaigning against animal experiments, I would deliver speeches that attempted to explain to audiences of ten or twenty old ladies – and to their pet dogs – the basis of scientific anti-vivisectionism. The thought that I was alone in going against the great majority of public opinion was discouraging, and equally distressing was the fact that I was a black sheep in a community of scientists, Nobel prizewinners and other acclaimed stars of the conference hall. Even more disturbing was the suspicion that perhaps I was wrong.

You can guess, then, what it means to me to see the growing legions of doctors who are now professing those same 'crazy' ideas in a more organized way. Considerable bodies of anti-vivisectionist physicians, veterinarians, biologists, and now lawyers, too, have been formed. These include Doctors and Lawyers for Responsible Medicine (DLRM), an international organization based in London; the German Vereinigung Ärzte gegen Tierversuche; the Italian Fondo Imperatrice Nuda; and the Medical Research Modernization Committee in America.

My feeling today is that anti-vivisectionists are entitled to be optimistic.

Appendix: ethical codes and statements

The Hippocratic Oath

The methods and details of medical practice change with the passage of time and the advance of knowledge. However, many fundamental principles of professional behaviour have remained unaltered through the recorded history of medicine. The Hippocratic Oath was probably written in the fourth century BC and was intended to be affirmed by each doctor on entry to the medical profession. In translation it reads as follows:

I swear by Apollo the physician, and Aesculapius and Health, and All-heal, and by all the gods and goddesses, that, according to my ability and judgment, I will keep this Oath and this stipulation – to reckon him who taught me this Art equally dear to me as my parents, to share my substance with him, and relieve his necessities if required; to look upon his offspring on the same footing as my own brothers, and to teach them this Art, if they shall wish to learn it, without fee or stipulation; and that by precept, lecture and every other mode of instruction, I will impart a knowledge of the Art to my own sons, and those of my teachers, and to disciples bound by a stipulation and oath according to the law of medicine, but to none other. I will follow that system or regimen which, according to my ability and judgment, I consider for the benefit of my patients, and abstain from whatever is deleterious and mischievous. I will give no deadly medicine to anyone if asked, nor suggest any such counsel; and in like manner I will not give to a woman a pessary to produce abortion. With purity and with holiness I will pass my life and practise my Art. I will not cut persons labouring under the stone, but will leave this to be done by men who are practitioners of this work. Into whatever houses I enter, I will go into them for the benefit of the sick, and will abstain from every voluntary act of mischief and corruption; and, further, from the seduction of females, or males, of freemen or slaves. Whatever in connection with my professional practice, or not in connection with it, I see or hear, in the life of men, which ought not to be spoken of abroad, I will not divulge, as reckoning that all such should be kept secret. While I continue to keep this Oath unviolated, may it be granted to me to enjoy Life and the practice of the Art, respected by all men, in all times. But should I trespass and violate this Oath, may the reverse be my lot.

The World Medical Association International Code of Medical Ethics

At the time of being admitted as a Member of the Medical Profession:

I solemnly pledge myself to consecrate my life to the service of humanity;

I will give to my teachers the respect and gratitude which is their due;

I will practise my profession with conscience and dignity;

The health of my patients will be my first consideration;

I will respect the secrets which are confided in me, even after the patient has died;

I will maintain, by all means in my power, the honour and the noble traditions of the medical profession;

My colleagues will be my brothers;

I will not permit considerations of religion, nationality, race, party politics or social standing to intervene between my duty and my patients;

I will maintain the utmost respect for human life from its beginning, even under threat, and I will not use my medical knowledge contrary to the laws of humanity;

I make these promises solemnly, freely and upon my honour.

(Declaration of Geneva, 1983 – spoken pledge)

Recommended reading

(The author is not necessarily in agreement with some aspects of the following works, but recommends them as overall views of the subject of scientific vivisection.)

Bard, S., B. Ganser and K. Raisch (1980) *Aktuelle Probleme der Tierversuche: Aufsätze zur gegenwärtigen Situation*, Munich: Salem-Forschungsinstitut, p. 60.

Fadali, M. A. (1977) *Animal Experimentation: A Harvest of Shame*, Los Angeles, CA: Hidden Springs Press.

Fano, A. (1997) *Lethal Laws*, London: Zed Books.

Illich, I. (1975) *Limits to Medicine – Medical Nemesis: The Expropriation of Health*, London: Calder and Brown.

Jacquinot, C. and J. Delaye (1984) *Les Trafiquants de bébés à naître*, Lausanne: Editions Pierre-Marcel Favre, p. 158.

Jakoby, W. B. and I. H. Pastan (1979) *Cell Culture*, Vol. LVII of S. P. Colowick and N. O. Kaplan, *Methods in Enzymology*, New York/San Francisco/London: Academic Press.

Page, T. (1996) *Vivisection Unveiled*, UKAVIS Publications.

Paul, H. B. (1975) *Cell and Tissue Culture* (5th edn), London: Churchill Livingstone.

Potelle, E. (1980) *Un Procès à instruire: la vivisection*, Editions de la Coalition Mondiale pour l'Abolition de la Vivisection.

Rambeck, B. (1989) *Der Mythos vom Tierversuch*, Frankfurt: Verlag Zweiausendeins.

Ruesch, H. (1980) *Die Fälscher der Wissenschaft: Technischer Rapport* (3rd edn), Munich: Hirthammer, p. 120.

Ruesch, H. (1988) *Imperatrice Nuda* (Slaughter of the Innocents), London: Futura Publications, p. 318.

Sharpe, R. (1988) *The Cruel Deception*, London: Thorsons.

Stiller, H. and M. Stiller (1977) *Animal Experimentation and Animal Experimenters* (trans. from German), Jenkinstown, PA: American Antivivisection Society.

Bibliography

Abercrombie, M. and J. E. M. Heaysman (1954) 'Observations on the social behaviour of cells in tissue culture. II. "Monolayering" of fibroblasts', *Exp. Cell Res.*, 6: 293–306.

Acheson, E. D., R. A. Cowdell and B. Jolles (1970) 'Nasal cancer in Northamptonshire boot and shoe industry', *Brit. Med. J.*, I: 385.

Aldridge, W. N. and M. K. Johnson (1977) *Proceedings of the 1977 British Crop Protection Conference: Pests and Diseases*, pp. 721–9.

Ames, B. N. (1971) 'Principles and methods for their detection', in A. Hollander (ed.), *Chemical Mutagens*, Vol. I, New York: Plenum Press, pp. 261–82.

Ames, B. N., W. E. Durstan, E. Yamasaki and F. D. Lee (1973) 'Carcinogens are mutagens. A simple test system combining liver homogenates for activation and bacteria for detection', *Proc. Nat. Acad. Sci. U.S.*, 70: 2281–5.

Angervall, L., U. Bengtsson, C. G. Zetterlund and M. Zsigmund (1969) 'Renal pelvic carcinoma in a Swedish district with abuse of phenacetin containing drug', *Brit. J. Urol.*, 41: 401.

Apert, E. (1906) 'De l'acrocéphalosyndactylie', *Bull. Soc. Méd. Hôp.*, Paris, 23: 1310.

Arnold, J. (1887) 'Über Teilungsvorgänge an den Wanderzellen, ihre progressiven und regressiven Metamorphosen', *Arch. Mikrosk. Anat.*, 30: 205–310.

Ballantyne, B. and Swanston, D. W. (eds) (1977) *Current Approaches to Toxicology*, Bristol: John Wright and Sons.

Bard, S., B. Ganser and K. Raisch *Aktuelle Probleme der Tierversuche – Aufsätze zur Gegenwärtigen Situation*, Munich: Forschungsinstitut.

Barkley, W. Emmet (1979) 'Safety considerations in the cell culture laboratory', in W. B. Jakoby and I. H. Pastan (eds), *Cell Culture*, Vol. LVIII of *Methods in Enzymology*, New York/San Francisco/London: Academic Press.

Barry, J. E. and D. M. Danks (1974) 'Anticonvulsivants and congenital anomalies', *The Lancet*, ii: 48–9.

Beddow Bayly, M. (1962) *Facts about Cancer Research*.

Bettero, A. 'Una nuova dimensione analitica', paper presented at Instituto Dermatologico Italiano, Monselice (IDIM) conference 'Cosmetica e farmacia', Punta Ala, CA, 17–23 May.

Biancifiori, C. and L. Severi (1966) 'The relation of isoniazid (INH) and allied compounds to carcinogenesis in some species of small laboratory animals', *Brit. J. Cancer*, 20: 528–38.

Blüchel, K. (1976) *Weisse Magier*, Fischer Verlag.

Bracco, G. (1981) 'Chiedono di divantare ricercatori', *Corriere Medico*, 39, 25–26 February.

Burach, R. (1970) *The New Handbook of Prescription Drugs: Official Names, Prices and Sources for Patient and Doctor*, New York: Pantheon.

Burnet, F. M. (1981) 'A possible role of zinc in the pathology of dementia', *The Lancet*, 8213/1 (24 January).

Burnet, J. (1942) *Medical World*, 3 July: 388.

— (1954) Editorial, *Medical Press*, 5 (May): 412.

Cahen, R. L. (1966) 'Experimental and clinical chemoteratogenesis', *Adv. Pharmacol.*, 4: 263–349.

Carrel, A. (1923) 'A method of physiological study of tissues *in vitro*', *J. Exp. Med.*, 48: 407–18.

Carrel, A. and M. T. Burrows (1910) 'The cultivation of adult tissue and organs outside the body', *J. Amer. Med.*, 55: 1379–81.

Clarke, G. D., M G. P. Stoker, A. Ludlow and M. Thornton (1970) 'Requirement of serum for DNA synthesis in BHK-21 cells: effects of density, suspension and virus transformation', *Nature*, 227: 798–801.

Clemmenson, J. (1965) *Statistical Studies in Malignant Neoplasms* (3 vols), Copenhagen, Munksgaard.

Clifford, P. (1970) 'A review of the epidemiology of nasopharyngeal carcinoma', *Int. J. Cancer*, 5: 287.

Cliver, D. O. (1973) 'Apparatus for changing tissue culture media', in P. F. Kruse and M. K. Patterson, Jr., *Tissue Culture: Methods and Applications*, New York/San Francisco/London: Academic Press, pp. 224–6.

Collins, J. M. et al. (1969) *Brit. J. Pharm.*, 36: 35–45.

Coleman, V. (1977) *Paper Doctors: A Critical Assesment of the Medical Establishment*, London: Temple Smith.

Cook, P. J. and D. P. Burkitt (1971), 'Cancer in Africa', *Brit. Med. Bull.*, 27: 14.

Corallo, S., R. Sega, A. Pirastu, G. Bozzi, M. Garimoldi, G. Broso and M. Castelfranco (1980) 'Ecocardiografia da sforzo in posizione seduta: studio della funzione ventricolare sinistra in 12 soggetti normali', paper presented at 5th National Congress of the Italian Society for the Study of Ultrasound in Medicine, Milan, 29–31 October.

Corbett, T. H., R. G. Cornell, K. Lieding and J. L. Endres (1974) 'Birth defects of children among Michigan nurse anesthetists', *Anesthesiology*, 41: 341–4.

Corriere Medico (1981a) Più esposte al cancro del polmone le mogli dei forti fumatori', *Corriere Medico*, 2 (25) (5–6 February): 19.

Corriere Medico (1981b) 'Sono cancerogeni i succhiottie per neonati?', *Corriere Medico*, 2 (28) (10–11 February): 16.

Crile, G. W., Jr. (1955) *Cancer and Common Sense*, New York: Viking.

Cunningham, D. D. and A. B. Pardee (1969), 'Transport changes rapidly initiated by serum addition to "contact inhibited" 373 cells', *Proc. Nat. Acad. Sci. U.S.*, 64: 1949–56.

Davis, L. E. (1979) *J. Am. Vet. Med. Ass.*, 175: 1014–15.

Danielsson, H. and B. Gustafsson (1959) 'On serum-cholesterol levels and neutral fecal steroids in germfree rats', *Bile Acids and Steroids*, LIX. *Arch. Biochem.*, 83 (2): 482.

D'Arcy, P. F. and J. P. Griffin (1979) *Iatrogenic Diseases* (2nd edn), New York/ Toronto: Oxford University Press.

Day, N. E. and C. S. Muir (1973) 'Aetiological clues from epidemiology', in R. W. Raven (ed.), *Modern Trends in Oncology. Part I: Research Progress*, London: Butterworth, pp. 29–59.

Delarue, F. (1977) *L'Intossication vaccinale*, Paris: Editions du Seuil.

Delort, M. (1962) Speech delivered at the inaugural session of the Academy of Bourges, France, 16 December.

Desjardins, A. (1925) in *Intransigeant*, 25 August, quoted in H. Ruesch, *Venditori di Malanni e Fabbricanti di Focomelie*, Rome: Edizioni CIVIS.

Desplaces, A. et al. (1963) 'Etude de la fonction thyroidienne du rat privé de bactéries (germfree)', *C.R. Acad. Sci.*, 257: 756–8.

Doell, R. G. and W. H. Carnes (1962) 'Urethran induction of thymic lymphoma in C57 bl mice', *Nature*, 194: 588–9.

Doll, R., C. S. Muir and J. Waterhouse (1970) *Cancer Incidence in Five Continents*, Vol. II, Berlin: Springer Verlag.

Donnai, D. and R. Harris (1978) 'Unusual fetal malformation after antiemetics in early pregnancy', *Brit. Med. J.*, 1: 691–2.

Draize, J. H., G. Woodward and H. O. Calvary (1944) *J. Pharm Exp. Ther.*, 82: 377–89.

Dulbecco, R. (1970) 'Topoinhibition and serum requirement of transformed and untransformed cells', *Nature*, 277: 802–6.

— (1971) 'Regulation of cell multiplication in tissue culture', in G. E. W. Wolstenholme and J. Knight, *Growth Control in Cell Cultures. A Ciba Foundation Symposium*, Edinburgh/London: Churchill Livingstone, pp. 71–87.

Dunlop, D. M. (1970) 'The use and abuse of psychotropic drugs', *Proc. Royal Soc. Med.*, 63: 1279.

Durant, W. (1963) *The Story of Civilization*.

Elsehove, J. and J. H. M. van Eck (1971) 'Congenital malformations, particularly cleft lip with or without cleft palate in children of epileptic mothers', *Ned. T. Geneesk*, 115: 1371.

Evans, V. J., J.C. Bryant, H. A. Kerr and E. L. Shilling (1964) 'Chemically defined media for cultivation of long-term strains for mammalian species', *Exp. Cell Res.*, 36: 439–74.

Fedrick, J. (1973) 'Epilepsy and pregnancy: a report from the Oxford Linkage Study', *Brit. Med. J.*, 2: 442–8.

Fell, H. B. (1965a) 'The application of organ culture to medical and biological research', in C. V. Ramakrishnan, *Tissue Culture*, The Hague: Dr W. Junk, pp. 17–26.

— (1965b) 'The technique of organ culture', in C. V. Ramakrishnan, *Tissue Culture*, The Hague: Dr W. Junk, pp. 9–16.

— (1972) 'Tissue culture and its contribution to biology', *J. Exp. Biol.*, 57: 1–13.

Fickentsher, K. (1980), *Diagnosen* (March), Pharmazeutische Universität Bonn.

Fischer, A., T. Astrup, G. Ehrensvard and V. Oelenschlager (1948), 'Growth of animal tissue cells in artificial media', *Proc. Soc. Exp. Biol. Med.*, 67: 40–6.

Flaks, A. (1965) 'The effect of 9,10-dimethyl-1,2-benzanthracene on young mice of low and high cancer strain', *Brit. J. Cancer*, 19: 547–50.

Florey, H. W. (1953), 'The advance of chemotherapy by animal experiments', *Conquest* (January): 12.

Friedman, R. M. (1979) 'Induction and production of interferon', in W. B. Jakoby and I. H. Pastan (eds), *Cell Culture*, Vol. LVIII of *Methods in Enzymology*, New York/San Francisco/London: Academic Press.

Ganguin, G. and E. Rempt (1970) 'Streptomycin in pregnancy and its effects on the hearing of children', *Ztschr. Laryngol. Rhinol. Otol.*, 49: 496.

Gantvik, K. M. and A. H. Tashjian, Jr. (1973) *Tissue Culture: Methods and Applications*, New York/ San Francisco/London: Academic Press, pp. 224–6.

Ghittino, P. (1970) *Piscicoltura e ittiopatologia. Vol. II: Epatoma della trota iridea*, Edizioni Rivista di Zootecnica, pp. 334–6.

Giardini, M. Chiara (1984) 'Il problema dei diritti degli animali nella letteratura recente', degree thesis, Faculty of Law, University of Florence.

Gilford, H. (1904) 'Progeria: a form of senilism', *Practitioner*, 73: 188.

Giornale d'Italia, Edizione di Milano, n. 44 (14 February).

Girard, R. Le Fruit de vos entrailles, Paris: Suger.

Goldberg, L. (1959) *Quantitative Method in Human Pharmacology*, London: Pergamon Press, p. 197.

Goldstein, S., J. W. Littlefield and J. S. Soeldner (1969) 'Diabetes mellitus and aging. Diminished plating efficiency of cultured human fibroblasts', *Proc. Nat. Acad. Sci. U.S.*, 64: 155–60.

Gordon, H. A. (1960) 'The germfree animal (its use in the study of physiologic effects of the normal microbial flora on the animal host)', *Amer. J. Digest Dis.*, 5: 841.

Gordon, H. A. and B. S. Wostmann, 'Morphological studies on the germfree albino rat', *Anat. Rec.*, 137 (1): 65.

Graham, A. F. and L. Siminovitch (1957) 'Conservation of RNA and DNA phosphorus in strain L. (Earle) mouse cells', *Biochem. Biophys. Acta*, 36: 427–8.

Green, M. and W. S. M. Wold (1979) 'Human adenoviruses: growth, purification and transfection assay', in W. B. Jakoby and I. H. Pastan, *Cell Culture*, Vol. LVIII of *Methods in Enzymology*, New York/San Francisco/London: Academic Press.

Greene, G. R. (1976) 'Tetracycline in pregnancy', *New Engl. J. Med.*, 295: 512–13.

Greenwald, P., J. J. Barlow, P. C. Nasca and W. S. Burnett (1971), 'Vaginal cancer after maternal treatment with synthetic estrogens', *New Engl. J. Med.*, 285: 390–2.

Griesemer, R. A. (1963) 'Congenital toxoplasmosis in gnotobiotic cats', paper presented at symposium on recent advances in germ-free animal experimentation organized by Amer. Inst. Biol. Sci., Amhurst 1963.

Griesemer, R. A. and J. P. Gibson (1963) 'The gnotobiotic dog', *Lab. An. Care*, 13: 643.

Grobstein, C. (1968) 'Developmental significance of interface material in epithelio-mesenchymal interaction', in R. Fleischmejer and R. E. Billingham (eds), *Epithelial–Mesenchymal Interactions*, Baltimore, MD: Williams and Wilkins, pp. 173–6.

Gross, D. R. (1979) 'Animal models in cardiovascular studies', in *Quantitative Cardiovascular Studies*, Baltimore, MD: University Press, p. 32.

Gustaffson, B. E. and C. B. Laurell (1960) 'Gamma globulin production in germfree rats after bacterial contamination', *J. Exp. Med.*, 110: 675.

Gustaffson, B. E. and L. S. Lanke (1960) 'Bilirubin and urobilins in germfree, ex-germfree and conventional rats', *J. Exp. Med.*, 112: 975.

Hadwen, W. R. (1926) *The Difficulties of Dr. Deguerre*, London: The C.W. Co.

Hall, D. A. (1976) *The Methodology of Connective Tissue Research*, Oxford: Johnson-Brouvers.

Ham, R. G. 1963) 'An improved nutrient solution for diploid Chinese hamster and human cell lines', *Exp. Cell Res.*, 29: 515–26.

— (1965) 'Clonal growth of mammalian cells in a chemically defined synthetic medium', *Proc. Nat. Acad. Sci. U.S.*, 53: 288–93.

Ham, R.G. and G. L. Sattler (1968) 'Clonal growth of differentiated rabbit cartilage cells', *J. Cell. Physiol.*, 72: 109–14.

Ham, R. G., L. W. Murray and G. L. Sattler (1970) 'Beneficial effects of embryo extract on cultured rabbit cartilage cells', *J. Cell. Physiol.*, 75: 353–60.

Hansson, O. (1979) *Arzneimittel-Multis und der SMON-Skandal*, Berlin: ATI Arzneimittel-Informationdienst.

Harlap, S., R. Prywes and A. M. Davies (1975) 'Birth defects and oestrogens and progesterones in pregnancy', *The Lancet*, i: 682–3.

Harris, J. W., H. H. Brewster, T. H. Ham and W. B. Castle (1956) 'Studies on the destruction of red blood cells. X. The biophysics and biology of sickle cell disease', *Arch. Intern. Med.*, 97: 145.

Hartinger, W. (1995) *Gentenchnollgie* (information bulletin of the Vereinigung Ärtze gegen Tierversuche e.V.) (September).

Hayflick, L. (1964) 'Advances in tissue culture methods important to viral disease problems', *Post Med.*, 35: 503–51.

— (1965) 'The limited *in vitro* lifetime of human diploid cell strains', *Exp. Cell Res.*, 37: 614–36.

Hayflick, L. and P. S. Moorhead (1961) 'The serial cultivation of human diploid cell strains', *Exp. Cell Res.*, 25: 585–621.

Heinonen, O. P., D. Slone, R. R. Monson, E. B. Hook and S. Shapiro (1977) 'Cardiovascular birth defects and antenatal exposure to female sex hormones', *New Engl. J. Med.*, 296: 67–70.

Herbst, A. L. and R. R. Scully (1970) 'Adenocarcinoma of the vagina in adolescence: a report of 7 cases including 6 clear-cell carcinomas (so-called mesonephromas)', *Cancer*, 25: 745–7.

Herbst, A. L., H. Ulfeloer and D. C. Poskanzer (1971) 'Adenocarcinoma of the vagina: association of maternal stilbestrol therapy with tumour appearance in young women', *New Engl. J. Med.*, 284: 878–81.

Herbst, A. L., R. J. Kurman, R. E. Scully and D. C. Poskanzer (1972) 'Clearcell adenocarcinoma of the genital tract in young females', *New Engl. J. Med.*, 287: 1259–67.

Higuchi, K. (1970) 'An impoved chemically defined culture medium for strain L. mouse cells based on growth responses to graded levels of nutrients including iron and zinc', *J. Cell Physiol.*, 75: 65–72.

Hill, D. W. (ed.) (1972) *Computers in Medicine*, London: Butterworth.

Hill, M. J., J. S. Crowter, B. S. Drasar, G. Hawksworth, V. Aries and R. E. O. Williams (1971) 'Bacteria and aetiology of cancer of large bowel', *The Lancet*, I: 95.

Hill, R. M. (1973) 'Teratogenesis and antiepileptic drugs', *New Engl. J. Med.*, 289: 1089–90.

Hiroyoshi Endo, Hideo Suzuki and Tetsuro Mohri, 'Effects of steroid hormones on HeLa cells' in C. V. Ramakrishnan, *Tissue Culture*, The Hague: Dr. W. Junk.

Holmes, R. (1967) 'Preparation from human serum of an alpha-one protein which induces the immediate growth of unadapted cells *in vitro*', *J. Cell Biol.*, 32: 297–308.

Hull, R. N. (1973) in A. Hellman, M. N. Oxman and E. Pollack (eds), *Biohazards in Biological Research*, New York: Cold Spring Harbor Lab., p. 3.

Hutchinson, J. (1886) 'Congenital absence of hair and mammary glands with atrophic condition of the skin and its appendages in a boy whose mother had been almost wholly bald from *alopecia areata* from the age of six', *Trans. Med. Chir. Soc. Edinburgh*, 69: 473.

Illich, I. (1976) *Limits to Medicine: Medical Nemesis – the Expropriation of Health*, London: Marion Boyars.

Inglis, B. (1981) *The Diseases of Civilization*, London/Sydney/Auckland/Toronto: Hodder and Stoughton.

Jacobs, J. P. (1966) 'A simple medium for the propagation and maintenance of human diploid cell strains', *Nature*, 210: 100–1.

Jackson, J. L., K. K. Sanford and T. B. Dunn (1970) 'Neoplastic conversion of chromosomal characteristics of rat embryo cells *in vitro*', *J. Nat. Cancer Inst.*, 45: 11–21.

Jacquinot, C. and Delaye, J. (1984) *Les Trafiquants de bébés à naître*, Lausanne: Editions P. M. Favre, p. 158.

Janerich, D. T., J. M. Piper and D. M. Glebatis (1974) 'Oral contraceptives and congenital limb-reduction defects', *New Engl. J. Med.*, 291: 697–700.

Jervis, H. R. and D. C. Biggers (1964) 'Mucosal enzymes in the caecum of conventional and germfree mice', *Anat. Rec.*, 148 (4): 591.

Johnson, M. K. (1977) *Arch. Toxicol.*, 37: 113–16.

— (1980) 'The mechanism of delayed neuropathy caused by some organophosphorus esters: using the understanding to improve safety', *J. Envir. Sci. Health*, B-15 (6): 823–41.

Jones, P. A. (1979) 'Construction of an artificial vessel wall from cultured endothelial cells', *Proc. Nat. Acad. Sci.*, 76 (4): 1882–6.

Jussawalla, D. J. and V. A. Deshpande (1971) 'Evaluation of cancer risk in tobacco chewers and smokers: an epidemiological assessment', *Cancer*, 28: 244.

Kapis, M .B. and C. G. Shayne (1933) *Non-animal Techniques in Biomedical and Behavioural Research and Training*, Lewis.

Kelsey, J. and S. Parker (1993) 'Epidemiology as an alternative to animal research', in M. B. Kapis and S. C. Gad, *Non-animal Techniques in Biomedical and Behavioural Research and Testing*, Lewis.

Kennedy, A., J. D. Donan and R. King (1981) 'Fatal myocardial disease associated with industrial exposure to cobalt', *The Lancet*, 1: 8217.

Kohler, P. O. and W. F. Bridson (1973) 'Enhancement of growth hormone production by cortisol', in P. F. Kruse and M. K. Patterson, Jr., *Tissue Culture: Methods and Applications*, New York/San Francisco/London: Academic Press.

Krugman, S., J. P. Giles and J. Hammond (1971) 'Viral hepatitis type B (Ms-2 strain) studies on active immunization', *J. Amer. Med. Ass.*, 217: 41–5.

Kruse, P. F. and M. K. Patterson, Jr. (1973) *Tissue Culture: Methods and Applications*, New York/San Francisco/London: Academic Press, p. 868.

The Lancet (1978) 'Clofibrate: a final verdict', *The Lancet*, ii, 8100: 1131–2.

Landsteiner, K. and A. S. Wiener (1940) 'An agglutinable factor in human blood recognizable by immune sera for Rhesus blood', *Proc. Soc. Exp. Biol. Med.*, 43: 223.

— (1941) 'Studies on an agglutinogen (Rh) in human blood reacting with anti-Rhesus sera and with human isoantibodies', *J. Exp. Med.*, 74: 309.

Langbein, K., H. P. Martin, P. Sichrovsky and H. Weiss (1983), *Bittere Pillen* (22nd edn), Cologne: Kiepenheuer und Witsch.

Larson, B. L. and C. R. Andersen (1973) 'Evaluation of milk protein synthesis', in P. F. Kruse and M. K. Patterson, Jr., *Tissue Culture: Methods and Applications*, New York/San Francisco/London: Academic Press, pp. 589–93.

Lenz, W. (1966) 'Malformations caused by drugs in pregnancy', *Amer. J. Dis. Child.*, 112: 99–106.

Lépine, P. (1967) interview in *Alsace*, 17 March.

Levine, P. and R. Stetson (1939) 'An unusual case of intra-group agglutination', *J. Amer. Med. Ass.*, 113: 126.

Levy, E. P., A. Cohen and F. C. Fraser (1973) 'Hormone treatment during pregnancy and congenital heart defects', *The Lancet*, i: 611.

Lichtfield, M. and S. Kentish (1974) *Bébés au feu*, Paris: Apostolat des Editions.

Liebelt, R. A., A. G. Liebelt and M. Lane (1954) *Cancer Res.* 24: 1869.

Ling, C. T., G. O. Gey and V. Richters (1968) 'Chemically characterized concentrated corodies for continuous cell culture (the 7-C's media)', *Exp. Cell Res.*, 52: 469–89.

Long, D. A. (1954) *The Lancet*, 13 (3): 532.

Loughnan, P. M., H. Gold and J. C. Vance (1973) 'Phenitoin teratogenicity in man', *The Lancet*, i: 70–2.

Lowe, C. R. (1973) 'Congenital malformations among infants born to epileptic women', *The Lancet*, i: 9–10.

McCann, J., F. Choi, E. Yamasaki and B. N. Ames (1975) 'Detection of carcinogens as mutagens in Salmonella microsome test. Assay of 300 chemicals', *Proc. Nat. Acad. Sci.*, 72: 5135–9.

McCarrol, A. M., M. Hutchinson, R. McCauley and D. A. Montgomery (1976) 'Long-term assessment of children exposed *in utero* to carbamazile', *Arch. Dis. Childh.* 51: 532–6.

McNeal, J. R. (1973) 'The possible teratogenic effect of salicylates on the developing fetus. Brief summaries of eight suggestive causes', *Clin. Pediat.*, 12: 347–50.

Macoschi, L. (1987) *Cavie Umane*, Florence: Edition LAN.

Mann, R. D. (1984) *Modern Drug Abuse: An Enquiry on Historical Principles*, MIP Press.

Martin, G. M., C. A. Sprague and C. J. Epstein (1970) 'Replicative life span of cultivated human cells. Effects of donor's age, tissue and genotype', *Lab. Invest.*, 23: 86–92.

Matsuoka, Y. (1973) 'Immunoglobins', in P. F. Kruse and M. K. Patterson, Jr., *Tissue Culture: Methods and Applications*, New York/San Francisco/London: Academic Press, pp. 611–17.

Mawdesley-Thomas, L. F. (1973) 'Present and potential use of tissue culture in toxicology', paper presented at seminar on potential humane non-animal research techniques, 14–15 March, London. Proceedings published as *Progress without Pain*, London: National Anti-Vivisection Society.

Meadow, S. R. (1968) 'Congenital abnormalities and anticonvulsant drugs', *Proc. Roy. Soc. Med.*, 63: 48–9.

Medical Research Council (Canada) (1977) *Guidelines for the Handling of Recombinant DNA molecules and Animal Viruses and Cells*, Ottawa: Medical Research Council.

Metcalf, D. and F. R. Stanley (1969) 'Quantitative studies on the stimulation of mouse bone marrow colony growth *in vitro* by normal human urine', *Aust. J. Exp. Med. Sci.*, 47: 453–66.

Miceli, J. (1981) 'Morire in pillole', *Epoca*, 1981 (25 September): 122–3.

Milham, S. and W. Elledge (1972) 'Maternal methimazole and congenital defects in children', *Teratology*, 5: 125.

Milkovich, L. and B. I. van den Berg (1974) 'Effects of prenatal meprobamate and chlordiazepoxide hydrochloride on human embryogenic and fetal developments', *New Engl. J. Med.*, 291: 1268–76.

Millar, J. H. D. and N. C. Nevin (1973) 'Congenital malformations and anticonvulsant drugs', *The Lancet*, i: 328.

Milunsky, A., J. W. Graef and M. P. Gaynor (1968) 'Methotrexate-induced congenital malformations', *J. Pediat.*, 72: 790–5.

Mitruka, B. M., H. M. Rawnsley and D. V. Vahedra (1976) *Animals for Medical Research: Models for the Study of Human Diseases*, New York: John Wiley and Sons.

Moffat, M. A. J. (1973) 'Some cell culture procedures in diagnostic medical virology', in P. F. Kruse and M. K. Patterson, Jr., *Tissue Culture: Methods and Applications*, New York/San Francisco/London: Academic Press.

Monaghan, J. M. and L. A. W. Sirisena (1978) 'Stilboestrol and vaginal clear cell adenocarcinoma syndrome', *Brit. Med. J.*, 1: 1588–99.

Moossy, J. (1979) 'Morphological validation of ischemic stroke models', in T. R. Price and E. Nelson (eds), *Cardiovascular Diseases*, New York: Raven Press, p. 7.

Moscona, A. and H. Moscona (1952) 'The dissociation and aggregation of cells from organ rudiments of the early chick embryo', *J. Anat.*, 86: 287–301.

Muir, C. S. (1971) 'Nasopharyngeal carcinoma in non-Chinese population with special reference to South-East Asia and Africa', *Int. J. Cancer*, 8: 351.

Müller, G. C. (1969) 'Biochemical events in the animal cell cycle', *Fed. Proc. Fed. Amer. Soc. Exp. Biol.*, 28: 1780–9.

Muoz, N. and R. Connelly (1971) 'Time trends of intestinal and diffuse types of gastric cancer in the United States', *Int. J. Cancer*, 8: 158.

Nagle S. C., Jr., H. R. Tribble, R. E. Anderson and N. D. Gary (1963) 'A chemical defined medium for growth of animal cells in suspension', *Proc. Soc. Exp. Biol. Med.*, 112: 340–4.

Nelson, M M. and J. O. Forfar (1971) 'Association between drugs administered during pregnancy and congenital abnormalities of fetus', *Brit. Med. J.*, 1: 523–7.

Newton, W. L. (1964) 'Absence of lethal effect of penicillin in germfree guinea pigs', *J. Bact.*, 88: 537.

Niswander, J. D. and W. Wertelecki (1973) 'Congenital malformation among offspring of epileptic women', *The Lancet* i: 1062.

Nora, J. J. and A. H. Nora (1975) 'Birth defects and oral contraceptives', *The Lancet*, i: 941–2.

— (1975) 'A syndrome of multiple congenital anomalies associated with teratogenic exposure', *Arch. Envir. Health*, 30: 117–21.

Oliver, M. F. J. A. Heading, J. L. Morris and J. Cooper (1978) 'A co-operative trial in the primary prevention for ischemic heart disease using clofibrate. Report from the committee of principal investigators', *Brit. Heart J.*, 40: 1069–1118.

Page, T. (1996) *Vivisection Unveiled*, London: UKAVIS Publications.

Pappworth, M. H. (1967) *Human Guinea Pigs: Here and Now Experimentation on Man*, London: Routledge and Kegan Paul.

Parascandola, J. (1981) 'Origins of the receptor theory', in J. W. Lamble (ed.), *Towards Understanding Receptors*, Amsterdam: Elsevier, pp. 1–7.

Parsa, I., H. Marsch and P. J. Fitzgerald (1970) 'Chemically defined medium for organ culture differentiation of rat pancreas anlage', *Exp. Cell Res.*, 59: 171–5.

Patterson, D. C. (1977) 'Congenital deformities: association with Bendectim', *Can. Med. Ass. J.*, 116: 1348.

Pedersen, K. O. (1944) 'Fetuin, a new globulin isolated from serum', *Nature*, 154: 575.

Peterson, J. A. and H. Rubin (1969) 'The exchange of phospholipids between cultured chick embryo fibroblasts and their growth medium', *Exp. Cell Res.*, 58: 365–78.

Pettifor, J. M. and R. Benson (1975) 'Congenital malformations associated with the administration of oral anticoagulants during pregnancy', *J. Pediat.*, 86: 459–62.

Pharoah, P. O. D., E. Alberman, P. Doyle and G. Chamberlain (1977) 'Outcome of pregnancy among women in anaesthetic practice', *The Lancet*, i: 34–6.

Pickering, G. (1964) *Brit. Med. J.*, 26 (December): 1615–19.

Pietra, G., H. Rappaport and P. Shubik (1961) 'The effects of carcinogenic chemicals in newborn mice', *Cancer*, 14: 308–17.

Pridan, H. and A. M. Lilienfeld (1971) 'Carcinoma of the cervix in Jewish women in Israel, 1960–1967', *Israel J. Med. Sci.*, 7: 1465.

Puck, T. T. and P. I. Marcus (1955) 'A rapid method for viable cell titration and clone production with HeLa cells in tissue culture. The use of X-irradiated cells to supply conditioning factors', *Proc. Nat. Acad. Sci. U.S.*, 41: 432–7.

Puck, T. T., S. J. Cieciura and A. Robinson (1958) 'Genetics of somatic mammalian cells III. Long term cultivation of euploid cells from human and animal subjects', *J. Exp. Med.*, 108: 945–55.

Quarti Trevano, G. M. (1981) 'Anche il caffè sospettato come fattore-rischio per l'insorgenza del carcinoma prostatico', *Corriere Medico*, 2 (20), 29–30 January.

Registry for Research on Hormonal Transplacental Carcinogenesis (1977) *Newsletter*.

Reid, L. M. and M. Rajkind (1979) 'New techniques for culturing differential cells: reconstituted basement membrane rafts', in W. B. Jakoby and I. H. Pastan (eds), *Cell Culture*, Vol. LVIII of *Methods in Enzymology*, New York/San Francisco/London: Academic Press.

Reines, B. (1985) *Heart Research on Animals*, Jenkintown, PA: American Antivivisection Society.

Rich, S. (1975) 'Senate vote to ban D.E.S.', *Washington Post*, 10 September.

Richards, I. D. G. (1972) 'A retrospective inquiry into possible teratogenic effects of drugs in pregnancy', *Advanc. Exp. Med. Biol.*, 27: 441–5.

Roe, F. J. and M. Walters (1967) 'Induction of hepatoma in mice by carcinogens of the polycyclic hydrocarbon type', *Nature*, 214: 279–300.

Rose, G. G. (1973) 'Dual-rotary-circumfusion system', in P. F. Kruse and M. K. Patterson, Jr., *Tissue Culture: Methods and Applications*, New York/San Francisco/London: Academic Press, pp. 283–91.

Rothblat, G. H. and V. J. Cristofolo (1972) *Growth, Nutrition and Metabolism of Cells in Culture*, New York/San Francisco/London: Academic Press, Vol. I, p. 471; Vol. II, p. 445.

Rotkin, I. D. and J. R. Cameron (1968) 'Clusters of variables influencing risk of cervical cancer', *Cancer*, 21: 663.

Roux, W. (1885) 'Beiträge zur Entwicklungsmechanik des Embryo', *Z. Biol.*, Munich, 21: 411–524.

Rudolph, R., J. J. Cohen and R. H. Gascoigne (1970) 'Biliary cancer among southwestern American Indians', *Ariz. Med.*, 21: 1.

Ruesch, H. (1976) *Imperatrice Nuda* (Slaughter of the Innocents), London: Futura.

— (1977) *Venditori di mallani e fabbricanti di focomelie*, Rome: Edizioni CIVIS.

Rumeau-Roquette, C., J. Goujard and G. Hull (1977) 'Possible teratogenic effect of phenothiazine in human beings', *Teratology*, 15: 57–64.

Russel, F. E. (1966) 'To be or not to be ... the LD50', *Toxicon*, 4: 81–3.

Russell, W. M. S. and R. L. Burch (1959) *The Principles of Human Experimental Technique*, London: Methuen.

Sabine, J. R., B. J. Horton and M. B. Wicks (1973) 'Spontaneous tumors in C3H-Avy and C3H-Avy of B mice: high incidence in the United States and low incidence in Australia', *J. Nat. Cancer Inst.*, 50: 1237–42.

Saachi, R., G. Reali and G. Rossi (1975) *Il Servizio Transfusionale*, Bologna: Patron Editore.

Safra, M. J. and G. P. Oakley (1975) 'Association between cleft lip with or without cleft palate and prenatal exposure to diazepam', *The Lancet*, ii: 478–80.

Sakakura, T., Y. Nishizuka and C. J. Dawe (1976) 'Mesenchyme-dependent morphogenesis and epithelium-specific cytodifferentiation in mouse mammary gland', *Science*, 194: 1439–41.

Sanford, K. K., W. R. Earle and G. D. Likely (1948) 'The growth *in vitro* of single isolated tissue cells', *J. Nat. Cancer Inst.*, 9: 229–46

Saxen, I. (1975) 'Associations between oral clefts and drugs taken during pregnancy', *Int. J. Epidemiol.*, 4: 37–44.

Saxen, I. and L. Saxen (1975) 'Association between maternal intake of diazepam and oral clefts', *The Lancet*, ii: 498.

Schardein, J. L. (1976) *Drugs as Teratogens*, Cleveland, OH: CRC Press.

Schär-Manzoli, M. (1980) 'Vaccino Sabin: il cancro sullo zucchero', *Orizzonti della Medicina*, Lugano, 5 (September).

Schenkel, B. and H. Vorherr (1974) 'Non-prescription drugs during pregnancy. Potential teratogenic and toxic effects on embryo and fetus', *J. Reprod. Med.*, 12: 27–45.

Schimmer, B. P. (1979) 'Adrenocortical Yl cells', in W. B. Jakoby and I. H. Pastan (eds), *Cell Culture*, Vol. LVIII of *Methods in Enzymology*, New York/San Francisco/London: Academic Press.

Schou, M., M. D. Goldfield, M. R. Weinstein and A. Villeneuve (1973) 'Lithium in pregnancy. I. Report from the Register of Lithium Babies', *Br. Med. J.*, 2: 135–6.

Scott, J. R. (1977) 'Fetal growth retardation associated with maternal administration of immuno-suppressive drugs', *Am. J. Obst. Gynec.*, 128: 668–76.

Seckel, H. P. G. (1960) *Bird-headed Dwarfs*, Springfield, IL: Ch. C. Thomas.

Seegmiller, J. E., F. M. Rosenbloom and W. N. Kelly (1967) 'Enzyme defect associated with a non-linked human neurological disorder and excessive purine synthesis', *Science*: 1682–4.

Segi, M. and M. Kurihara (1963) *Trends in Cancer Mortality for Selected Sites in 24 Countries (1959–1960)*, Sendai, Japan: Department of Public Health, Tohoku University School of Medicine.

Sell, S. (1964) 'Gamma globulin metabolism in germfree guinea pigs', *J. Immunol.*, 4 (92): 559.

Shayne, C. G. (1933) 'Structure-activity approaches as an alternative to animal testing for predicting toxicity in man', in M. B. Kapis and C. G. Shayne, *Non-animal Techniques*, pp. 63–71.

Signori, E. (1981) 'Prescrivere ogni giorno mezzo litro di latte', *Corriere Medico*, II (21) (30–31 January): 5.

Simons, P. J. (1980) 'An alternative to the Draize test', in A. N. Rowan and C. J. Stratman, *The Use of Alternatives in Drug Research*, London: Macmillan.

Simpson, H. C. R., R. W. Simpson, S. Lousley, R. D. Carter, M. Geekie, T. D. R. Hickaday and D. M. Mann (1981) 'A high carbohydrate leguminous diet improves cell aspects of diabetic control', *The Lancet*, 1 (8210): 1–5.

Sjöstrom, H. and R. Nilsson (1972), *Thalidomide and the Power of the Drug Companies*, Harmondsworth: Penguin.

Smith, M. I. and E. Elvove (1930) *Public Health Reports*, Washington, DC, 45: 1703–16.

Smithells, R. W. (1976) 'Environmental teratogens of man', *Brit. Med. Bull.*, 32: 27–33.

South, J. (1972) 'Teratogenic effects of anticonvulsivants', *The Lancet*, ii: 1154.

Speciani, L. O. (1984) *Di Cancro si Vive*, Masson Italia Editore, p. 214.

Speidel, B. D. and S. R. Meadows (1972) 'Maternal epilepsy and abnormalities of the foetus and newborn', *The Lancet*, ii: 839–43.

Stanley, E. R., W. A. Robinson and G. L. Ada (1968) 'Properties of the colony factor in leukaemic and normal mouse serum', *Aust. J. Exp. Biol. Med. Sci.*, 46: 715–26.

Starrveld-Zimmermann, A. A. E., W. J. van der Kolk, J. Elshove and H. Meinardi (1975) 'Teratogenicity of antiepileptic drugs', *Clin. Neurosurg.*, 77: 81–95.

Sullivan, F. M. (1979) 'The teratogenic and other toxic effects of drugs on reproduction', in P. F. D'Arcy and J. P. Griffin (eds) *Iatrogenic Diseases* (2nd edn), New York/Toronto: Oxford University Press, pp. 437–58.

Sweetman, P., C. Bauer Jr. and C. Maura (1933) 'In vitro techiques for use in drug discovery', in M. B. Kapis and C. G. Shayne, *Non-animal Techniques*, pp. 43–61.

Tarro, G. (1988) *Metodi Alternativi alla Vivisezione nella Cancerogenesi*, Ginevra: Congresso OIPA (Organizzazione Internazionale Protezione Animali).

Tashjian, A. H., Jr. (1979) 'Clonal strains of hormone-producing cells', in W. B. Jakoby and I. H. Pastan (eds), *Cell Culture*, Vol. LVIII of *Methods in Enzymology*, New York/San Francisco/London: Academic Press.

Temin, H. M. (1969) 'Control of cell multiplication in uninfected chicken cells and chicken cells converted by murine sarcoma viruses', *J. Cell. Physiol.*, 74: 9–16.

Thilly, W. G. and D. W. Levine (1979) 'Microcarrier culture: a homogeneous environment for studies of cellular biochemistry', in W. B. Jakoby and I. H.

Pastan (eds), *Cell Culture*, Vol. LVIII of *Methods in Enzymology*, New York/San Francisco/London: Academic Press, pp. 184–94.

Thompson, E. B. (1979) 'Liver cells', in W. B. Jakoby and I. H. Pastan (eds), *Cell Culture*, Vol. LVIII of *Methods in Enzymology*, New York/San Francisco/London: Academic Press, p. 544.

Todaro, G. J., G. K. Lazar and H. Green (1965) 'The initiation of cell division in a contact-inhibited mammalian cell line', *J. Cell. Comp. Physiol.* 66: 325–33.

Transactions of the Birmingham Philosophical Society, 20 (4): 1882, Declaration by Sir Lawson Tait at the Scientific Academy of Birmingham, quoted in H. Ruesch (1977), *Venditori di Malanni e Fabbricanti de Focomelie*, Rome: Edizioni CIVIS.

Trevan, J. W. ((1927) 'The error of determinatin of toxicity', *Proc. Roy. Soc. Med.*, 101: 483–514.

Treves, F. (1898) B*rit. Med. J.*, 5 November, quoted in H. Ruesch (1977), *Veditori di Malanni e Fabbricanti di Focomelie*, Rome: Edizioni CIVIS.

Tsubaki, T., Y. Honma and M. Hoshi (1971) 'Neurological syndrome associated with clioquinol', *The Lancet*, i: 696–7.

Tulinius, H. (1970) 'Frequency of some morphological types of neoplasms of five sites', in R. Doll, C. S. Muir and J. Waterhouse (eds), *Cancer Incidence in Five Continents*, Vol. II, Berlin: Springer Verlag.

Tuyns, A. (1971) *International Agency for Research on Cancer Annual Report 1970*, Lyon: IARC, pp. 28–9.

Van Wezel, A. L. (1967) 'Growth of cell-strains and primary cells on micro-carriers in homogeneous culture', *Nature*, 216: 64–5.

Venning, G. R. (1983) *British Medical Journal*, 14 January: 199–202.

Veronesi, U. (1986) *Un Male Curabile* (3rd edn), Milan: A Mondadori Editore, p. 211.

Vojta, M. and J. Jirasek (1966) '6-azauridine induced changes of trophoblast in early human pregnancy', *Clin. Pharmacol. Ther.*, 7: 162–5.

Wagner, J. C. (1971) 'Asbestos cancer', *J. Int. Cancer Inst.*, 46: 5.

Walker, G. (1979) 'Role of pKM-101 in the Salmonella tester strains', paper presented at NATO Advanced Research Symposium, Monte Carlo, 22–28 September.

Wallraff, G. (1985) *Ganz Unten*, Cologne: Verlag Kiepenheuer and Witsch.

Warburg, O. (1930) *The Metabolism of Tumours*, London: Constable.

Warkany, I. (1975) 'A warfarin embryopathy?' *Amer. J. Dis. Child.*, 129: 287–8.

Warrel, D. W. and R. Taylor (1968) 'Outcome for the fetus of mothers receiving prednisolone during pregnancy', *The Lancet*, i: 117–18.

Waymouth, C. (1965) 'The cultivation of cells in chemically defined media and the malignant transformation of cells *in vitro*', in C. V. Ramakrishnan, *Tissue Culture*, The Hague: Dr. W. Junk, pp. 168–79.

Weil, C. S. and R. A. Scala (1971) 'Study of intra- and interlaboratory variability in the results of rabbit eye and skin irritation tests', *Toxicol. and Appl. Pharmacol.*, 19: 276–360.

Weiss, P. and A. C. Taylor (1960) 'Reconstitution of complete organ from single-cell suspensions of chick embryos in advanced stages of differentiation' *Proc. Nat. Acad. Sci.*, 46: 1177–85.

Werner, O. (1904) *Über Katarakt in Verbindung mit Sklerodermie*, Kiel: Schmidt und Klaunig.

White, P. R. (1949) 'Prolonged survival of excised animal tissues *in vitro* of precisely known constitution', *J. Cell Comp. Physiol.*, 34: 221–41.

Wiebel, F. and R. Baserga (1969) 'Early alteration in amino acid pools and protein synthesis of diploid fibroblasts stimulated to synthetize DNA by addition of serum', *J. Cell. Physiol.*, 74: 191–202.

Wilson, H. V. (1907) *J. Exp. Zool.*, 5: 245.

Yeh, J. and H. W. Fisher (1969) 'A diffusible factor which sustains contact inhibition of replication', *J. Cell. Biol.*, 40: 382–8.

Yoshikura, H. and Y. Hirokawa (1968) 'Induction of cell replication', *Exp. Cell Res.*, 52: 439–44.

Zollinger, Lindon, Filler, Corson and Wilson (1964) *New Engl. J. Med.*

Index